STAR-STICKS

★

Dec 7, 1980

To Tom Duffy —

I hope you enjoy Star-Sticks

Best wishes!

Gene Finstey

Copyright © 1979 by Summer House Publications   Second Printing, March 1980

All rights reserved. No part of this book may be reproduced or transmitted in any form or by any means, electronic or mechanical, including photocopying, recording, xerography, or any information storage and retrieval system, without permission in writing from the publisher.

Manufactured in the United States of America

Summer House Publications, Baltimore, Maryland 21210

Library of Congress Catalog Card Number 79-64888

ISBN-0-935736-27-1

r-Sticks was designed and produced by Brushwood Graphics.

STAR-STICKS

Eugene M. Fusting

Summer House Publications
Baltimore, Maryland 21210

Contents

Introduction	vii	Page	129
		Radebaugh	137
Attack	1		
Corcoran	3	**Defense**	145
Duquette	8	Devine	147
French	14	Kane	156
Fusting	20	Keigler	161
Griebe	40	Schardt	170
Long	48	Starsia	178
O'Neill	55	Waldvogel	190
Tickner	65		
Warfield	75	**Goalie**	199
		Beroza	201
Midfield	83	Blick	205
Arena	85	Chadwick	212
Darcangelo	93	Creighton	217
Henrickson	100	Krongard	222
Huntley	107	Mackesey	228
Lichtfuss	116	Mahon	237
Marino	121		

v

Richard Scalera

Introduction

Unlike most other books on lacrosse, *Star Sticks* is neither a history of the game nor a description of its rules. Instead it's a collection of personal narratives *written to help you improve your playing.* Whether you're a fan, a beginning player or an experienced club ball player, the chapters of *Star Sticks* will give you new insights into how you can improve your game. Each of the contributors is an outstanding example of the best of today's lacrosse players. There are other superstars who I either couldn't reach or who were unable to commit the time required to answer the detailed questions which formed the basis for each chapter. To those who did contribute, I want to express my deep appreciation. Their motivation was to pass along to future players their love and understanding of the game; their only reward is in seeing lacrosse grow in popularity throughout the United States.

Not all of the players who play a certain position handle the same situation in the same way. What I suggest is that you try some of the different approaches and see whether they feel right to you and your style of play. But remember, before you try the unusual play or technique, you need to master the fundamentals. Take from each player what you find you can use successfully on the field.

Several common themes run throughout the four sections of *Star Sticks*. One is the absolute necessity of teamwork. It's especially significant that these players, each a star in his own right, are the first to see the importance of team play. Each knows that he can't hog all the glory; each knows *his* own success depends on the efforts of all the rest of the team.

Another common theme is that each player recognizes his own limitations. Some admit to being slow; but, rather than stand around complaining about their lack of speed, they discuss how they've developed a style of play that allows them to work around or with their limitation. Not everyone can be excellent in all phases of the game, so you have to fully develop what skills and advantages you feel you do

Introduction   viii

possess.

A third common theme is the necessity for communication. While good communication is especially important to goalies and attackmen, all the players recognize that you must keep your teammates informed of where you are, what you're doing and what the offense or defense is doing. Good communications is one of the hallmarks of the winning lacrosse team.

Each of the players in this book makes a personal statement concerning his overall philosophy of playing his position, then goes on to discuss exactly how he handles various field situations, offensive and defensive plays and other technical aspects of play unique to his position. Read not only the articles on your own position, but those on the opposition. For example, if you're an attackman, you need to study what the defensemen in this book say about how they try to neutralize your favorite moves and what the goalies have to say about defending your feeds and shots.

In addition to our superstars, there are many others who contributed to making this book possible. Special thanks goes to Jay Elliott, director of the Lacrosse Hall of Fame, whose advice and direction were a real help in putting the material together. In fact, the entire staff of the Hall of Fame was most cordial and helpful. I also want to thank Henry Ciccarone at Johns Hopkins and Ritchie Moran at Cornell for their assistance.

I owe a large debt of gratitude to Susan Bowden, whose generous spirit and knowledge of the world of printing were invaluable. I want to thank my wife Judy, whose total interest and incredible help was the key, always with an eye to keeping the book affordable. Marie Jones, who designed the book and drew the diagrams, was an able assistant. Special thanks to Carol Offut whose artwork graces the cover.

Bruce Innes, my editor at Summer House, spent countless hours working over the manuscripts, mastering the terminology and concepts of lacrosse, and learning to read my illegible handwriting.

As with any book, there's a group of unsung heroes who need to be mentioned —in this case, it's the photographers. I want to encourage and say thanks to all photographers who help to convey to an ever-widening audience the excitement and thrill of lacrosse.

Finally, I'd like to dedicate this book to its primary audience—the future stars of lacrosse.

—Eugene M. Fusting

Introduction

Dallas Weigel

Richard Scalera

Attack 1

Attackmen usually are thought of as loners who don't really need the rest of the team. High-scoring and fast-moving, they're the envy of both fans and the other players. But, as you'll see, it's not quite that way, at least not for the great attackmen. These players realize that first and foremost they must be team players. They can't score without a lot of effort and help from the middies and the defensemen, and all their goals can go for nothing if their team's goalie can't stop the opposition. In fact, their primary job is not necessarily to score but to *create* scoring situations for someone on the team.

Although each player devotes a lot of space to talking about the critical skill of shooting, each also points out that being good at playing attack involves a lot more than just getting the ball and shooting. Ball *control* is what they stress. If you can't control the ball, you'll never get a chance to bang one into the net.

While the goalie directs the defense, it's up to the attackman to direct the offense. He has to be as good at communicating and seeing the overall picture as the goalie. He has to know when to speed up or slow down the pace of the game. He has to be able to coordinate the rest of the players into an efficient, unstoppable offensive unit.

Each attackman in this book has his individual style of play. While some of the moves discussed are only for players who have completely mastered the basics, taken as a whole, this section presents a complete look at playing successful attack lacrosse.

Attack

Jeff Wagner

Terry Corcoran

EDITOR'S INTRODUCTION

Terry Corcoran has been the backbone of Jerry Schmidt's Hobart team for the last three years. At 6'2" and 180 lbs., Cork ended his illustrious career with 296 points highlighted by a convincing 23–13 win over Washington College for a second straight Hobart championship. Cork contributed 5 goals and 3 assists to the Hobart talley.

A three-time All-American, he also twice received the Hero's Attackman of the Year award. He was voted the Most Valuable Player of the 1977 Superstars game. Cork plans to play club lacrosse and help coach a college team.

PLAYER'S INTRODUCTION

Since the age of 15, when I started to play in high school, the game of lacrosse has been an important part of my life. I love the competition, the pressure and the fun. The game also has given me championships, awards and celebrations; it has taught me how to deal with success as well as develop a distaste for failure. It enabled me to make lasting friendships during high school and college. It gave me a chance to become closer to my younger brothers as they knocked me around our backyard with defensive and goalie sticks. But perhaps the greatest thing the game of lacrosse gave me was the opportunity to become a source of pride to my parents and family.

Philosophy of Attack

I have always felt that an attackman must be both a dodger and a feeder. Pure dodgers can be neutralized by double teaming and pure feeders can be aggressively overplayed while their cutters are face guarded. Hence, my concept of an outstanding attackman is one who dodges to the goal while looking to feed to his cutters as he drives.

Technique

When I have the ball behind the goal, I like to take my defenseman right to the cage, while being aware of both cutters and defensemen (or midfielders) sliding to double team. In addition to driving from behind the cage, I like to drive from the wing areas. To stop a hard drive, a defenseman usually has to overplay which gives you the opportunity to take advantage of his poor positioning. By driving high above the plane of

Corcoran

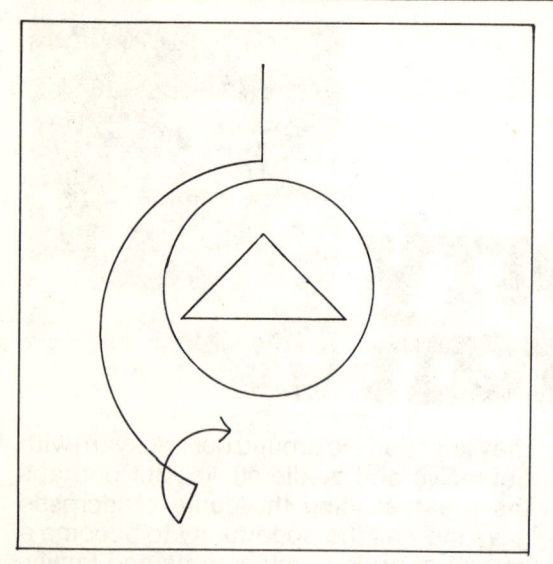

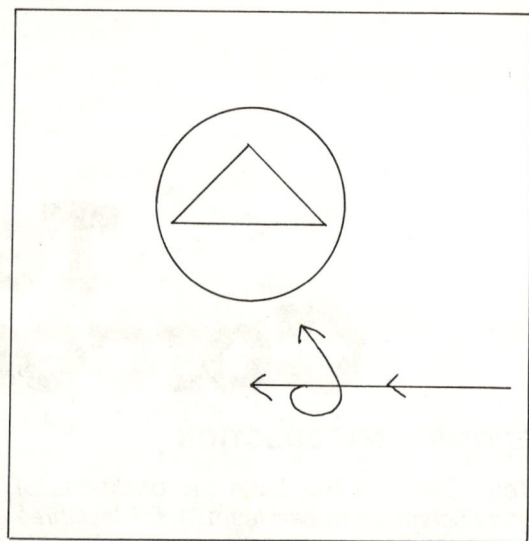

Diagram 1: Drive high for a shot or inside roll.

Diagram 2: Drive across for shot or inside roll.

the goal, you have an opportunity for an inside roll. (See Diagrams 1 and 2.) *[By driving high, Cork not only has an opportunity for an inside roll but frequently he forces the defense to slide in order to cover him. This is exactly what he wants to happen because, as soon as the defense slides, he can flip the ball to the open man.—G. F.]*

Diagram 2 represents my favorite move, though I add a rather unorthodox twist. I like to lean into my defenseman, drive tight around the crease, dive in front of the cage, and shoot a one handed shovel shot. *[Very few players do this one handed shovel shot as successfully as Terry. As he leans into his defenseman, the defenseman's natural reaction is to start pushing him. This is exactly what Cork wants him to do because it allows Cork to beat him. Then he dives, giving himself a better shooting angle. It's almost impossible for the defense to back up; he comes in so low that the defense can't get him in time.—G. F.]*

When driving to the cage, I like to use either the basic roll dodge or split my defenseman by bringing my stick quickly across my face as I change hands and direction, thereby avoiding a poke check.

To prevent a defenseman from going over my head to take away the ball, I tuck my stick in tight under my free arm when he goes over. To protect against wrap checks, you also can block by using your free arm outstretched with the palm turned out and the thumb pointed down.

Feeding

I've found that you can feed from almost anywhere on the field, though the best places are on the wings of the goal and the worst is directly behind the goal because the goalie can pick off the ball. When feeding, you always should be moving to prevent yourself from being poke checked. To prevent a defensive poke check, feed coming out a roll dodge. *[If you feed like Cork* does, you'll create a real problem for your defenseman. Your defenseman is told that his job, as the attackman comes up to a feeding position, is to take away the attackman's strong hand. As he tries to do this, you turn back, go the opposite way, and look for the cutter—all while the defenseman is still trying to recover from missing you. You can set up this play by driving hard one way thus forcing the defense to play up (to prevent your taking him to the goal) and then rolling back. If your cutters know this is what you're going to do, they can time their cuts accordingly.— G.F.] If someone is open, I try to get the feed off in any way possible—underhand, overhand, or sidearm. As I feed I usually look at the cutter and make my pass to the spot where the cutter should be.

In addition to not feeding from directly behind the goal or while you are stationary, you should not carry the stick in two hands prior to the feed. It's too easy for the defenseman to disrupt your pass with a poke check if you have both hands on the stick. You also should not force the feed itself. [In addition to not forcing the ball, there are a few other points to remember when feeding. Don't feed if you don't have complete control of the ball, if there's no open lane, or if there's an opponent between you and your teammate (unless he's so close to you that you can use a little flip pass that can go around him). Feed when you're set and ready. Accurate feeding takes a lot of practice and perfect timing.—G. F.]

Playing Off the Ball

When a midfielder has the ball and is making a move to the cage, be prepared to be a release in case your defenseman slides to the ball. Also be prepared to back up the goal if the middie shoots. When another attackman has the ball behind the goal, I

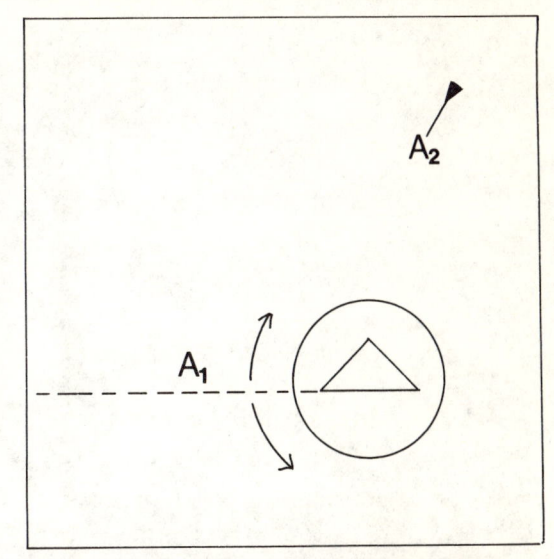

Diagram 3: Position when ball is behind.

like to position myself on the plane on the opposite side of the goal. This enables me to swing in front of the goal for a feed or swing to the point to serve as a release for the other attackman. (See Diagram 3.) [This also occupies your defenseman. He has to watch you, which takes him out of the backup position. If A2 goes left and your man slides across the crease to help out, take two or three steps behind and you're open for a pass. Now your defenseman is trapped. He's in front and you're behind with the ball.—G. F.]

After I've thrown the ball to a teammate, I like to cut back door in order to be in position to receive a feed. Sometimes, I'll just cut to prevent my defenseman from backing up on the pass receiver.

Shooting

When shooting, I go for *any* open part of the goal. Usually, I look to the goalie's off stick side. I like to fake the goalie if I have him

Corcoran

one on one, but I'll usually shoot anyway even if the fake doesn't work when I'm within ten yards.

Playing Ground Balls

After goals scored, ground balls are undoubtably the next most important statistic in a lacrosse game. Usually, the team that recovers the most ground balls wins. You should always pick up a ground ball with your back hand low on the stick, parallel to the ground; move hard and decisively and bring your stick up close to your head in order to protect it. *[Cork is so right here. Loose balls are extremely important. The problem is that with the new lighter sticks, many players stab at the ball, only to miss it. The surest way to capture a ground ball is to bend over when trying to pick it up. If you keep two hands on your stick, you'll find that you must bend over.—G. F.]*

Tom Duquette

EDITOR'S INTRODUCTION

Tom started playing when he was eight years old and by the time he was ten was playing with the Dumbarton League, which his father runs. He played all four years of high school and then went on to the University of Virginia where he was named All-American for each of his four years of college play. He also set a career goal record at Virginia of 107 goals. He was voted the Most Valuable Player in the 1973 North-South college game with 4 goals and 4 assists and played on the World Team in 1974.

Tom played for the championship Mt. Washington team in 1977 and now plays for TJ's. He also coached four seasons at St. Annes Belfield and was named coach of the Year in 1976.

He is presently getting a masters degree in Sports Psychology at the University of Virginia and serves as assistant lacrosse coach.

Tom is not only a great player but has a real ability to get inside a player's head—whether his own or his opponent's—and think through the proper move. To the casual observer, it looks as if Tom is playing strictly by reflex; but, as his article makes clear, a lot of practice and a lot of mental effort go into his play.

Philosophy of Attack

Ask any beginning lacrosse player what position he would like to play and his most likely answer would be attack. What makes this position so appealing? The reason I think is simple: The heroes of modern sports are those who score the most points. Attackmen are perceived as goal scorers; hence the desire to play the position.

The word "attack" implies forceful, offensive action, and when applied to lacrosse, offensive action means goal scoring. An attackman's major function is to score goals or to assist in getting them scored.

There are a number of ways in which an attackman can approach his role. These include seeing himself primarily as a shooter, dodger, feeder or cutter, or, in the case of the great attackman, a combination of all of them. *[As Tom suggests, seeing yourself actually perform the task, holding a mental picture down to every last detail will go a long way in helping you make yourself into the kind of player you want to be. Perfect the things that you can do well and you'll find that your confidence will improve and along with it your overall ability.—G. F.]*

Attack

Duquette

But, no matter what the orientation, the ability to handle a lacrosse stick is fundamental to success. Other natural abilities, such as size, speed, quickness, etc., may be necessary for success; but, without stickwork, these other qualities mean little. This may seem like an overstatement, but stickwork is not a native ability. Through practice, it can be learned and refined. Put simply, practice means hard work, which, while it may be a cliche, is not a bad place to start your lacrosse career.

Time spent working both right and left handed on a wall, playing catch, and shooting at the goal make the stick a natural extension of the arm. An extension so natural that in competition the ball can be caught and directed on target without conscious effort.

This may seem to be an oversimplification, but it's basic to my philosophy of attack. The stickwork I developed outside the confines of any team practice has been largely responsible for much of the success I have had in the game. *[Duke has developed tremendous skill in handling his stick; and, as he says, he did it after regular practice. Doing this makes it easier to concentrate on other areas of play because you don't have to waste any concentration thinking about whether you can catch and throw properly. You'll also have more self-confidence if you know you have good stick work.—G. F.]*

Once good stickwork is mastered, the foundation has been laid for success in any of the areas—shooting, feeding, dodging or cutting. In most players, at least two of these roles are paired, and the best offensive players are adept at all four.

In a developmental sense, I was a shooter first. I learned to move without the ball as a creaseman, then to get the ball in a position to shoot. Feeding developed as an afterthought when the game ceased to be a one on one confrontation. Others have come to play the attack position equally well or better through a different sequence. The specific order of skills' mastery in itself is immaterial; what *is* important is that the skills build on each other so that eventually all four elements are present.

Shooting

The bottom line of all offensive play has to be shooting. The ball does not find its own way into the goal; it must be propelled there. Shooting in lacrosse is a practiced art. Given shots from given positions become almost automatic. In the flow of the game, these shots are called up without hesitation. Good shooters have a sense of where they are on the field and where the goalie should be when the ball is in a given position. They shoot the practiced shot to take advantage of where the goalie should be. If he is not there, they can alter their shot to score the goal. Good shooters challenge the goalie.

As with developing good stickwork, the key to good shooting is practice. The proper kind of practice is important. Standing still shooting at the goal from five yards away does not accomplish anything. Shooting the shot on the move and from those positions from which the shots will be taken during the game does achieve the purpose. Also, when practicing all shots should be taken at full speed. Holding back your motion for accuracy will only hurt you when you're in a game situation.

Many coaches stress hitting anywhere within 6' x 6' goal, but the great shooters shoot for practiced portions of this area. Some shoot high, others low, and some mix it up by aiming for the corners. But, during a game, they score because, thanks to hours of practice, they can hit a *precise* spot

Attack

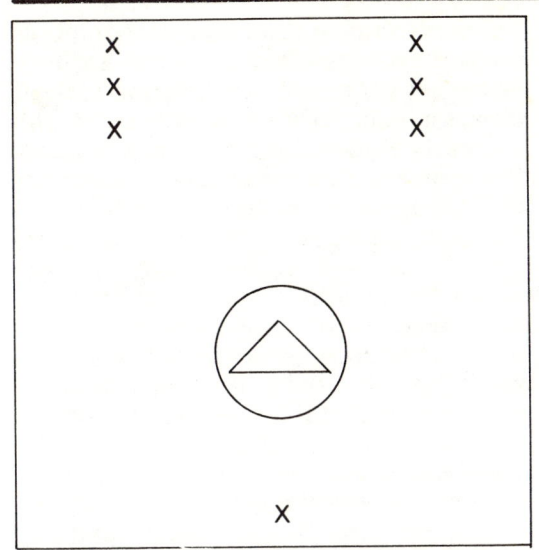

Diagram 1: Shooting Drill for Creaseman: Six attackmen, each with a ball line up three on a side behind. The creaseman breaks left, right, left, right, etc., cutting to the ball as the attackmen come around. After you've run through this drill, bring the feeding lines closer together and add cuts away from the ball.

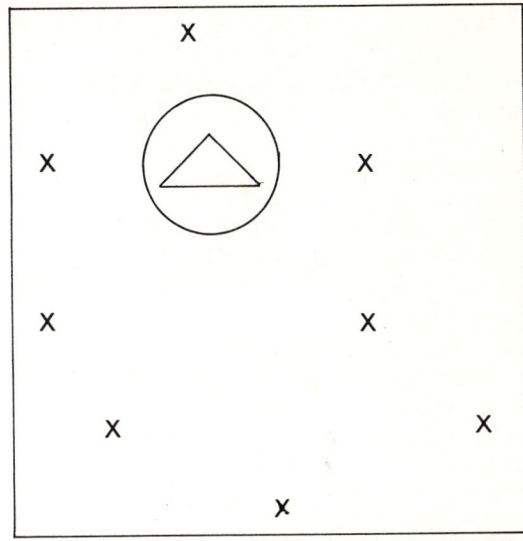

Diagram 2: Shooting Drill: Scatter 8–12 balls within the box area and have a teammate serve as backstop. Practice scooping up the ball and shooting without stopping your movement.

within the goal.

Mechanically, the key to good shooting is to have your weight moving towards the goal. This affords maximum power; and, with practice, this power can be directed toward the proper spots in the cage. (Diagrams 1 and 2 present my favorite shooting drills.)

Dodging

Until the '60's, the attackman's role as a dodger had been very limited. Jimmy Lewis, who played for Navy (1964, '65 and '66), revolutionized attack play by adding dodging as another distinct component of the game. When he had the ball, he was a threat not only as a feeder but also because he could take the ball to the goal and score himself. This has been the trend in modern attack play—with the ball in your stick, make yourself as dangerous as possible. Just as good shooters challenge goalies, good dodgers challenge their defensemen.

A dodge is initiated for two purposes: To maneuver yourself into a position for a shot or to draw a backup in order to drop the ball off to someone else who is in a position to shoot. Either way, the dodger's purpose is to get the ball to the goal as directly as possible. (In Diagram 3, there's a good dodging drill for those who want to improve this skill).

Feeding

Traditionally, feeding has been the attackman's major activity. Team offenses were designed to revolve around him and his possession of the ball. The attackman maintained possession behind the goal while midfielders, creasemen and the

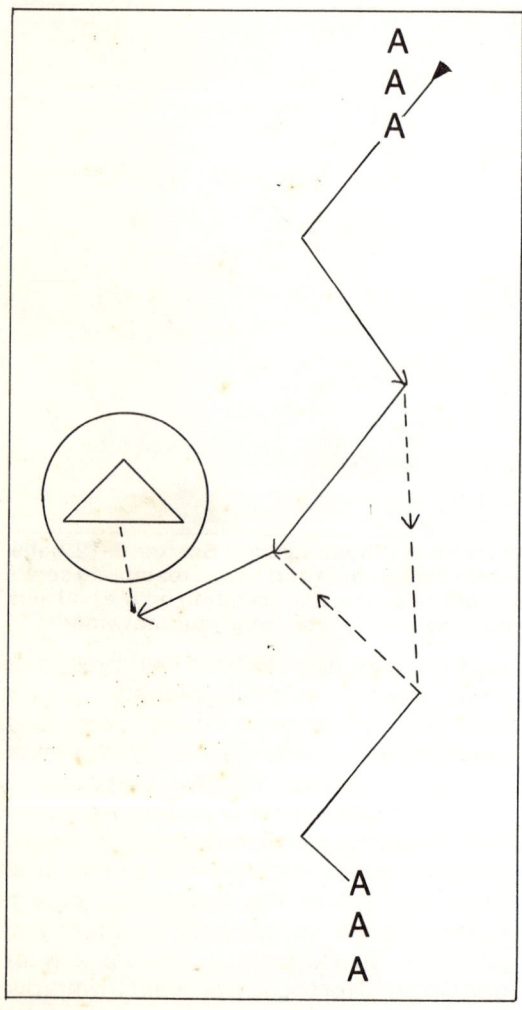

Diagram 3: Dodging Drill: Place pylons as indicated; move from pylon to pylon, use rolls twice, faces twice, half & half twice. The next man starts when the man before him hits the first pylon. Stress stick protection, foot work, solid planting and smooth change of hands.

There are several factors that contribute to success in feeding. First, the ability to move with the ball with complete confidence in your ability to hang on to it. This allows all of your attention to be devoted to the area of the field in which the cutters are moving. Second, the ability to release the ball quickly and accurately once a cut has been initiated. Third, the ability to anticipate when a player is going to cut and when he is going to be open. This involves having a sense of how, when and where the cutter wants the ball. Unlike shooting or dodging, it is difficult to get a true feel for feeding outside the game situation. The angles and the interplay of the 13 players on the offensive side of the field cannot be duplicated with one person feeding and one person cutting on the practice field. *[Learning what your teammates like to do and can do will go a long way toward developing a sound team. Lacrosse is a team sport so communication is extremely important.—G. F.]*

Cutting

Probably the most underrated and underused element of an attackman's repertoire is cutting, that is, moving without the ball. The easiest way to score a goal is to free yourself for a wide open shot on the crease. An attackman in a settled situation can execute this move in a variety of ways. First, you can work with the other attackmen, picking and rolling while the ball is on the midfield. Second, after relinquishing possession of the ball, you can initiate a give and go situation. Third, anytime your defenseman leaves to back up or turns his attention away from you, you can go back door.

other attackmen, moved off the ball trying to get open. Only when overplayed did the feeder go to the cage.

Remember that beating a man once or twice without the ball makes him that much

Attack

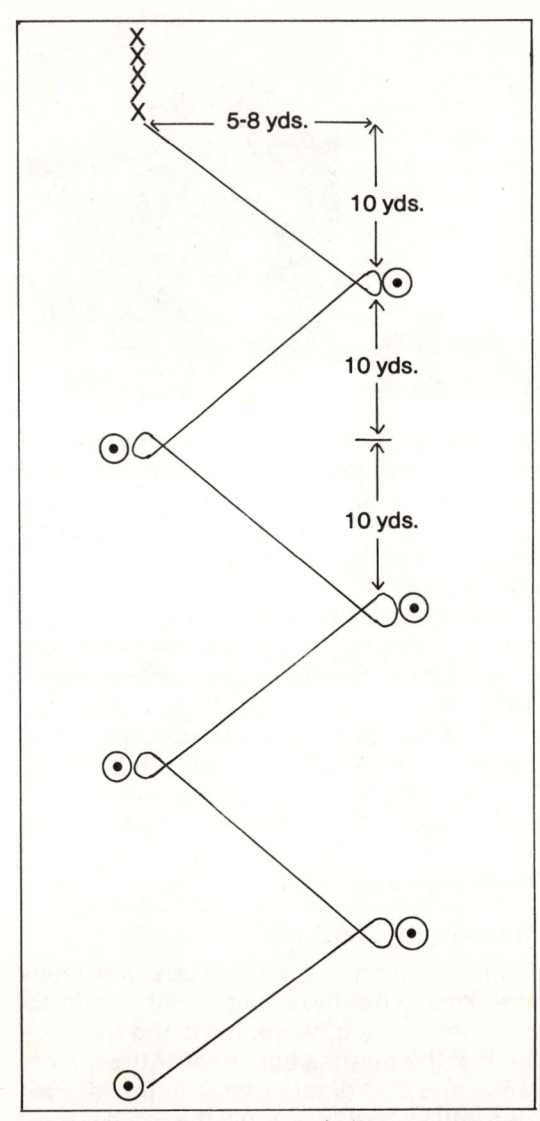

Diagram 4: Back Door Cutting & Give and Go Drill. Ball should change sides after two minutes.

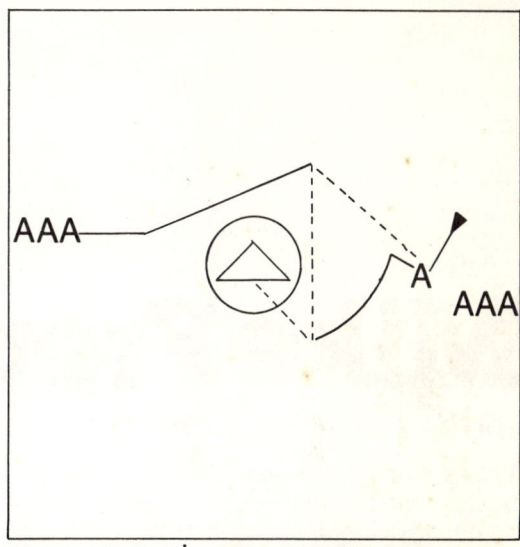

Diagram 5: Cutting & Feeding Drill. After a complete run, move to the opposite side and repeat.

However, Diagrams 4 and 5 illustrate two variations of a drill which will help you improve both your cutting and feeding skills.

Team Play

Lacrosse *is* a team game. An individual's skills must be integrated with the skills and goals of the entire team. Fast breaks, extra man, and 6 on 6 settled offense are all *team* endeavors with individual skills important to their execution. But the individual cannot try to dominate the team without doing irreparable harm to the overall effort.

easier to beat when you have the ball. As with feeding, good cutting skills are acquired by necessity in game situations.

Mike French

EDITOR'S INTRODUCTION

A three-time All-American, Mike is one of the most prolific scorers in NCAA history. He led the country in total points in 1974, 1975 and again in 1976. Evidence of his scoring ability was his outstanding performance in the 1976 Championship Game where he exploded for 7 goals and 4 assists to lead Cornell over Maryland 16–13 in overtime.

This strapping 6'2", 190 lb. attackman, who would like to see lacrosse return to the Olympics permanently, was the quarterback of Richie Moran's Cornell teams. Mike was voted the Best and Fairest player in the 1978 World Championship game after he led his home country, Canada, to their first title since the games began. He's currently working as a management consultant with Laventhol & Horwath, a large CPA firm in Philadelphia, and, in his spare time, working to promote field lacrosse in Canada. He has already been selected to play on the Canadian National Team for 1982.

PLAYER'S INTRODUCTION

Lacrosse has always been my love, and it has opened doors for me to meet tremendous people, many of whom are now my best friends. It also has opened my eyes to opportunities that I was unaware of back home in Canada, opportunities which include business ventures and the chance to travel in Europe, Canada, the United States and Australia.

The people I have met in lacrosse circles are unique. They know the game, enjoy it, and appreciate a good contest. However, most lacrosse people also have diverse interests and are very successful in careers and ventures outside the sport. Talking with lacrosse people has helped tremendously in broadening my horizons and getting me involved in a variety of different interests.

Philosophy of Attack

From the point of view of an individual attackman, his most important job is to coordinate the offense. He is the quarterback of the offense and must settle the offense and coordinate between the attackmen and midfielders. From the team standpoint, his job is to keep the ball moving (in the air because the ball moves faster in the air than on foot). This forces the defense to constantly adjust. [This can't be stressed enough—movement of not only the ball but

YOU.—G. F.] Movement behind the goal also is important, especially if the strength of your team is in crease cutting and midfield cuts. If you have good dodgers in the midfield, then the ball should be relayed out front so picks opposite and isolations can be set up. It is important for an offensive team to thoroughly scent the weaknesses of the opposition so that they can implement an offensive strategy which best takes advantage of those weaknesses.

Control is important; the stick must always be moving. A stationary feeder is subject to any number of defensive checks. The stick should be vertical and protected by the helmet. The attackman must assert himself and take control. Remember that your middies have just played defense; give them a chance to catch their breath. Be patient! Wait for the defender to overcommit. When he does, a drive to the goal will initiate a slide; and, with the double team, an offensive player always will be open for a feed and an unmolested shot on the goal.

Playing Behind

When I have the ball behind the goal, I hold the ball so the middies can time their cuts to the goal. As a quarterback, I call out the offensive plays and coordinate the movement of all the offensive players on the field. I prefer to start plays from a settled situation. (If a play doesn't work, I pull out, and start again.) *[Patience is the hardest thing to learn. It's so tempting to force the ball. Accept that your opponents will shut you down at times. Just regroup and start over.—G. F.]*

Dodging

Before I dodge, I force my defenseman to try to take the ball from me and then take advantage of his commitment by an inside roll or power drive to the cage. Many times I like to encourage my defenseman to try an over the head or wrap check. Going over the head involves a total commitment by the defenseman; and, if he misses, I have a clear passage to the cage for a shot or a slide and feed to the crease.

Driving a defenseman to close quarters at the cage often forces him to wrap. This can give me the option of an inside roll and a drive to the goal for a quick shot.

The most dangerous defenseman is the one who plays physically, yet honestly, without overcommitting himself. It's hard to bait this type of opponent. But a defenseman who gambles, while he may steal the ball occasionally, is often likely to get burned for a goal.

Behind the cage, I keep my defenseman moving with frequent changes of direction to get him off guard. Then I drive inside or outside to the cage.

My favorite move involves driving my defenseman to the outside and then using an inside roll or sweep from out front with an attack-midfield inversion. But each move is unique because how each one goes depends on the sequence of events. I think the important thing for an attackman, or any player for that matter, is to take advantage of defensive lapses and use the right move (fall dodge, roll dodge, etc.) at the right time. Avoid double teams and congestion; control and protect the ball and you will keep the ball. *[As you can see, Mike's move is aimed at counteracting what his defenseman does. This takes a great deal of preparation and thought. Watching various defensemen and seeing what other attackmen do against them will go a long way toward helping you learn what you should do in similar circumstances.—G. F.]*

French

Jeff Wagner

Attack

Feeding

I feed from the right and left hand sides of the cage because if the pass is missed, it can be backed up in the midfield. When I feed, I'm always moving. Never feed standing still. It's too easy for the defense to check you or block the feed. To get free of my defenseman prior to feeding, I use several techniques: constant movement, switching hands to the left, driving to the left and turning back to the right, etc.

Most of my feeds are overhand or sidearm. Perhaps because of my box lacrosse background, I feel that wrist action plays the most important part in passing and shooting. Personally, I feel that passing from the shoulder is most accurate and gives the feeder the best line of sight to his target. *[If you stick with Mike's philosophy and feed overhand, you're certainly better off. I know that at times you will have to feed side arm or underhand. Remember, it takes an experienced player to see such feeds coming and then to be able to catch them.—G.F.]*

I'm always looking for the cutter! However, it is up to the cutter to time his cut to the cage so that he cuts when I have a step on my defenseman and am moving toward the front of the goal. You should feed to a passing zone, especially if you know the cutter, his strong hand, and where he likes the feed for the quick stick.

Most unsuccessful feeds can be traced to impatience, forcing the ball, not keeping the stick up so the cutter can see where the feed is coming from, or failure to keep moving when feeding.

Playing Off the Ball

When a middie has possession of the ball, break in and break out for the ball. Don't get in the way of the ball carrier because you don't want to double team him. If a one on one situation occurs and the middie dodges his man, be prepared for the defenseman to double team. Go *back door* and call for the pass. Then drive to the cage.

If another attackman has the ball, rotate with the third attackman, moving to the crease and picking to free the crease attackman so he's open for a feed and shot. Or, set picks and flips behind the goal to ensure that the ball is always moving. Don't stand still and wait for the feeder behind to make his move—create an opportunity or scoring situation.

If you've just passed off to a teammate, break away from the ball to an open area or to the cage (give and go) or set picks for the crease attackman or the middies. You may also break to the attackman for the return pass or flip. Create confusion but don't get caught in a double team. Break in and break out.

Shooting

When I shoot, I don't aim at any particular area of the cage. What I do is shoot for the area where the goalie isn't. It's a big net, and there is lots of open area. The best shot is a low bounce to the opposite side of the goalie's stick. (This is a good shot on both natural and artificial turf.)

Don't give the goalkeeper the opportunity to use his stick. Waist high shots are effective also, especially on the bounce. I don't fake a shot unless I'm in a one on one situation. A fake usually takes up too much time and causes you to get checked. So, don't measure it, waffle it. (In a one on one situation, I fake to draw the goalie out of position. But there is usually enough goal area open that a fake isn't really necessary.) *[Mike played box lacrosse for 10 years, so when he says it's a big net, he's used to shoot-*

French

ing at a 4' by 4' goal. Naturally, a 6' by 6' looks tremendous. How would you feel if you suddenly were in a game where the goal was 8' by 8'? Do you think it would make scoring a little easier?—G. F.]

My favorite shooting style is sidearm because I feel it gives me the advantage of (1) shooting around the goaltender when in close and (2) shooting around a defender while on the move which catches the goalie off guard and often allows me to use the defender as a screen. I shoot whenever I can. But there is no 30-second clock, so be patient and wait for the best shot. If a teammate has a better opportunity, dump off to him.

Cutting & Picking

I usually cut from in front of the cage. I try to run my defender into a screen or pick in the crease area and then cut off in the opposite direction, left or right. I like to cut when the feeder is driving toward the cage for two reasons: (1) he has a better idea of my position, and (2) my man may try to slide and double team, leaving me unmolested.

When picking, always remain stationary. Don't move for your teammate with the ball; it is up to him to run his man off of your tail. Try to pick or set a stationary screen where your teammate can see you but his defender cannot. Picks behind the goal, with the person setting the pick cutting from behind for a feed and shot, are a good way to create confusion for the two defensemen involved. (See Diagram 1.) In this diagram, the defensive players are not sure whether they should switch or fight off the pick. At that moment of confusion, the man off the ball makes a strong cut to the cage. He will be open for a feed and shot. Keep the head of your stick close to your body when you pick. That way you'll always be ready to help out in case of a double team.

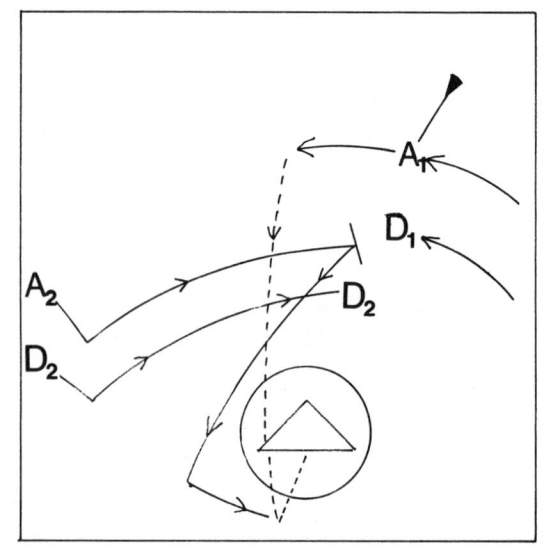

Diagram 1

My favorite play involves working off flips and picks behind with the three attackmen always rotating. (See Diagram 2.) This basic rotation was what Jon Levine, Eamon McEneaney and I concentrated on during every practice and used effectively in our games. The play proved especially effective in NCAA playoffs. All three men act as feeder, pickman and shooter; no one man performs just one task. (Sometimes we added midfield cuts and sweeps to give us additional options.)

Role of the Coach

Attitude is probably the most important part of the game. And I believe (especially in a team sport) that the coach is the key. As far as I am concerned, Richie Moran is the best coach I've ever played for in any sport. He is one hundred percent behind his players, both on and off the field—and it's what he does off the field or when you're not affiliated with lacrosse that makes him

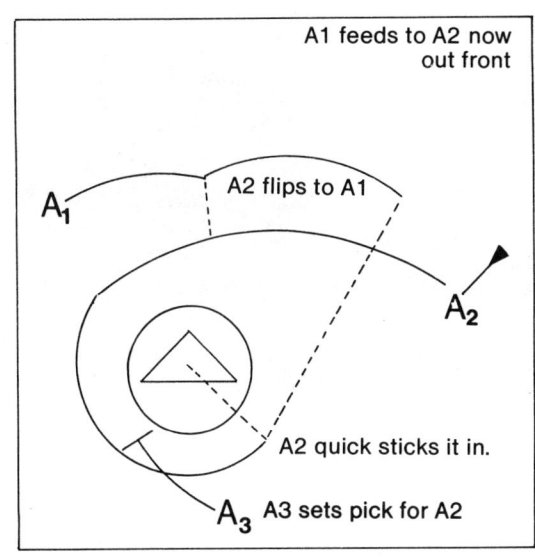

Diagram 2

- A1 feeds to A2 now out front
- A2 flips to A1
- A2 quick sticks it in.
- A3 sets pick for A2

so respected. He prepares harder and works harder than any of his players for each game, and it makes you want to work harder.

In my mind, a coach's attitude is a team's best motivator. I have been with Richie in both victory and defeat, and *never* have I seen a more humble winner or a more gracious loser. The right coach can convey his attitudes to his team and create a special closeness. When this occurs, regardless of how much talent you have, and when you feel the guys on your team are like your brothers, a cohesiveness results that makes you invulnerable.

Future of Lacrosse

I hope to see the game spread to other sections of the U.S. and get more national exposure. I think (and I certainly hope) that the field game will not go professional. However, professional box lacrosse might be a future possibility if the rules are moderated and compromised to make it universally acceptable, if it is promoted stressing the skill and finesse involved rather than the roughness and physical demands, and if it's played in air conditioned indoor facilities at a time of year when it does not have to compete against already popular summer or fall sports.

As for the field game, I assume there will be rule changes and different strategies. I hope that the game can be sped up in a manner that will not eliminate any of its most attractive characteristics (man-up and man-down plays).

I would like to predict that lacrosse will spread internationally with the ultimate result that it becomes a *permanent Olympic sport.* I do not think I'll ever forgive my home country, Canada, for not having its national sport as even an exhibition sport in the 1976 Olympics.

Gene Fusting

Dallas Weigel

EDITOR'S INTRODUCTION

Gene Fusting started playing in high school as a sophomore while attending Baltimore's Boys Latin School. He was named All-Maryland in his Junior and Senior years as a midfielder. He went on to star as an attackman for Washington College, where he led the country (NCAA) in total points scored. In 1967, he represented the United States in the World Championship Games.

Gene has both played and coached club lacrosse. He presently serves on the United States Coaches Association's Executive Committee. He's played in every North-South Club All-Star game and was voted the Most Valuable Player in the 1972 game. The record he set in that game for individual points scored (6 goals and 4 assists) still stands.

For the last several years, in addition to selling life insurance, he has been coaching the Mt. Washington Lacrosse Club. Gene was named Coach of the Year for 1977. This former All-American has played or coached in 10 championship games, eight of them on the winning side during his 13 seasons of club ball.

Playing Attack

During my career, I've seen many players who had natural ability, who were very competitive and even had tremendous spirit. But they lacked two crucial skills and so never became exceptional players. These two skills are field vision and knowing what to do when you don't have the ball.

If you can master these two points and accurately catch and throw, not only will you become an exceptional player, but you'll have more fun. And that's what lacrosse is all about.

These two skills are important no matter what position you play, but here we'll concentrate on offense. Good field vision means total awareness, knowing where every player on the field is at all times and being able to anticipate their every move. The player with the ball must know what his other five offensive men are doing—who's cutting, who's picking, what the defense is doing, where the goalie is, who's open for a pass, whether there's a back up, etc.

The second important skill, playing without the ball, will be covered in more detail. For now, remember that to be a really ex-

21
Attack

Keating

Fusting

ceptional player you have to BE AWARE and KEEP MOVING.

In order to have an effective and exciting offense, you need to learn when and how to move. This means moving the ball and, more importantly, moving yourself. You must always be trying to create an offensive situation, either through preplanned or freelance play or countering, or taking advantage of a defensive mistake or maneuver.

Let's set up an offensive situation and discuss the various movements of each player to see how these two basic skills are important in real playing situations. We want the man with the ball to have the option of either dodging, feeding, passing or throwing an outlet pass. The men without the ball have their jobs cut out for them also. They must know how and where to cut, pick, be open for an outlet pass, and keep their defensemen from backing up on the man with the ball. In Diagram 1, A3 starts with the ball. He passes to A1. Any time you move the ball, you still want to be dangerous. Remember this rule, "You throw, you go!" When you pass to a teammate, all eyes are focused on the ball transfer. This is the best psychological moment for you to break into a more advantageous position to receive a return pass.

Let's look at each player's option. Following our rule, A3, having passed the ball, must move from his present position. Where should he go?

A3: Seeing A1 come toward him, A3's first option is to cut across the crease. This does two things. It takes his defenseman out of the way of A1, who is coming around, and it creates an offensive threat. A3's defenseman now has to make a decision. If he stays to help back up, A3 will cut behind him and get an easy feed from A1. If he goes with A3, then there is no back-up. His uncertainty creates an offensive advantage. It is all made possible by A3 cutting across. If A3 had stayed where he was, he would have made it easy for his defenseman because A3's defenseman could guard his man and back up at the same time.

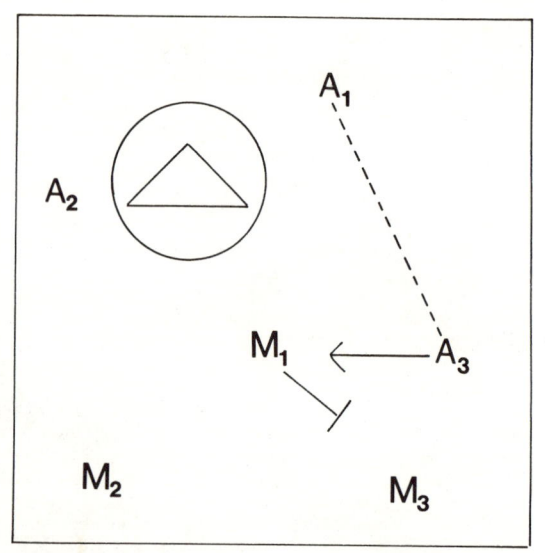

Diagram 1

A3's other options on this play include picking for A1, picking for M1, or faking going across the crease and then coming back and picking for M3. In our example, let's move A3 across the crease. Since M1 already is on the crease, A3 will clear all the way through.

I should note here that whenever it's possible, get your defenseman moving in a direction *opposite* to that which you plan to go. This rule is especially important when you're cutting or picking for a teammate. It will make your defenseman work harder and make him think only of you. Done properly, he won't be able to back up and it will be easy to pick him off because he's so busy concentrating on you, he won't see the pick coming. As you're reading what follows, assume that you'll do this each time you make a move.

A2: Notice that A2 is not behind the goal. The weakside attackman (the one on the opposite side of the goal from the ball) should stay up around the pipes because his defenseman is taught to stay up to help back-up. In this position, A2 can either break in front or behind for the ball. In our example, A2, seeing A1 going around the goal and A3 coming across, must move. He must go behind the goal for two reasons. First and most importantly to back up the goal, and second to be in a position to catch an outlet pass from A1.

M1: If the ball is out front, M1 should screen or pick for someone low. If the ball is behind, he should pick for someone out front. As A1 receives the ball, M1 starts moving out to pick for either M2 or M3, keeping an eye on A3, who may pick for him. Drifting out will make it easier for A3 to pick, because M1's defenseman will have to go with M1 and won't be able to see the pick coming. In our diagram, M1 picks for M3 as A3 goes across.

M3: M3 sees M1 coming out and picking. M3 then knows he has to cut. He will exercise one of three basic options, depending on what the defense does or what he can get his defenseman to do. (As we discuss each of M3's options from the point of view of M3, also consider them as if you were the feeder.)

M3—Option 1: The first thing M3 wants to do is see what his defenseman is going to do. Is he playing too far off him? Is he turning his head too much? In our example, M3 should realize that M1's defenseman is going to tell his defenseman to "watch the pick" causing M3's defenseman to stand behind M1 and wait for the cut. So M3 acts as if he's going to cut hard but, as he reaches the pick, he stops, jumps back, takes the feed, and shoots. (See Diagram 1a.)

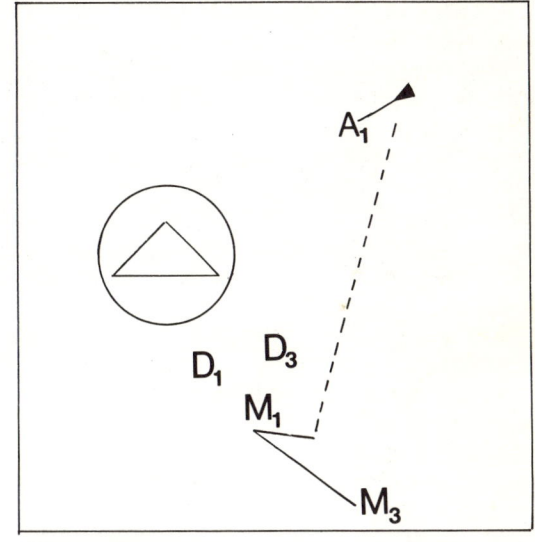

Diagram 1a

M3—Option 2: Here M3's defenseman is playing M3 above the pick so M3 fakes cutting left but breaks right, making sure his shoulder rubs his teammate (M1) to prevent his defenseman from getting past. (Diagram 1b.)

M3—Option 3: This is the reverse of Option 2. M3 cuts right and comes back left looking for the feed inside. This presents a problem, doesn't it? If M3 goes inside, then D1 may switch off his man and play the cutter. The offense must turn this into an advantage. They can do it by having M1 cut straight down to the goal. (See Diagram 1c.) The key here is that D3 is *behind* M1, making it easier for M1 to cut. (After all, the whole object of picking and cutting is to get the defensive man behind you.)

In addition to these basic options, M1 could have picked for M2, giving M2 the same set of options. After a cutter goes by, M1 replaces him because if M1 stays in, he would clog up the middle.

M2: If M1's option was to pick for M2, M2

Fusting

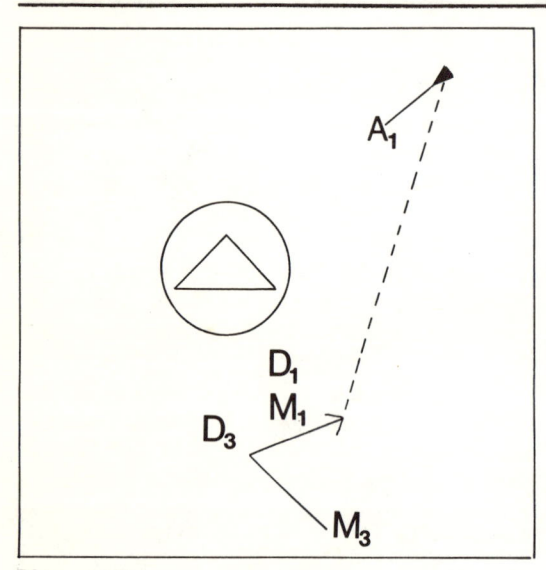

Diagram 1b

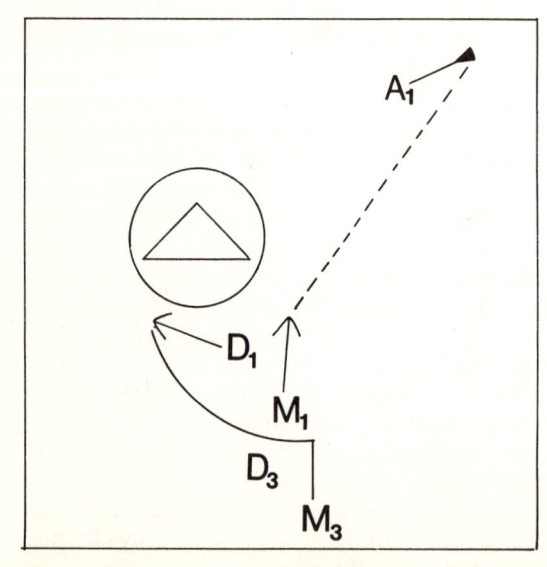

Diagram 1c

would have the same options as M3 had. Since M1 picked for M3, M2 has his job cut out for him. He has to get into a position to back up the feed by moving over to his right. He also will be an outlet pass for A1.

You can see that every player without the ball has made a real contribution to the offense. Now, let's discuss the man with the ball, A1.

A1: After A1 receives the ball, his first look should be to the man who threw it to him in case he's open for a shot at the goal. If A3 isn't open, what options are available? A1 could dodge. A3 has taken his man out of the back-up position and M1 also moved, pulling his defenseman away from the ball.

A1 could feed. He could feed to A3, who is cutting across. He could feed to M1, if A3 picked for him. He could feed to M2, if M1 picked for him. Or, he could feed to M3, if M1 picked for him.

Because his teammates are moving and not standing still, the man with the ball has plenty of scoring opportunities. If A1 doesn't have a play, he can release it to his outlet—A2 breaking behind the goal or M2 breaking to his right out front.

Let's take a look at the total picture on this play. Our objective was to have total movement; everyone doing something to create a good offensive situation. Everyone is involved, not just the ball carrier. Because of this movement, the man with the ball always has the option of throwing to one of his teammates.

We've kept our offense in complete balance. The players are in the same formation in which they started, except that the individual players have shifted. (See Diagram 1d.) We can continue this movement in any direction (and should do so) to keep the defensive players moving, not giving them a chance to get set up or be able to back up.

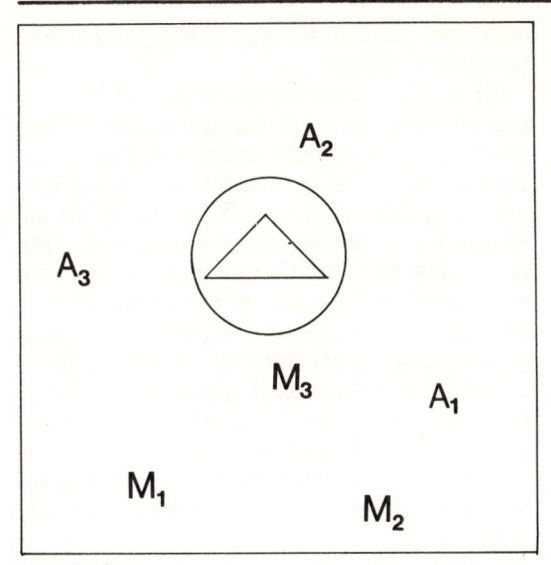

Diagram 1d

Involving everyone in the action makes for exciting lacrosse. The short, precise passing which this concept encourages will instill additional confidence in the offensive team. You will be where you want to be—utilizing a total team concept.

The offensive situation we've been discussing shows every possible move. Review again each player's move to see why he did what he did. Imagine yourself at each position, and see what you would do in each case.

Now that you have an idea of what to do when you don't have the ball, let's go over some individual techniques to use when you are in possession of the ball. This is important because your team can't progress unless you learn how to get and keep the ball.

Shooting

Shooting is a skill that can and should be mastered by every player. And the key to being a good shooter is to KNOW WHEN TO SHOOT AND WHERE TO SHOOT. How hard you can shoot is important, but I've seen many shooters who stood outside and fired one shot after the other *over* the goal. Learning to be accurate will make you more of a threat than being a strong but inaccurate shooter. (Ultimate perfection, of course, is a result of both strength and accuracy.) In addition, you need to master a variety of different shots so you can vary your delivery depending on the circumstances.

The present day stick is getting lighter and lighter all the time, but so is your defenseman's, making it easier for him to wrap you, go over your head, intercept a feed, check you, pick up a loose ball, and poke. In addition, more and more teams will go to a zone defense from time to time making double teaming more effective. But even if you beat the field defensemen, you still have to get the ball past the goalie. And it seems that every year there are more and more good ones.

Let's take it from the top. The first thing you must learn is to protect your stick from your defenseman. The way to do this is to "choke-up" on your stick. If you are playing right handed, hold your hand anywhere from the throat of the stick to between three or four inches down. Slide your bottom (left) hand to within 10 or 12 inches of your top hand. (See Figure 1.) There are some excellent reasons for this rather untraditional method of holding the stick:

1. It can give your feeder a better target to aim at.
2. It's easier to catch bad feeds.
3. It lets you use your body as a shield between your defenseman and your stick.
4. Your shooting will be more accurate.
5. It makes it easier to play with your weak hand.

Fusting 26

Traditional Grip   Fusting "Choke" Grip

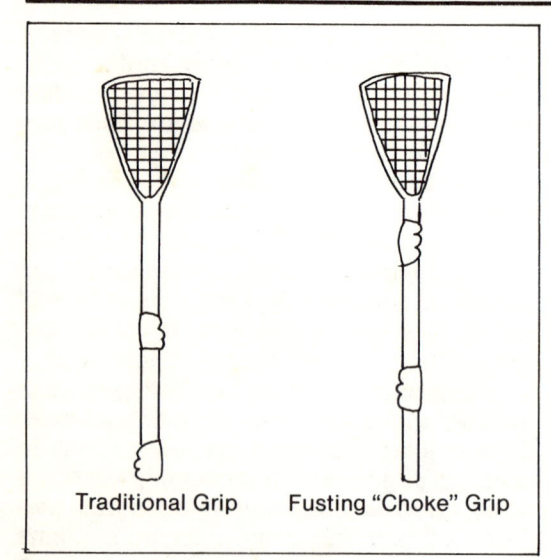

Figure 1

Let's discuss each of these five points.

Good Target: As you cut, hold your stick upright. This gives the feeder an excellent target right above your shoulder. You may think the feeder would have the same target if you held your stick in the traditional method (bottom hand on the butt end of the stick). This is true, but the problem with the traditional grip is that even if you beat your man on a cut, his long defense stick can check you. Holding the stick close to your body makes this more difficult because less of the stick is exposed above your shoulder.

Bad Feed: Most feeds will be bad. If you know this ahead of time and plan on it, you'll be prepared. If the feed is thrown on the opposite side of your body and you're holding your stick conventionally, you'll find it virtually impossible to catch the ball. But if you've choked up on your stick, you'll find it's very easy to bring the stick across your face, catch the ball, bring it back, and be able to shoot.

Using Your Body as a Screen: This is my favorite move and although it takes much practice, anyone can master it. Choke up on your stick; but, instead of holding it at your side, move your left arm (playing left handed) behind you. Twist your body slightly so it's between your stick and your defenseman. The secret of this move is to not move a muscle until the ball is past your defenseman and almost to you. Don't telegraph the move with your body movements. You can see you don't have much time to react. The other thing to be careful about is your eyes; they're a dead giveaway and guess who knows it—your defenseman. Watch any shooter; his eyes automatically open wider when the ball comes toward him. You must learn to control your facial expression as the ball comes to you.

When you catch the ball, let the defenseman check you before you shoot. (He's going to anyway—either he saw you catch the ball or he heard his goalie yell "check.") What usually happens is that a player catches the ball and thinks he has to shoot right away. As he shoots, his defenseman checks him. This is why most shots never get to the goal. But, since you know the defenseman is going to check you anyway, you're going to let him do it. After he does it and misses (because your stick is still behind you), he'll do it again. But, in order for him to do it again, he has to pull his stick back to get enough power to blast you. As he pulls back his stick, you shoot. (You may think this procedure is a lot different than you're used to. However, if you think about it, it's the same thing you would do if you were behind the goal and were checked. In that case, you protect your stick and, when your defenseman pulls his stick off you, you feed.)

The real advantage of letting your defenseman check you before you shoot is that it forces you to take your time. Always remember this: YOU HAVE MORE TIME TO SHOOT THAN YOU THINK. The only way you're going to see how much time you do have is in practice. Deliberately try to hold the ball before you shoot. See how much time you really do have. (Another second, right?) Even if you're surrounded, you have more time than you think.

Controlling Your Shot: How many times have you seen a player catch a feed and be so close to the goal that he can't shoot? How many times does a shooter try to jam the ball past the goalie only to see the goalie nonchalantly catch the ball? Why does this happen? Because the shooter is holding his stick in the traditional grip and, when he shoots, the ball in the stick is being held so high over the goal that he can't get it in unless it's an absolutely perfect shot. Using my "choked up" method, the stick is low (shoulder high) after you catch the ball. Taking your time, pick your spot in the goal and, using your wrists, let it go. When you shoot this type of shot "punch" with your top hand and pull (toward your body) with your bottom hand to give you a quick release. After you shoot, pull your stick back instead of following through. The end result is much like cracking a whip.

If you find yourself too far in after you cut, don't run out with the ball, thinking you don't have a shot. Make one fake with your stick to freeze the goalie and the defense. (When you're in so close, the defenseman will think you're going to quick stick, especially if you fake. Many times he won't follow through with a check.) Now, take two or three steps backward toward the midfield to give yourself a better angle. Look at the goalie's leg (he'll be holding his stick high) and shoot anywhere between his waist and his ankles.

Weak Hand: If you are a strong right handed player, playing choked up will allow you to develop a good left hand in a matter of minutes. Think of the head of the stick as if it were a baseball glove. (After all, right handed baseball players always catch with the left hand.) Put your left hand all the way up at the throat of the stick, just as if you had a baseball glove on your left hand. If the ball is thrown high on your stick side while you're choked up, simply loosen up on your top hand and let the handle of the stick slide through while you're pushing up with your bottom hand.

When to Shoot

SHOOT WHEN *YOU'RE* READY. I can't emphasize this enough. When you shoot, make sure you do it when you want to; you don't have to force it or quick stick every time you get a feed. You should have a full second after every cut. The key is learning to protect your stick to make sure you get that extra second.

Shooting After a Check: After a defenseman has checked you, he will pull his stick off before he hits you again. Shoot when he pulls off. Some defensemen will come at you with their body, but, if so, they'll have to come on your stick side. If this happens, roll the opposite way (with your back to the goal) and either shoot backhand or change hands and shoot low.

Goalie's Eyes: When you are out front or on the side and dodging, feeding, or ready to pass off, make sure you know where the goalie is. Sometimes he will be screened

Fusting

either intentionally by your teammate or unintentionally by his own defenseman. Look for his eyes. If you can't see them, he can't see you. Let it go.

Goalie Turns His Head: The goalie's job is to know where every player is at all times. He directs his team. Frequently, I've seen the goalie take his eyes off the man with the ball because he thinks you are too far out to shoot or have a bad angle. As he's checking the other players' positions, fire.

I remember one of the best examples of this I've ever seen. It was during a Mt. Washington-Chesapeake game. Attackman Joe Cowan had just beaten two midfielders to a loose ball. The middies, seeing Joe was too far out (he was about 15 yards from the side line) turned their backs on him and dropped in to play defense. Cowan looked at the goalie and, noticing that he was checking up getting his defense ready, fired. The ball rifled over the goalie's shoulders. The look on the goalie's face was one of unbelief. This was one of the best shots I've ever seen. It wasn't *where* Joe shot it but *when* he shot that counted.

Shooting When Defensemen Slide

This is an excellent time to shoot. All defensemen practice sliding and backing up on the offensive player if one of their men gets beat. Take advantage of it. As you come in for the shot, the goalie directs his defense to slide to pick you up. The defenseman comes rushing at you. The goalie has really helped you by creating a screen for you. As the defenseman charges, hold your stick so the goalie can't see its head. (Whether you hold your stick side arm, three quarters, or over hand will depend on the position of the onrushing defenseman.) When the defenseman is in a straight line with the *head* of your stick and the goalie, take a step toward the goal and, at the last possible moment, shoot around the defenseman (but as close to him as possible in order to use as much of the screen as you can). On this type of shot, I prefer to aim anywhere from the goalie's ribs on down. Since the goalie has his stick high it's hard for him to stop a low ball when he only sees it coming at the last second.

Now, I know what you're thinking, "Here's this 6'3" locomotive coming at me, and you want me casually to take my time when I shoot." That's right! That's exactly what I want you to do. However, after you shoot, hold your stick perpendicular across your chest. If the defenseman continues to come at you (most of them will), jump into the air as he hits you. The defenseman may force you back two or three feet, but at least you'll still be standing up.

Shooting on Unsettled Situations

There will be times when you have the ball behind the goal and your defenseman is in front. You're in a feeding position, and, since you're not covered, you have to force the play. To do so, you have to come around. As you come, you want your opponent thinking you're going to feed, so hold your stick in your normal feeding position. Then the defense will have to freeze because they all know that if one of them charges, you'll simply drop the ball to your open teammate for an easy goal. As you're coming around, you're almost walking. Defensemen know that attackmen don't walk around the goal to score, but that's what you'll be doing. As you come, eventually you'll be in a position where you are on a line with the pipes. At this point, fake a feed to hold the defense for a split second more.

Attack

Then, take a quick step inside toward the goal. Watch the goalie's legs and let it go. This same play can be done on extra man offense. Some teams play a zone defense and don't send their defensemen behind the goal, making it five on five out front. In this case *you* must force the action since you're the extra man.

Shooting When the Goalie Overcommits

You must learn to capitalize on the goalie's weaknesses. Even the best ones, especially in the excitement of the game, will make a mistake. You have to learn where he is at all times, particularly on fast breaks and unsettled situations. Here are two examples.

Example 1: You receive the ball and you're the man who's going to shoot. The goalie knows this; and, since he may charge you, you must be prepared. Before you ever receive the ball, though, you must know where the goalie is. As soon as you receive the ball, turn your head to see what he's going to do. (Remember, you're protecting your stick with your body.) If the goalie is almost on you, he will be coming stick on stick. (Don't fake; you won't have time.) At the last possible second, drop your stick and shoot underhand right by his legs. It's almost impossible for a goalie running full speed with his stick up to drop his stick all the way down when you shoot low. The trick is to get as close as possible to him before shooting.

Example 2: Sometimes a goalie will come out by mistake and then hesitate. He knows he's overcommitted but he's not sure what to do. (He shouldn't have come out because you were too far away.) Take your time; pull him farther out, and lob the ball over his head.

Shooting In Close

When you're coming in hard from the side or have just dodged using an inside roll, the two things to look for before shooting are the goalie's stick and his legs. If you're coming left handed, look at the goalie's right leg. As you're coming in, he will step toward you with that foot. When he steps, fire. There is absolutely no way he can get the ball. Even if he doesn't step toward you, use the same shot. (See Diagram 2.)

After you master this maneuver, you will want to learn a technique that I almost guarantee will mean that you'll never miss this shot. As you're shooting (still playing left handed), twist your stick so the head turns completely over. This will put "spin" on the ball which makes the shot curve and also makes it bounce very high. When you

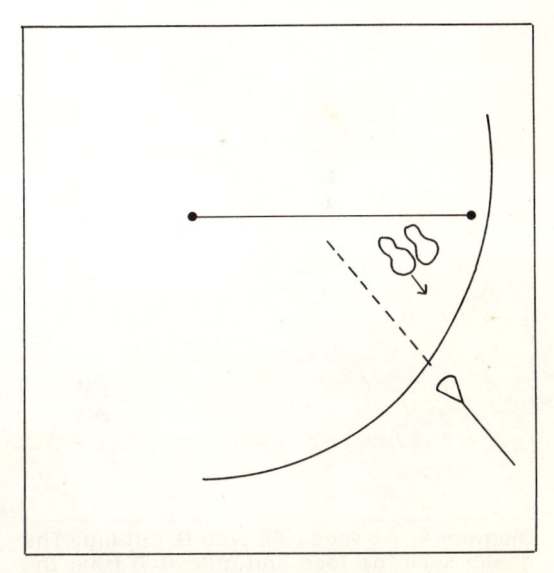

Diagram 2: (Looking straight down on the goal) Shoot as the goalie steps toward you. Aim from his knees on down.

Fusting

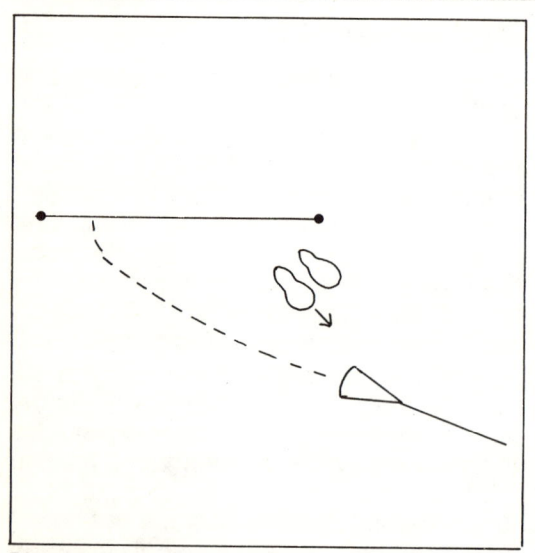

Diagram 3: Bounce Shot: Spin causes ball to curve after hitting ground.

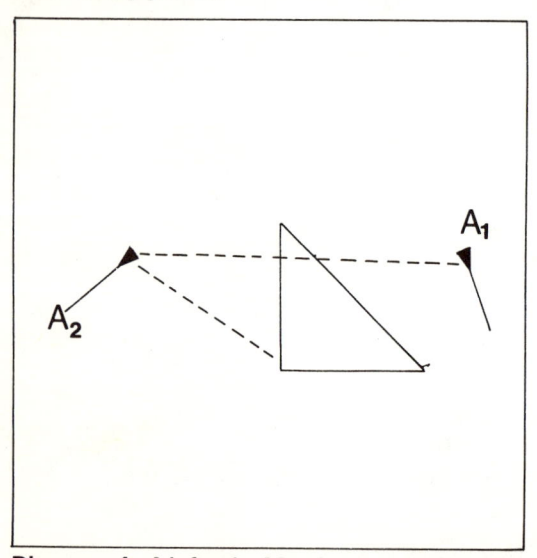

Diagram 4: A1 feeds A2 who is cutting. The goalie sees the feed and follows it from the feeder's stick to the cutter's. The goalie's stick will be the same height as the ball. To stop the goalie from making an easy save or throwing the ball into his stick, A2 shoots low. Remember: Always shoot on an opposite plane.

shoot, the ball curves back into the goal instead of missing the goal as it would if it had been a straight shot. Once you master this, the goalie can have perfect position on you and feel certain you can't get it by him only to wonder how you managed to score. (See Diagram 3.)

Another advantage of a spin shot is that the spin causes the ball to rise as it travels through the air. Thus, when the goalie sees you're going low, he moves down into position only to watch the ball sail over his shoulder into the cage.

Where Not to Shoot

Many times you'll see a player shoot the ball hard only to have the goalie catch it and look like a hero. To avoid this, there is one rule to follow: *Don't shoot on the same plane that you received the ball on.* For example, if you receive the ball from the feeder shoulder high, don't shoot shoulder high. The goalie has followed the feed from the feeder's stick to yours. His stick will be exactly the same height as the ball. Therefore, always shoot on an opposite plane; in this case, shoot low. (Diagram 4.)

Cutting

Now that you can protect your stick and catch the ball under pressure, you must learn how to cut. The best time to cut is when your defenseman turns his head to see where the ball is. The problem is that while *you* may be open, the man with the ball isn't ready to feed you. But there are some cutting techniques that will buy you some time so you can stay open until you can get the ball. Keep in mind that it takes much patience and practice to become a good cutter; you must learn not only *how* to cut but *where* and *when* to cut.

Diagram 5

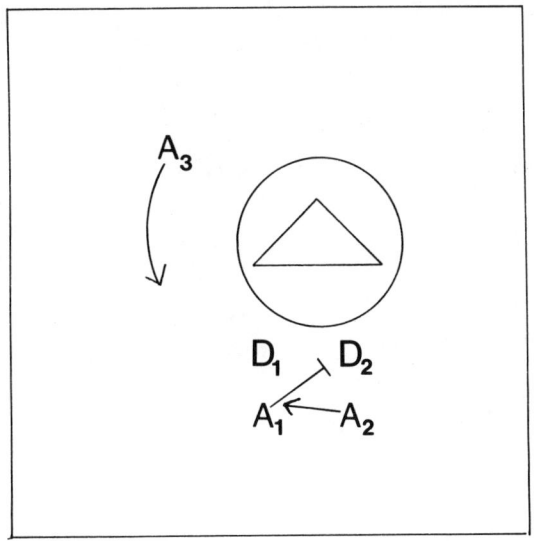

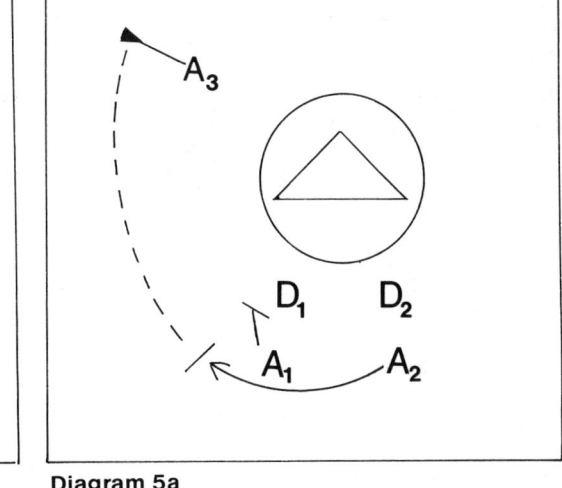

Diagram 5a

Let's start with an example in which you are the cutter. (Also see what you would do if you set the pick.) A3 has the ball and is coming around; A1 will want to pick. The most common mistake is that A1 picks D2. If this happens, A2 cuts to the ball only to be checked by D1. (See Diagram 5.) The correct move is for A1 to pick D1. When he does, A2 has two men picking for him (A1 and D1) because now D2 can't get through. As shown in Diagram 5a, D1 has unintentionally blocked his own man.

Bad Cuts

Learn to take advantage of a middie making a bad cut. For example, you are on the crease and go out to pick for the middie. He cuts by you and so does his man. Always act as if, when the behind attackman feeds the ball, he is really throwing to you. Even though in Diagram 6 A1 is feeding M1, think he's throwing to you. Then you'll get

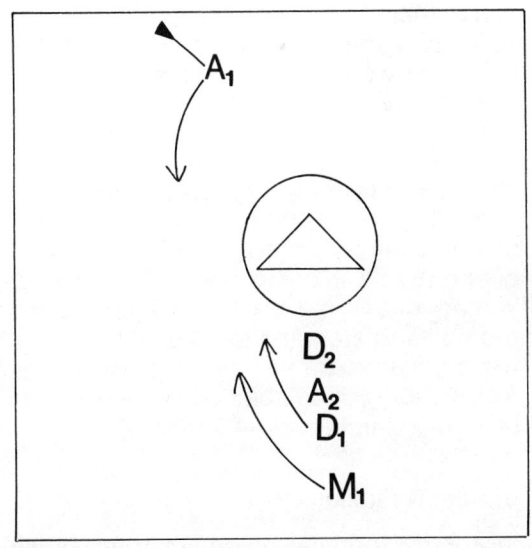

Diagram 6

Fusting

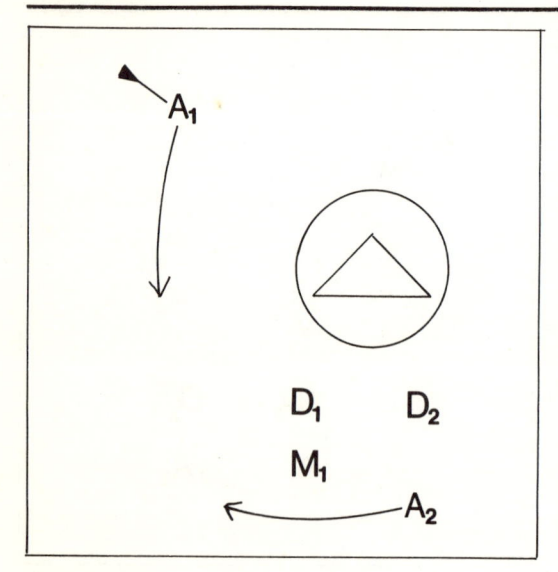

Diagram 6a

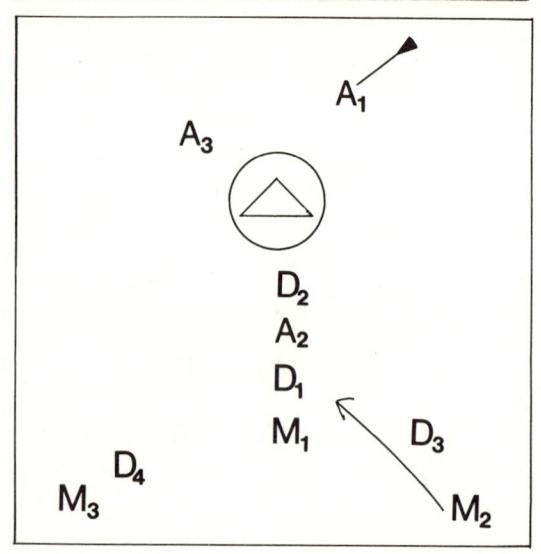

Diagram 7

yourself in position to receive the pass after M1 has cut by you. Diagram 6a shows A2 stepping left after D1 and M1 go by. If D1 checks M1's stick or it's a bad feed, you're there to receive the pass. (This is the same play that we just ran in which D1 is forced to pick off his own teammate, D2. See Diagrams 5 and 5a.)

Once D2 is blocked, you pop out for the feed. You'll be surprised how many easy shots you can get this way even though you weren't the intended shooter. Many coaches will tell you to go the other way (to cut right) and, in some cases, it may be advantageous to cut right. But, by watching the ball and stepping left, you'll help your team get an extra five or ten goals a year. All because you're able to take advantage of a very simple screen strategy!

Cutting & Picking

In a 2-2-2 formation (see Diagram 7), we can create many scoring situations by

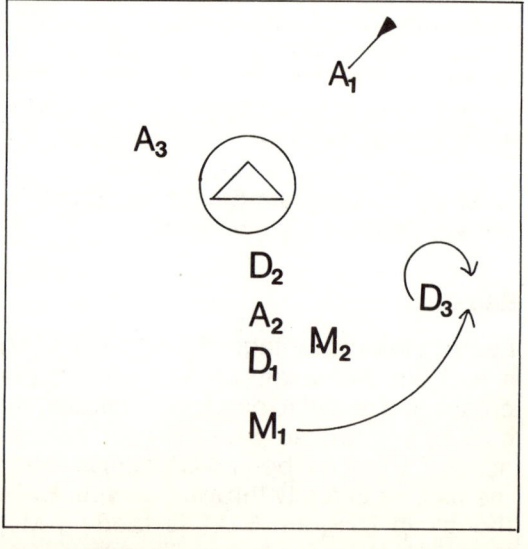

Diagram 7a

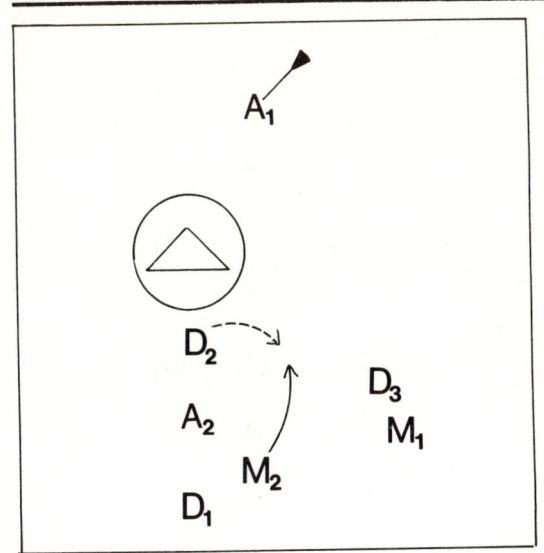

Diagram 7b

Diagram 7c

taking advantage of any switching that the defense may do. In Diagram 7a, M2 is going to pick for M1, so he runs and stops right next to D1. As he does, M1 comes right handed for the feed. This looks like an easy set up, but D3 will switch to keep M1 from making a sure goal. The key is the positioning of M2. M2 is being played by D1; but where is D1? Behind him! So, when M1 cuts and sees D3 switching on to him, he goes wide. M2, now with his man behind him, cuts for the feed. (Diagram 7b.) If D3 tries to get back to M2, M1 will still be in a position to shoot. But what if D2 slides over and takes him? That's okay because A2 can cut straight down or to the back side. (Diagram 7c.) There isn't anyone to stop him because D1 is still behind him.

Let's set up another offense utilizing the pick. In Diagram 8, we'll use a 2-2-2 offset. Here M1 throws to A2. M1 breaks hard and runs right to A3's defenseman and stops.

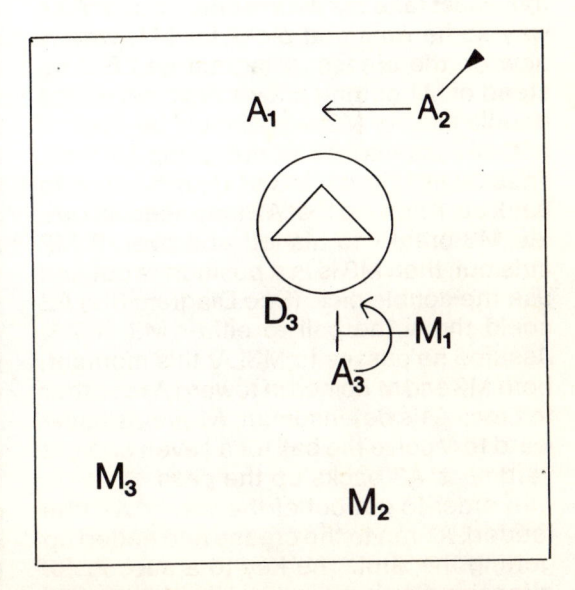

Diagram 8

Fusting

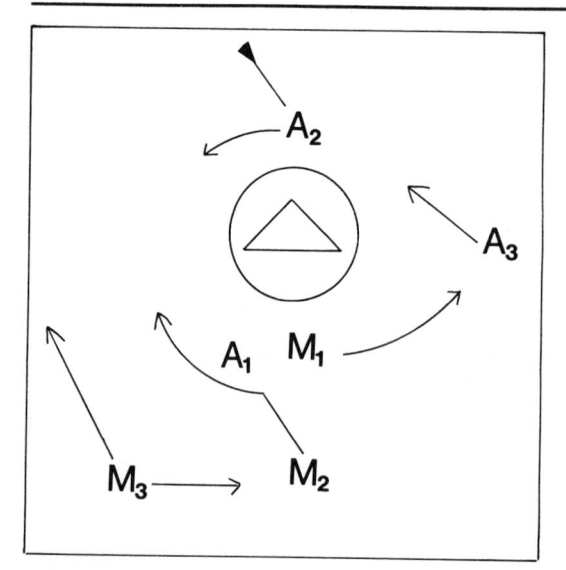

Diagram 8a

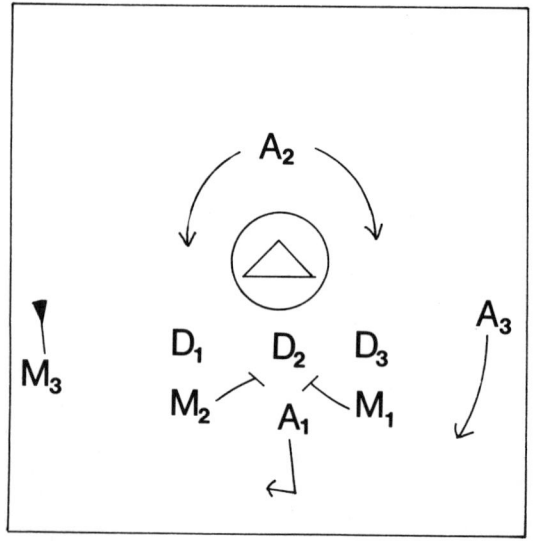

Diagram 8b

A3 cuts and looks for the ball. Let's assume that this is covered. He then clears out and A2 starts to his right. A1, seeing this, must take his defenseman out of A2's way so he runs and picks for M1, who is now on the crease. (Diagram 8a.) But instead of M1 cutting off, we have set a nice double pick for M2, who should be open. If not, M2, seeing A2 is not going to feed, lines up next to A1. M3's first move was to back up. Knowing that A2 may need an outlet, M3 breaks to his left and over. If M2 cuts out, then M3 is in a position to cut and use the double pick. (See Diagram 8b.) A2 could throw the ball to either M3 or A3. Assume he passes to M3. At this moment, both M2 and M1 pinch in toward A1 in order to block A1's defenseman. A1 jumps backward to receive the ball for a seven or eight yard shot. A3 backs up the pass.

In order to get out of the way of A2 (the feeder), A1 ran to the crease and ended up getting the shot. The key to a successful offensive play is movement. If A1 had stayed where he was, the entire play would have failed through lack of teamwork.

It may seem that the crease is crowded with three offensive players on it, but it seems to happen so often that you should learn to take advantage of it. Remember that each defenseman is taught to play in a triangle formation (ball—his man—goal), so none of them will be in a position to stop this play. In addition, your shot is coming off a double pick, making it impossible for the defenseman to get through.

In a well-balanced, total movement offense, the man with the ball at times can't see who is open or what may be happening. You should designate another man who is more removed from the action to call out some kind of code that tells the man with the ball what's happening. This will let the ball carrier move the ball faster and disconcert the defense. In Diagram 8b, M3 and A3 can see the play developing faster than A2; either one could serve as the caller.

Attack

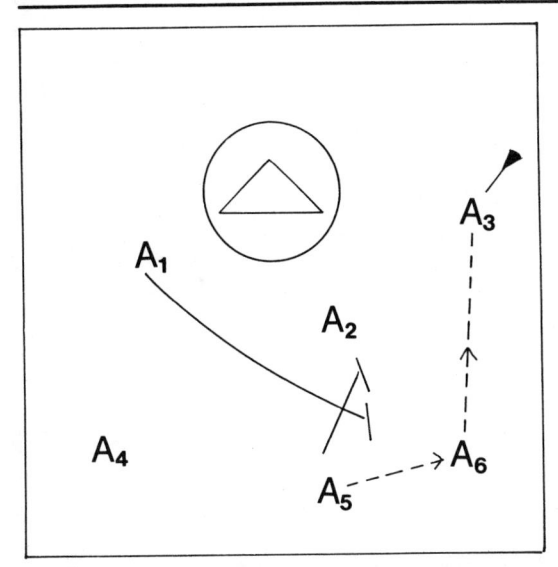

Diagram 9: Positions on this play—A3 has the ball; A2 is on the pipe, looking for the ball; A1 is cutting and forcing his defenseman to get on the side of the ball; A5 is cutting down to the ball, forcing his defenseman to follow.

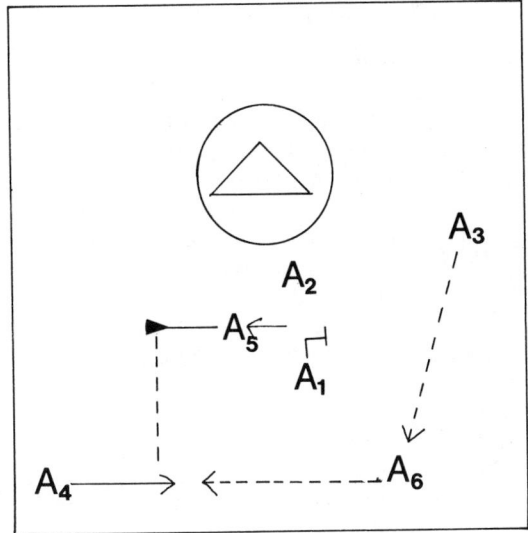

Diagram 9a

Set Plays

In set plays everyone must be included in the action or it will be easy for the defense to back up. Consider the following all-even situation. There are three men out front, one on the crease and two behind. (See Diagram 9.) As the whistle blows, the two behind attackmen move up to the pipes creating a 3-3 offense.

A5 has the ball; he passes to A6, who throws to A3. A5 cuts down, yelling for the ball. A1 cuts to the ball, looking for the pass but making sure there is enough room for his defenseman to get through. (You'll see why later.) In fact, A1 is a decoy and his job is to get his defenseman on the side of the ball. (See diagram 9a.)

All defensemen are now on the side of the ball which is exactly what we want. A2, A1 and A5 are all stacked in a row. With everyone looking at A3 for the ball, A3 throws hard back to A6, who throws to A4 coming toward A6. As A4 receives the ball, he immediately throws inside to A5, who has stepped left and is looking for the over-the-shoulder pass. (See Diagram 9a.)

A5 always will be open because as A5 steps left, A1 steps down to pick off A5's defenseman. This is not a moving pick because A1 steps down and to his left, giving him enough time to stop. The reason A2 lined up on the pipe was to give A5 a good angle shot when he receives the ball.

The key is acting. Good acting will get your defensemen to play as they are taught—between their men and the ball—which is exactly where you want them in this play. I like the double pick play because it makes it almost impossible for the defense to get by and opens up many different scoring possibilities.

Fusting

Cutting Without the Use of Picks

Many times you're in a situation where one of your teammates has beaten his defenseman. Now the defense shifts to back up. When your defenseman goes, you go, too. Follow your defenseman and get into a position so that the man with the ball can get it to you. In other words, don't let your defenseman play between you and the ball. In diagram 10, M1 beats his man. As D1 goes to pick up M1, A1 follows him and cuts inside for the pass. This looks simple, but let's envision what might happen to complicate the play and why it works if you (A1) do the right thing.

First, a good attackman won't play behind the goal when the ball is out front. So don't make it easy for the defense by going behind. You can always go behind if necessary. Second, you always want to be able to take advantage of a defensive maneuver, so you must always cut when your defenseman does. Third, when you come around, make sure you come far enough. If you don't, you'll rush your shot and have a bad angle. The best thing to do is *get yourself in front of the goalie.* This is an almost guaranteed goal and here's why.

The first thing M1 is going to do is look for the shot himself. But, now that you're in position, (with your stick protected and ready for the feed), he will throw it to you. When you catch it, you can take as much time as you like before shooting. The goalie is forced to freeze; he can't come out and check you. (If he does come out and check your stick, the ball will go into the goal since you're in line with the goal and the ball.) After you catch the ball, turn, pick your spot and let it go.

If you're on the crease, use the same move. Follow your defenseman and step in a position to be open. In Diagram 10a, A1

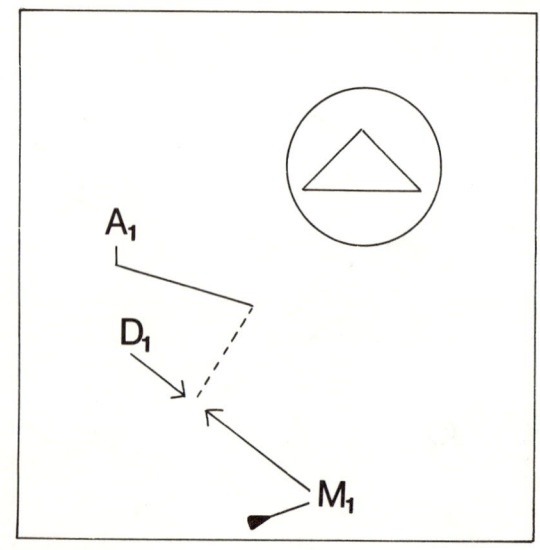

Diagram 10

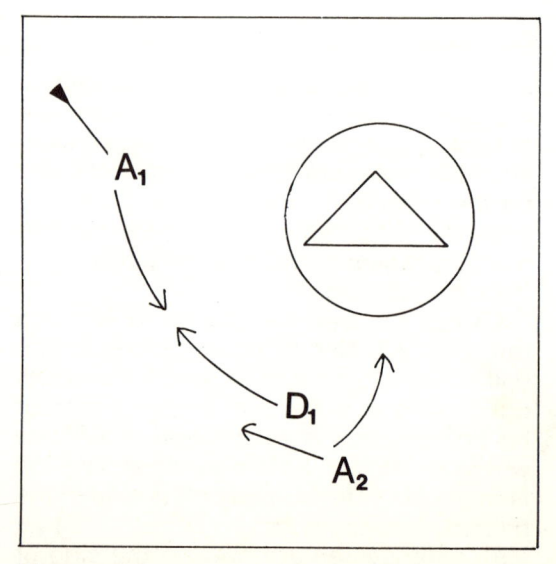

Diagram 10a

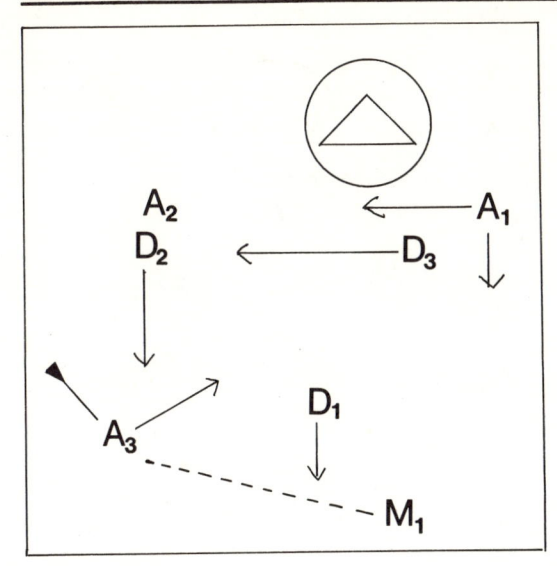

Diagram 10b

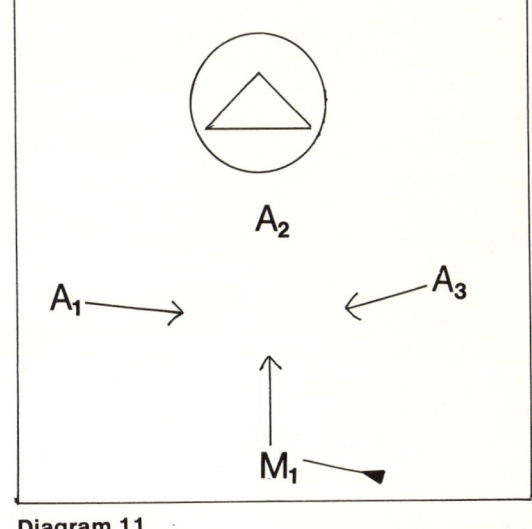

Diagram 11

has dodged his man; D1 goes to back up; A2 follows and breaks either left or inside. (Since it's a short shot, many times it's advantageous to go left because if you go right another defenseman may be able to pick you up while you're sliding across the crease.)

In Diagram 10b, the point man (A3) receives the ball and, knowing that D2 is charging, steps toward the middle, hoping to create a 3-on-2. Let's examine A1's moves. All he has to do is watch his defenseman, D3. Often D3 chooses to go across. If this happens, A1 follows him and gets into a position to receive the ball, hopefully in front of the goalie. If D3 doesn't go across, A1 would go high, making it easier to receive the ball. The important thing to remember is to get into a passing lane so that the ball carrier can get the ball to you and so that neither a defenseman nor his stick can get you.

Fast Breaks

The quickness of lacrosse causes many fast breaks so we must be prepared for them. Many times the ball is picked up in the middle of the field and the attackmen can't get set in the traditional box setup. Let's set up a play for a 4-on-3 break. (This play also makes an excellent practice drill because it will improve your stick work and help you learn where to go when you don't have the ball.)

As the middie brings the ball down the field, the attack sets up in a triangle with A2 directly in front of the goalie and A1 and A3 close enough to make the defensemen think about them but wide enough so the defense can't get them if either receives a pass. (See Diagram 11.)

As M1 brings the ball down, A1 and A3 will break toward the middle of the field and out toward M1. M1 has the option of throw-

Fusting

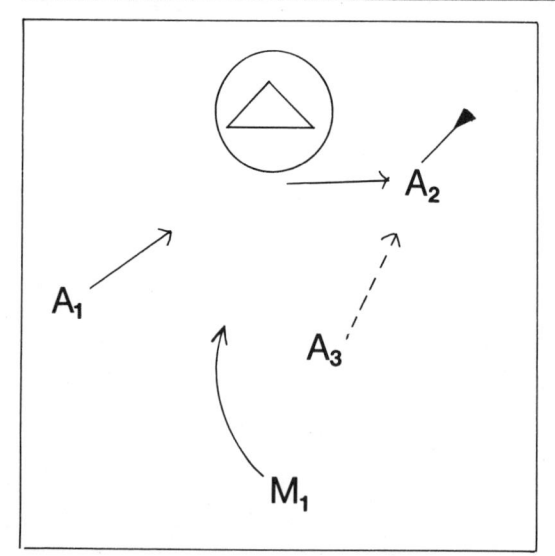

Diagram 11a

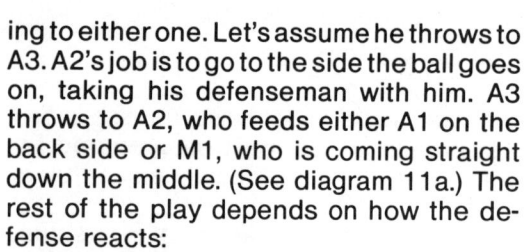

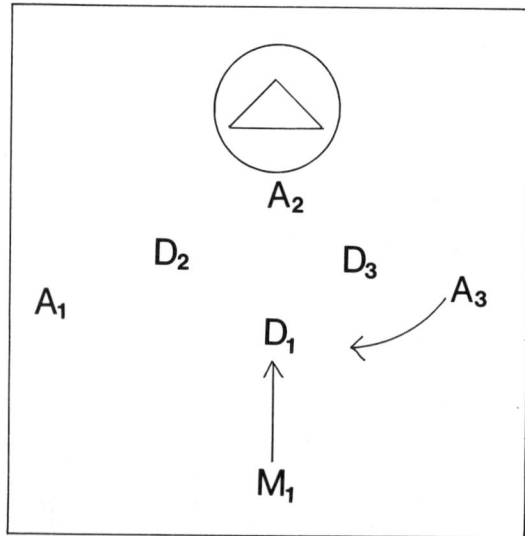

Diagram 11b

ing to either one. Let's assume he throws to A3. A2's job is to go to the side the ball goes on, taking his defenseman with him. A3 throws to A2, who feeds either A1 on the back side or M1, who is coming straight down the middle. (See diagram 11a.) The rest of the play depends on how the defense reacts:

Option 1: M1 brings the ball down and goes as far as possible to draw his defenseman. If the three attackmen are being played, A1 and A3 drop back; M1 walks in and shoots.

Option 2: M1 brings the ball down. A1 and A3 cut toward him. If D2 and D3 go, M1 feeds A2 on the crease. (This option usually works the first time it's used in a game.)

Option 3: M1 brings the ball down, throws to A3. (At this point D1 is on M1; D3 must pick up A3 or A3 has a clear shot.) A2 breaks to the side for the pass. The man who is playing him is D2, who is splitting A1 and A2 but favoring A2. (See Diagram 11b.) A2 won't have any trouble getting the ball because D2 is behind him. If D2 doesn't pick up A2, A2 walks in and shoots, therefore D2 must go with A2. This leaves A1 wide open for the back side cut. The only possible man who can get to him is D1, but as he goes, M1 cuts straight down for the shot. It's impossible for the defense to cover him but D3 (who is the only possible man who has a chance) gives it a try. As he goes, A3 is left standing free for a return pass and an easy shot. A2, as the feeder, simply picks the man who is open by watching what the defense does.

The reason I like to use this particular play for drill work is that it shows you that in any situation all you have to do is see what the defense is going to do and react to their movement.

Drill

This drill helps you concentrate more on the ball than on your man. In addition, it will teach you to protect your stick by keeping

Attack

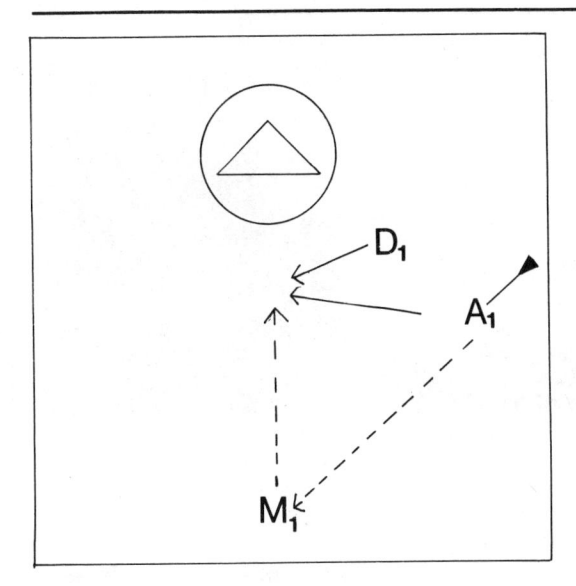

Diagram 12

your body between tne stick and your defenseman. In Diagram 12, A1 starts with the ball and throws it to M1 and then cuts across the crease for the return pass and shot. D1 is the key. He puts his stick down and, as A1 cuts across, grabs him with his hands on his back and pushes A1, trying to make A1 think of him and not the ball. Many times you'll see a player cut across the crease and drop an easy pass or miss it altogether. The reason is that he is thinking of the defensive player and not concentrating on the ball. Each time you do this drill, increase the intensity of the defenseman's play until you simulate game conditions.

Bob Griebe

Tom McFarland

EDITOR'S INTRODUCTION

Bob Griebe has won every award that it's humanly possible for a lacrosse player to win. He went from a high school All-American at Deer Park to one at Towson State, where he piled up 229 career points. Bob has played club lacrosse for only three years but was voted the Hero's Award as the Best Attackman in Club Lacrosse for two of them. An inspirational leader, he is one of the most unselfish players playing today. He's led the Maryland Lacrosse Club to two divisional titles, played on the 1978 USA National team, and was Most Valuable Player in the College-Club Superstar game of 1978, with 7 assists.

Bob is a sales representative for STX, Inc., so, as he puts it, "Just about my whole life revolves around lacrosse."

PLAYER'S INTRODUCTION

The game of lacrosse has given me the opportunity to compete against some outstanding athletes. Every phase of the game from the time I step into the locker room to the time the game is over, is total enjoyment and fun. Lacrosse also gives me the opportunity to run and stay in good physical shape.

By working hard and watching others to correct my weaknesses, I feel I have become a more able and knowledgeable lacrosse player. The success I have found in lacrosse also helps me in my job as a salesman with STX. As both a player and a salesman, I deal with a lot of different types of people from many areas of the country. This not only broadens my horizons but gives me contacts and friends who surely will be helpful to me throughout my life.

Philosophy of Attack

An attackman should be the ball controller of a team's offense. Since a midfielder must concentrate offensively and defensively on both ends of the field, it is unlikely that when he does get the ball on the offensive end of the field, he can determine whether the team needs to control the ball or force the ball to the goal. But an attackman has time to analyze the team's needs while the ball is down on the defensive end of the field.

Since an attackman is the ball controller of the team, he must be able to sense when to dodge and when to give up the ball by passing off to an open man.

41   **Attack**

Jeff Wagner

Griebe

Basic Technique

When I have the ball behind the goal, I try to keep moving at all times. Constant movement keeps my defenseman from overplaying me, making it possible to pass to an open teammate. I am constantly looking for midfielders cutting into an area from which they can score. I try not to hold onto the ball too long. If there are no open cutters or no opportunity for me to dodge, I pass off the ball and continue my movement without the ball. *[Not holding onto the ball is a characteristic of the exceptional player. Bob knows that holding it slows down the offense and makes it easier for the defense to back up or slide.—G. F.]*

By moving when you don't have the ball, you keep your defenseman busy, giving another player the opportunity to get open. When a middie has the ball, cut from behind the goal across the top of the crease looking for a pass from him. (See Diagram 1.) When another attackman has the ball, look to set a pick for him behind the goal. A pick can sometimes free your attack teammate for a one on one situation with the goalie.

If you're getting ready to feed or shoot, try to make sure you're not checked. *[This comes with experience. One helpful hint—as your defenseman pulls his stick back to check you, make your move.—G. F.]* To avoid a defenseman who tries to go over your head, keep your stick in a vertical position close to your body. As he comes over your head with his stick, pull your stick in as close to your body as possible and drive past the defenseman's hip which is closest to you. (Without the use of his stick, he is at a definite disadvantage.)

If a defenseman tries to take the ball away from you by using a wrap check, use a basic roll dodge. As you feel the pressure

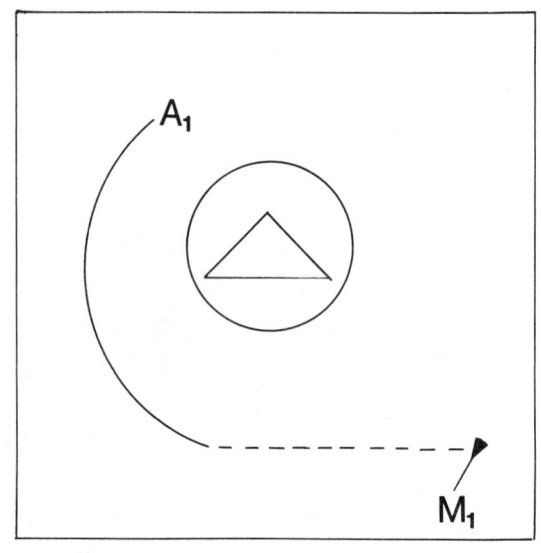

Diagram 1

of the defender's stick wrapping around you, pivot off your leg which is closest to your defenseman. Turn your back into him and roll away in the opposite direction from which his check is coming. It is often helpful to switch hands while you roll away from your defender. This prepares you in case you need to get off a quick shot or pass. *[This is excellent advice, especially if you're quick like Bob. If not, do exactly what he suggests except, as you pivot and change direction take your bottom hand off the stick and hold it out to absorb the blow and, in effect, block your defenseman's stick.—G. F.]*

Dodging

When a defenseman tries to play you too aggressively, constantly trying to take away the ball, it's time to dodge and go to the goal. To position yourself for a dodge, try to maneuver your defenseman to an area of the field where he alone is guarding you.

Attack

Try to avoid a situation where a second defenseman can leave his man and double team you. *[If the area you're in looks crowded, it may be because the defense has slid. If so, this is a perfect time to forego the dodge and move the ball to whoever is open on the other side of the field.—G. F.]*

If a defenseman runs at you from a distance at top speed, dodge because it's very difficult for him to make a quick change of direction while running full speed. But do not make your move too early. Wait until he makes his final lunge for the ball. When he does, use either a quick face dodge or roll dodge.

My Favorite Play

The move I most prefer can be used very effectively by an attackman taking the ball from out of bounds directly behind the goal. In this move, which is similar to a face dodge, you start off with two hands on the stick. If right handed, hold the stick with the head section directly in front of your body. The first step is to run straight at your defenseman at approximately three-quarter speed. Step two begins when you are approximately one defensive stick length away from your defenseman. As you approach, take your right foot and step as if you were going to run to your right. Take your stick and move it from a two handed grip to holding it only with your right hand. Step three is to push off your right foot and accelerate to full speed while pulling the stick across your body and into your left hand. Drive around the left side of the goal for the shot. (See Diagram 2.)

Attitude

Attitude is one factor which cannot be measured by physical performance. In fact,

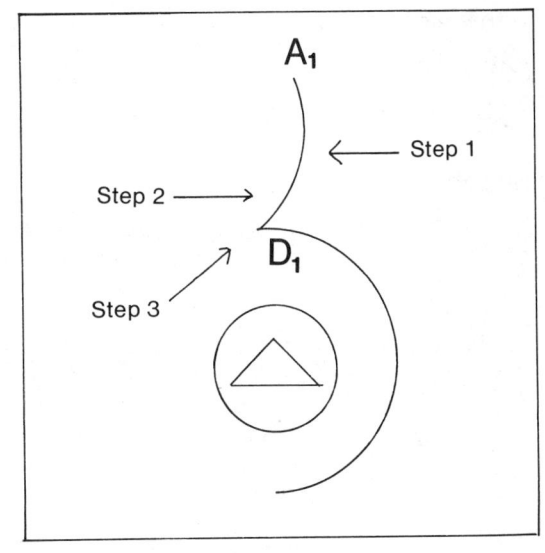

Diagram 2

a good attitude can help compensate for physical weakness. Good attitude makes you want to work as hard as you can on your shortcomings until you can perform adequately in a game situation. Good attitude makes you want to go out and push yourself harder than your opponent. If you have a win-each-game attitude, it should rub off on any player who doesn't feel as strongly about trying to beat a competitor who is supposed to be really tough.

Drills

While every player will develop his own favorite drills, be sure to drill with a defenseman or an attackman in order to simulate actual game conditions. One thing you should practice constantly is having a defenseman play you one on one. Start from behind the goal and drive around the goal, practicing taking shots with defensive pressure on you. Remember to practice with your weak hand as many times as with your strong hand. A player equally adept with both left and right hand shots will be a tougher opponent.

Shooting

In shooting, always go for the top or bottom corners of the goal on the goalie's off stick side. This is the area that is usually least protected. An especially tough shot for a goalie to stop is one which is aimed at the hip opposite his stick. *[Bob brings up a good point. In order for the goalie to block a hip shot, he has to either bring his stick over his head or use a sweeping motion from the ground up. In both cases, it's very difficult for him to make the save.—G. F.]*

When approaching a goalie, you can fake a shot to any area of the net, forcing the goalie to move to cover your fake, and then shoot to another area. However, the method I've found to be the most effective is not to fake at all. Instead, always have a set area in mind that you are going to shoot at. When you don't fake, the goalie tends to remain stationary, making it difficult for him to make a quick move to where your shot is taken. *[Faking too many times gets the goalie moving, and he may get in the way of your shot. Keeping your stick high forces the goalie to keep his stick high, making it easier for you to shoot to one spot.—G. F.]*

To be a good shooter you should be able to shoot with both your left and right hands. You must work to master all types of shots using both sidearm and overhand movement.

CUTTING

Cut away when the man with the ball is in a good position to feed you. Only cut to an area on the field where it is possible to receive a pass. A common mistake made by many players is to cut to an area where it is impossible to receive a pass. In that case, the cut is wasted.

The two most frequent cutting situations for an attackman are shown in Diagrams 3 and 4. Diagram 3 shows attackman A1 cutting off the crease attackman's pick toward the midfielder with the ball (M1). As A1 receives the pass, he looks for a shot at the goal. Diagram 4 shows attackman A1 cutting off the crease attackman's pick toward the attackman with the ball (A3). As A1 receives the pass, he looks for a shot at the goal.

There are many other cutting situations which could be illustrated but these are examples of common cuts used throughout a game by all attackmen. *[When Bob doesn't have the ball, he's constantly in motion—attacking the goal, keeping his defenseman occupied, and looking for an opening for a return pass.—G. F.]*

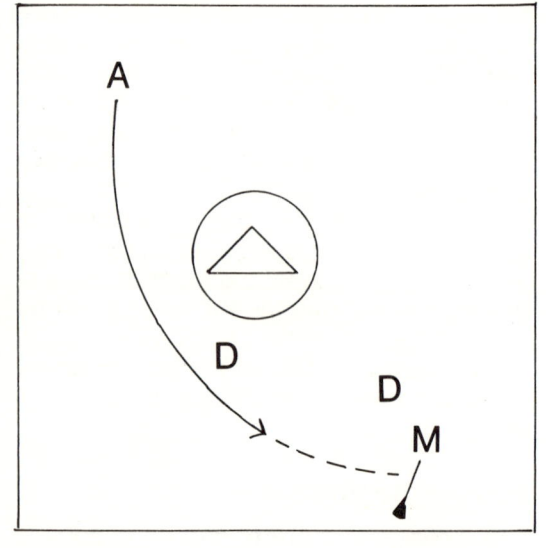

Diagram 3

Attack

Diagram 4

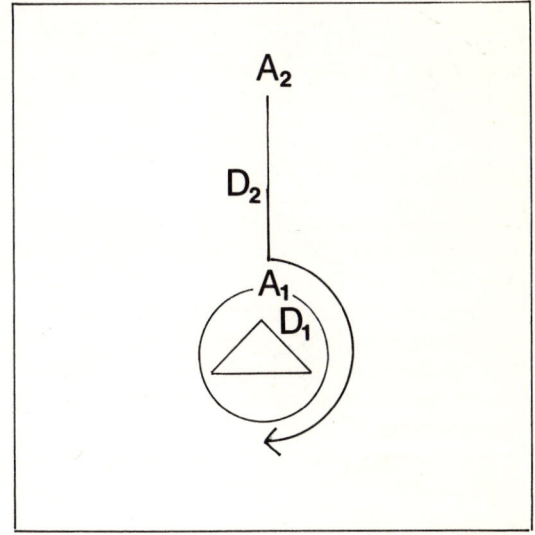

Diagram 5

Picking

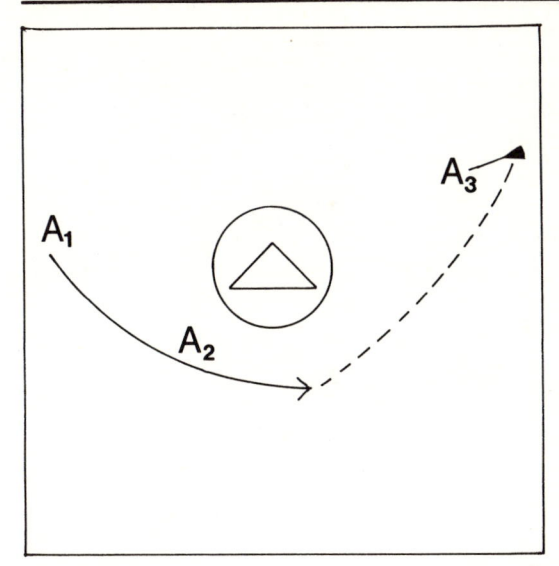

The proper way to pick is to remain stationary with your stick in a vertical position close to your body. When picking, your stick cannot be parallel to the ground. Diagram 5 shows the most common pick used by an attackman behind the goal. Notice that the pick man (A1) stands right on the back of the crease line; this is his correct position.

A player who runs off of a pick behind should take the route of A2 in Diagram 5, running off of A1's hip. By doing this, A2 forces his defenseman to be picked off by A1.

Feeding

I feel there are certain areas from which to feed because they allow easier and more successful passes. These areas are shown in Diagram 6. Areas A1 and A2 are an attackman's prime locations for feeding. By feeding from these areas, you are in a position where a defenseman usually does not play you overaggressively, because you are not in a scoring position. By feeding from these areas, you can feed an open cutter without worrying about your defenseman checking your stick.

If you are a right handed attackman, you can feed all right handed cutters from area A1. If there are no open men, keep moving behind the cage until you approach area A2. Here you can look to feed all left handed cutters. [This is not a technique I recommend for the novice player. Bob's skill in feeding from the corners has been perfected during many, many hours of practice and real game situations. You also have to have worked for a long time with your cutters so that they understand what you are going to do and you know how to anticipate their moves. Bob's rather unorthodox move gives him one advantage in that it forces his defenseman to play him much tighter farther out. This makes it

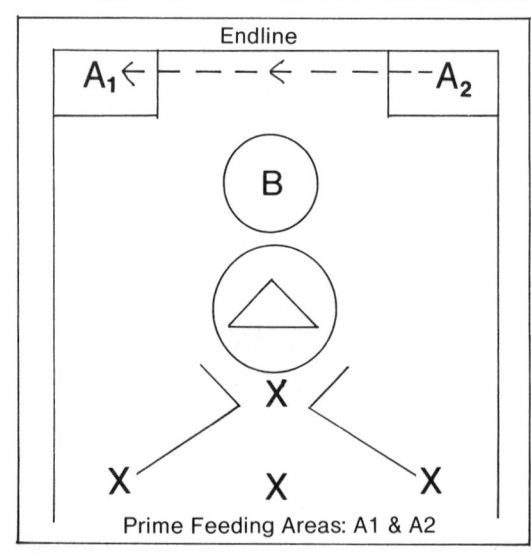

Diagram 6

Prime Feeding Areas: A1 & A2

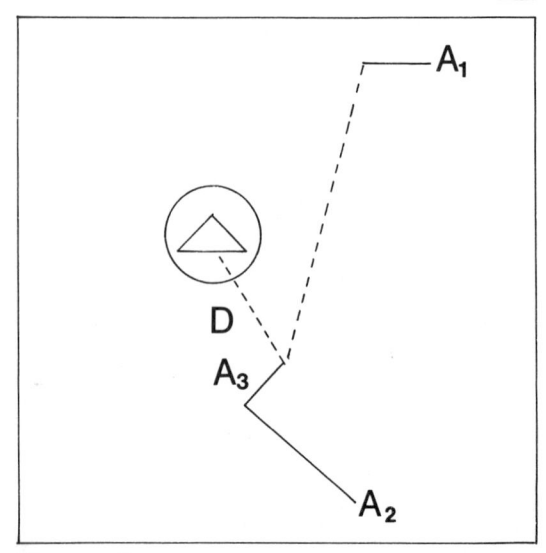

Diagram 7

easier for Bob to beat his man.—G.F.]

Contrary to what many players believe, feeding from area B should not be encouraged because (1) you must get the ball past the goalie's stick, and (2), in this area, a defenseman plays an attackman very tightly which makes it difficult to feed accurately.

My favorite attack plan, probably one of the most basic plays in lacrosse, uses one of the prime feeding areas as its starting point. If done correctly, this play will score many easy goals. (See Diagram 7.) Attackman A1 starts with the ball in the corner of the field behind the goal and moves toward the back of the goal. At the same time, attackman A2 cuts across toward the crease attackman (A3) and then pops back out looking for a pass from A1.

When you're not in one of the back corners and need to get free of your defenseman to feed, one of the best ways is to try, early in the game, to dodge past him and go to the goal. Whether you get by the defenseman or not doesn't matter at this point. What does count is that by forcing the dodge, your defenseman most often will play off you in anticipation of a dodge. This makes it easier for you to feed throughout the game.

A feed should not be attempted by winding up as if you were taking a shot. This allows a defenseman time enough to easily check your stick and send your feed off target. A correct feed should be taken three-quarter arm, because it allows your pass to curve around the defenseman's body. The less accurate sidearm feed should be used only as a last resort, but you *should* still learn it because at times it will be the only possible way to feed. A feed should be accomplished by a quick, flicking motion which propels the ball at the speed needed to get it to your receiver.

Before you feed, try to get a perspective of the entire field. By doing this, you can see all the cutters at the same time. As you play with the players on your team, you will get to know each individual's cutting tendencies. By learning their habits, you will be able to anticipate where your cutter will be coming from and how fast he will get to a certain spot on the field. You then can pass to that spot, confident that the ball and the cutter will come together.

However, do not force feed a ball into a crowd of players. At all times, try to feed a cutter on the same side of the field as you are. There are times when you will find men open on the opposite side of the field, but passes across field must have more velocity on them to get past the defenders' sticks. They are, therefore, harder to control and harder to catch.

Future of Lacrosse

In the next five or ten years, I see the game of lacrosse spreading into areas of the U.S. which are not currently playing lacrosse. The game will speed up due to the introduction of such rules as running time, keeping the ball in constant play, and fewer timeouts. I feel fairly certain that the rules will change so that substitutions will have to be made on the fly. The overall game will speed up, and there will be fewer settled situations.

Jeff Long

EDITOR'S INTRODUCTION

Jeff Long has to be the smoothest attackman who has played for the Naval Academy in the last ten years. His excellent stick work coupled with his superior team play are ample reasons why he was not only a three-time All-American but a true leader in the traditional sense.

The Longman is one of the most consistent play makers in the game today. He holds a number of records at the Naval Academy, including total career points—233 with 149 assists. No one who was there in the stands will ever forget his tremendous effort against Hofstra in a come-from-behind win. Jeff finished that game with 2 goals and 9 assists. He's passing on his skills to a new group of midshipmen at the Academy, where he's coaching lacrosse, teaching Physical Education and recruiting for Navy's lacrosse team.

A member of the 1978 USA National team, Jeff looks at the attackman's role from many angles. He feels the main responsibility is to control the tempo of the game and be in complete command of the offense.

PLAYER'S INTRODUCTION

The game of lacrosse has probably been the most important part of my life for the last nine years. Lacrosse got me into a great college and enabled me to really progress as a person. It has been the kind of outlet for me that others find in skiing or sailing. During my years at the Naval Academy, I would be in class all day, leading a fairly disciplined life. If I had a bad day, I would go out to the lacrosse field after classes and lose myself shooting on the goal or practicing field work.

Lacrosse has enabled me to meet many people who have become very close friends. The lacrosse community is like one big fraternity and sorority mixed together. On the field, two opposing teams can be at each other's throat; but, once the final whistle blows, everyone gets together and the hostility quickly disappears. A common bond that cannot be described seems to exist among lacrosse players.

Probably one of the most enjoyable months of my life was during the World Championship of 1978. For 32 days, I played, lived and partied with 22 players and 3 coaches who were, in my opinion, the best in the world. Never have I been surrounded by a better group of individuals.

Philosophy of Attack

Ideally, the attack position is the last in a series of connected movements. Like the

Attack

Long

anchor man in a relay race, the attackman is responsible for finishing the job that the goalie, defensemen, and midfielders have begun. It is the attackman's responsibility to know when to slow down the pace or when to pick it up, to act as quarterback on the field, to take control of the game, and to make things happen for his team.

The attackman can look at his role in the game from many angles. I feel his main responsibility is to control the tempo of the game and to be in complete command of the offense. A good attack unit will constantly be on the move and be working with each other as well as coordinating their movements with the middies. The attackman must have excellent field sense! By this I mean he should be able to read the situation and take advantage of it. He must know when there is a fast break and when to force a fast break. On the other hand, he must be able to tell if the middies need a blow and be able to slow down the pace. The worst thing that can happen to a team is to have the middies running up and down the field because of a turnover due to the attackman having tried to force a play that wasn't there. *[As Jeff says, this is very frustrating. Not having the ball for a few minutes can make most attackmen pretty anxious but again patience must be observed. Some teams like to attack the goal when it's 3 on 3 or 4 on 4, but this strategy has to be worked out before the game so the middies know what to expect.—G. F.]*

Of course, to effectively play the position, the attackman must be a good feeder and shooter, the hardest part of which is knowing who and when to feed or shoot.

One of the most important skills that separates a good attackman from an outstanding one is the art of riding. A good riding attack unit usually can account for three or four goals a game. Defensemen and goalies are not used to constant harassment when they have the ball. Usually, you can force the ball to the weak link in the clearing team and then work on him until he makes a mistake. Constant pressure with a lot of talk among the riders is necessary. There must be a lot of movement because a ride is basically a 3 on 4 situation.

I feel that to have a championship team, you *must* have a good attack unit. However, the team consists of ten players, and all ten must stick together to win. A superior attack unit can be completely neutralized if it does not work well with the other seven players. Lacrosse is a team sport. Without team play, the most outstanding individuals can be reduced to next to nothing.

Playing Behind

When taking the ball behind, the primary objective is to beat your defenseman to the goal and get off a good shot. Usually, the defense will try a double team; many goals result from the attackman passing off to the man whose defenseman left to double team the ball carrier. Effective moves behind the goal include the quick change of direction dodge and running directly at the defenseman and then giving one quick burst to get to one side of the goal. When dodging from behind, it is very important to wait until you have a good angle before shooting. A very common mistake is to shoot before taking one or two steps past the plane of the goal. Remember that if you shoot too soon, your angle will be very bad. *[Longman brings up an interesting point. Many players coming around the goal shoot too soon. They think that because a defenseman is beating on them they're covered. This is not true. Remember as he's beating on you, he must pull his stick off in order to hit you* again. *This is when you shoot. The best way to make sure of your shooting angle is to mark an "X" in the dirt or drop some lime if you're playing on astroturf; when you come around the goal don't shoot until you reach your mark.—G.F.].*

Feeding

You can feed from anywhere on the field; however, I do not recommend feeding directly across the cage because everyone sags into the middle so that many times the feed will get knocked down or picked off before it reaches its destination. Also, there will not be many players in a position to back up a feed across the cage.

One basic rule for feeding: always be moving when feeding! Standing flatfooted and feeding allows the defenseman to check at will as you feed. To give yourself room to feed, run at the defenseman or run laterally with him, then step back or aside as you get ready to feed.

Any way you can get the ball off accurately when feeding is okay, but the easiest feeds (in order of preference) for the cutter to handle are as follows: First, overhand because it comes directly to the cutter. Second, underhand because it tends to rise in flight. Least preferable, sidearm because it is harder for the shooter to control the accurary of his feed. *[These are good points. Jeff is right when he says that it's really hard to see sidearm and underhand feeds. Another problem is that the feeder is faking with his stick to avoid his defenseman so it's hard for the cutter to know when and where the actual feed will come.—G.F.]*

When feeding it is bad to telegraph your feed. Get into the habit of seeing the whole area of play and being able to pick out an open cutter without fixing your eyes on him.

When feeding a teammate, you must read the situation. If a man has a defender close to him, it is better to spot feed him. This type of feed is very common around the crease area. The art of good feeding depends to a large degree on being able to anticipate your teammates' moves. A lot of practice will help.

Shooting

Good shooting depends very much on the tendencies and habits of the goalie and how much you can discover about him early in the game. For example, you have to find out if he's right or left handed because you always want to shoot to his off side. A very effective shot is one that is waist high and to his opposite hand. Many goalies have a tendency either to chop or pop up no matter where the shot is coming from. This is the ideal time to pop a fake, get the goalie moving one way and shoot against his motion. Any time there is time enough to pump a fake, I recommend it because, if you can get the goalie moving, you have a greater chance of scoring.

The most effective shot in the game seems to be the overhand bounce shot. When taking this shot, you should try to bounce the ball near the crease line. This gives the shot a high bounce, and the goalie has a hard time following its motion. Another very successful shot for me has been a low underhanded shot (or worm burner) that skims at just about ground level to the off side low corner.

Avoiding Checks

When a man goes over my head a lot, I like to use it to my advantage. I like to bait him to go over; then, just as I feel him coming up, I tuck the stick and roll *opposite* from the

Long

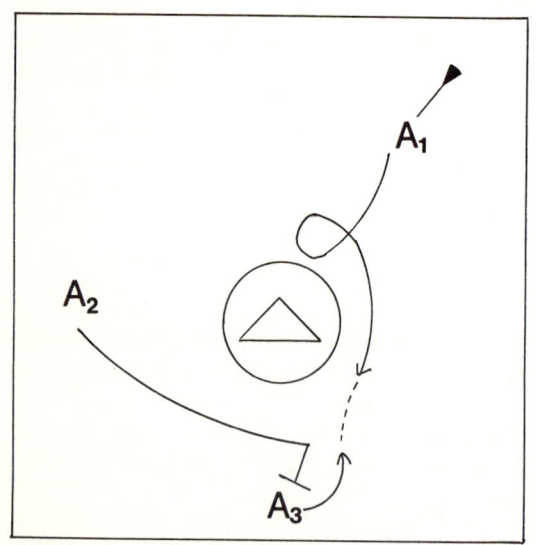

Diagram 1: A2 sets a backdoor pick for A3, who looks for a feed from A1.

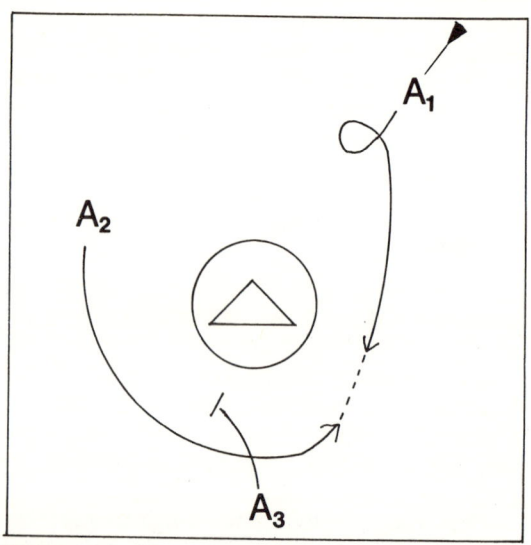

Diagram 2: A2 looks as if he will set a pick for A3. But as A2 gets two or three steps from A3, A3 steps toward A2 and sets a pick. A2 accelerates right, off A3's pick, and looks for a feed from A1.

way his stick is coming. This leaves him behind me with my body between him and my stick.

A wrapping defenseman gives me more problems than any other type of defender. The best way to counter a wrap is to tuck the stick to the body and roll the opposite way. Many times I make the mistake of letting my stick hang on my roll, allowing the defender to check my stick. But if you protect the stick with your body, you can avoid being checked.

Dodging

Dodging is one aspect of the game that every attackman treats in his own way. I truly feel that the attackman has the edge every time he wants to dodge. After all, he knows what he wants to do, and the defenseman has no idea. I never know what dodge I'm going to use until I get close enough for the defenseman to commit himself one way or the other.

Two things to look for when preparing to dodge are (1) what hand the defenseman has his stick in; and (2) whether he guards you straight on or shades you right or left. The golden rule of dodging is—*Take advantage of your defender's mistakes!* [Jeff has mastered different types of dodges in order to take advantage of his defenseman's weak point. Watching and studying your opponent will go a long way toward deciding your final move. As the Longman says, let your defenseman make your decision for you.—G. F.]

My Favorite Move

My favorite move is to take the ball to the side or out front. From there, I run straight

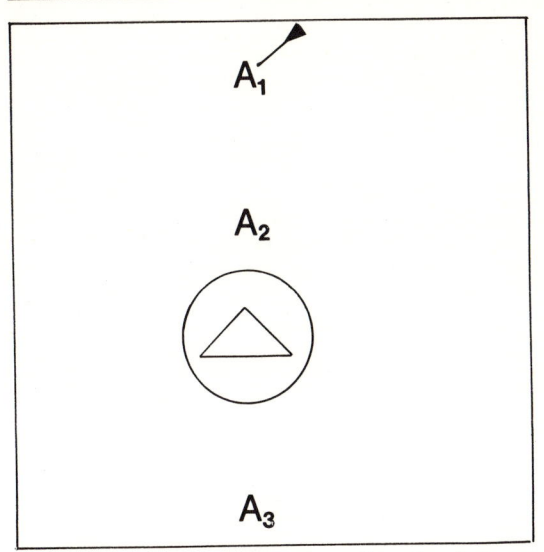

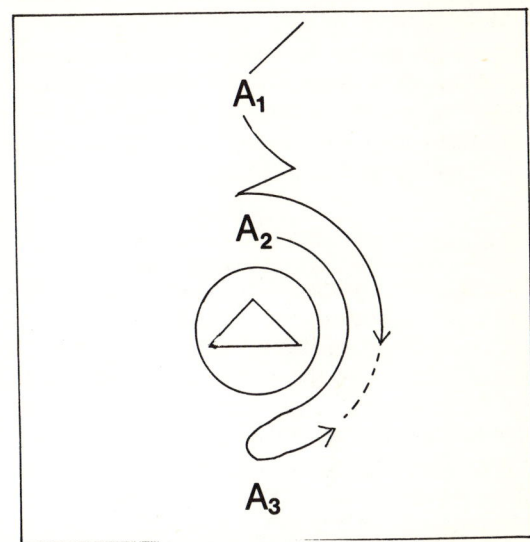

Diagram 3 and 3a: A1 changes direction twice as he comes up to the plane of the goal. A2 goes up the same side A1 will feed from and makes it look as if he will pick for A3, who is off the pipe about 8 yards out. A2 then quickly rolls back toward A1, who spot feeds A2 about 5 or 6 yards out.

at the defender and attempt to get him to back pedal. As soon as he does, I break right or left in one quick move. I always keep the stick in feeding position so that if I get doubled, I can dump the ball off to the open man. Because I am dodging into the center, I usually get doubled early. It is the responsibility of the other offensive players to pop out to receive my feed as soon as I get doubled.

Diagrams 1, 2, 3 and 3a show the three basic attack plans that I have found to work especially well.

Playing Off the Ball

When the ball is out front with the middies, the attackman should be moving all around the goal area. Many times the defender will turn his back for a split second, and that is time enough to make a move to the goal looking for a feed from the middie.

When the other attackman has the ball, I try to work with him and force a double by the defenders. This can be done by setting a pick or flipping the ball behind. If the other attackman wants to go to the goal, I try to stay on the off side pipe to give him a large area in which to dodge and lose his man. The *worst* thing I could do without the ball is to stand still and allow my defenseman to double.

As soon as I throw the ball to a teammate, I cut to the goal or to a spot where I can receive the ball and then go to the goal. The give and go play is still one of the most worthwhile and valuable moves in the game.

Ground Ball

Control of loose balls and ground balls is the key to any good lacrosse team. When the ball is on the ground, the team that takes posession most often usually seems to win the game. As soon as a ground ball is picked up, I always look to dump it to a teammate who is farther up the field. Remember that the fastest way to advance the ball upfield is in the air.

Cutting

The cutting game, if done correctly, can give an opposing team nightmares. Most cuts come from the midfield down to the goal. I feel it is the cutter's responsibility to use the pick to get open. (Some people think the opposite—that the picker has that responsibility.) I have found the most effective cut is to run directly at the picker and, just as I get a step away from him, to quickly go one way or the other. The cut must be very sharp; you should rub shoulders with your picker.

Future of Lacrosse

In the next five or ten years, I definitely foresee a transition to the International Rules that we played under when the USA team went to England for the world championship. The faceoff rule after goals will be put back into the game within the next year or two. I do not see too many drastic changes in the game other than attempts, like the adoption of the International Rules, to speed up the game.

Attack

Mike O'Neill

EDITOR'S INTRODUCTION

Just as Joe Cowan was all-everything for Johns Hopkins in the late 60's, so Mike O'Neill accomplished the same feat in the late 70's. Mike has had a brilliant college career. Ever since his first game for Hopkins as a freshman when he exploded for 5 goals against Virginia, he has proven to be a versatile and accomplished attackman. His coach, Henry Ciccarone, summed up his career by saying "Mike was just a special kind of player." In recognition, he was a four-time All-American, and he closed his Hopkins career by being named Most Valuable Player in the 1978 NCAA Championship Game, which saw the Blue Jays beat a tough Cornell team for the title.

Even though Mike had 233 career points, he also was an outstanding rider and was devastating on loose balls. Fans will long remember the great game he had against Navy when he piled up 4 goals and 5 assists while also picking up 12 ground balls and was all over the field helping his team pin back a tough Navy defense. In addition Mike won the Turnbull Trophy twice as the best attackman and last year won the award as the best player in Division 1. Mike will soon be coaching lacrosse at the University of Delaware and playing club lacrosse with the highly-talented Chesapeake Club.

Philosophy of Attack

The function of attack play is to control the offense. This doesn't mean just call out plays or dodge your man, but to read the situation and do what is appropriate. For instance, if your midfielders have just been playing a lot of defense, it is the attack's job to break out and get the ball and, more importantly, to control it. On the other hand, if the situation is unsettled and you have a 4 on 3 or a 3 on 2 situation, you have to force the play and make something happen. Go to the goal; if you draw a defenseman, dump the ball off to the open man.

Playing With the Ball

When I have the ball behind the goal, I try to move my defenseman. I never stand still or jog with the ball. I always make my defenseman work to cover me. I do this by changing directions quickly and unexpectedly as shown in Diagram 1.

While working a defenseman, wait for him to make a mistake. For example, if he

Richard Scalera

Attack

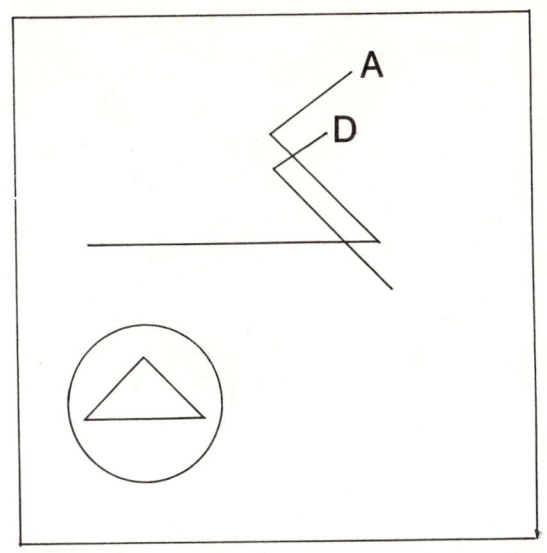

Diagram 1

overplays your stick side, it's a great time to plant and go the other way. You can force your defenseman into making mistakes by baiting him—hold your stick so he tries to go over your head and take the ball; then, when he commits, pull your stick into your body and go to the goal.

While you are doing these maneuvers, your head should be up and your eyes always looking for an opening (on the crease, a cutting middie, or your other behind attackman). *[This is a really good point. Keep your head up and your eyes looking. Too many players are overly concerned with their defenseman. You must always feel you can beat him and look for the right opportunity.—G.F.]*

Dodging

There are many times when a dodge is especially effective. My favorite is to take the ball from out of bounds either directly behind the goal or at the side of the pipes (coming from the sideline). These plays are effective because if you run right at the defenseman, he has got to give you something. You can run right by him because you're running at top speed and he's standing still. If he takes away your stick side, pull the stick across your body and go the other way. Remember that the purpose behind dodging is to make your defenseman move one way while you go the other, that is, you force him to take away one side of the goal. A good way to do this is to use as much one on one play as possible; practice patterns that force your defenseman to move. Hopefully, you can get him to cross his feet. Once he does that, plant and go the other way.

My favorite move here is the face dodge. I run my defenseman hard one way, making him think I'm going to continue to go that way. When he moves in that direction to cover me, I plant my foot (if you are running with the stick in your right hand, plant and push off with your right foot and vice versa) and go the other way. As I am planting my foot to change directions, I am simultaneously changing hands with the stick. In Diagram 2, I would start off with the stick in my right hand and switch it to my left hand when I make the cut. When switching the stick, I pull it right across my face, parallel to my body. I do it either one handed or two handed, keeping my upper hand (when I'm holding the stick with two hands) as high up on the throat of the stick as is comfortable. The higher up your hand is on the throat of the stick, the more control you have in pulling your stick across your face.

Avoiding Checks

To avoid having the ball stolen away by a defenseman going over my head, I pull the stick into my body and hide the head of my stick behind my head. An important point to

O'Neill

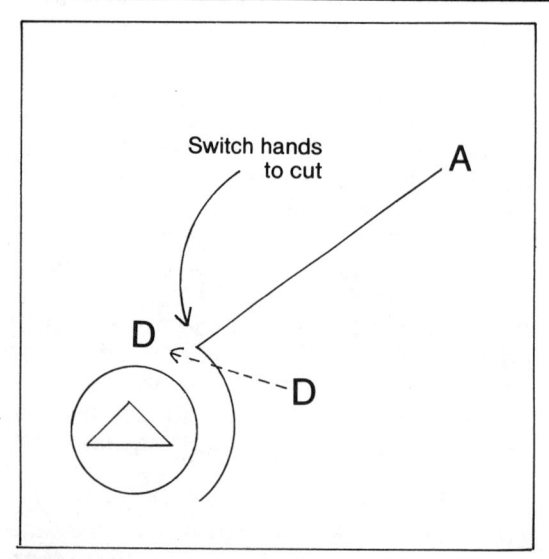

Diagram 2

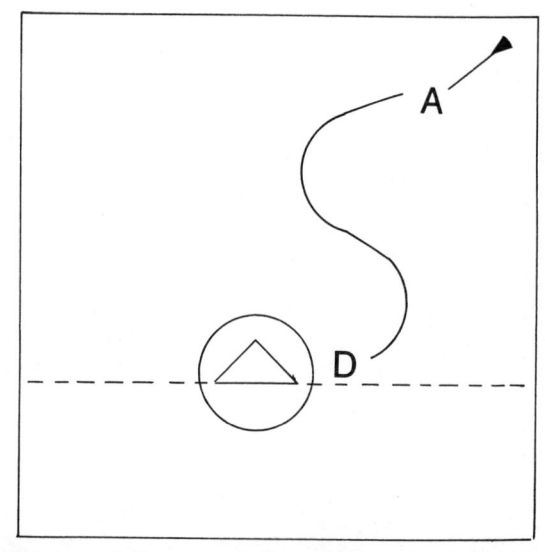

Diagram 3: As you reach goal line extended, put stick in left hand (away from D). Get your right arm and shoulder out in front to protect your stick and absorb the blow.

remember is that you should stand upright and not crouch as the defenseman is going over your head. It's obvious that the taller you stand, the harder it is for him to go over your head. Also, don't slow down or come to a halt; if anything, accelerate and run away from the pressure.

I can usually feel a wrap check coming. My defenseman will get his body real tight to mine, usually at the goal line extended. If I feel a wrap coming, I turn my upper body into the check so I take the blow on my off-stick shoulder. (See Diagram 3.) Then, I try either to run through the check or bounce out and get away from the pressure. At first, these movements are very awkward; but, the more you practice against the wrap, the easier they become.

Feeding

Diagram 4 shows what I think are the best areas from which to feed. From anywhere

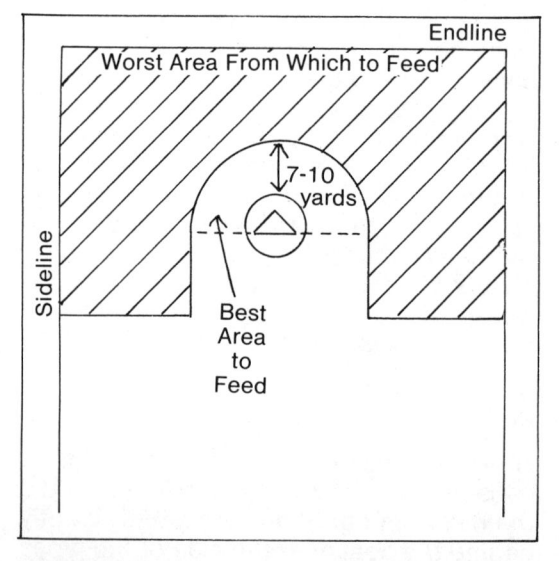

Diagram 4

within this semicircle, you can pretty much see the whole offensive action, plus your feeds will be short. The longer the feed, the more chance of error; the less accurate the feed, the more time the defense has to recover. (Many coaches and players feel you should not feed from directly behind the goal because the goalie can knock it down. I do not agree because you can fake the goalie away or throw the ball past him. Most goalies are more concerned with following the ball than trying to knock down feeds.)

The worst areas from which to feed are also shown in Diagram 4. These areas are too far out. I made a point to shade the areas higher than the goal line extended because it is really tough to have a good feed-and-shoot hookup for jamming in the ball from the angles you have when you receive a feed from those areas. In addition, the man you are feeding can't cut directly to the goal. Instead, as shown in Diagram 5, he has to cut toward you to meet and catch the ball and therefore has to shoot the ball across his body to get it into the goal. In addition, you force him to catch the ball in an area of the field where there is already a lot of congestion. [*Most players catch the ball coming from behind the goal and shoot right away. But as Mike says it's difficult to just turn and shoot. It takes a lot of practice and shouldn't be done until you're sure of your timing, reflexes and accuracy.—G.F.*]

To feed well, it is essential that you first get away from your defenseman. You cannot do this by standing still. Standing still (with or without the ball) is the worst thing an attackman can do. You must be able to feed while running, and you must be able to do it both left and right handed.

To get the cushion you need to feed, run your defenseman one way, plant and, as

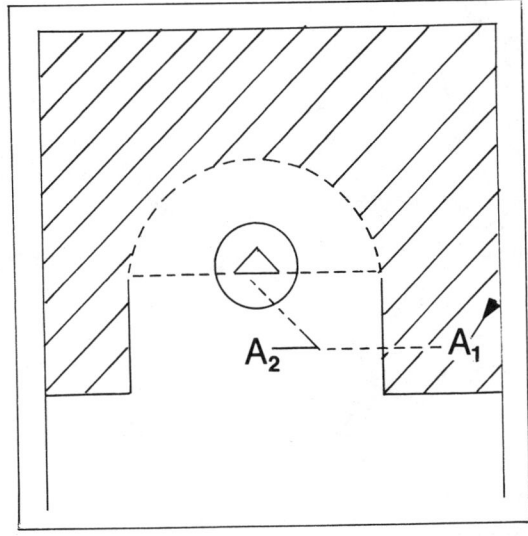

Diagram 5: Feed from bad feed area forces A2 to cut toward A1 instead of toward the goal to receive pass.

soon as you turn, come back the other way. Be looking to feed off your cut.

The plant and turn sequence is a way of negating your defenseman's ability to take away your dangerous hand. Since his job is to turn you back, he gets up on your dangerous side to prevent you from beating him to the goal. This is when you should plant and come back.

A second method I like to use to get a feeding cushion is to pretend I'm driving my man to the goal, and then step away from him—almost jumping back. I cock my stick, look inside and then fire. (See Diagram 6.)

As shown in Diagram 7, one of the easiest ways to get some time to feed is to come off a pick and step back.

There are several ways to feed successfully; however, the most consistently accurate and easiest feed for the cutter to

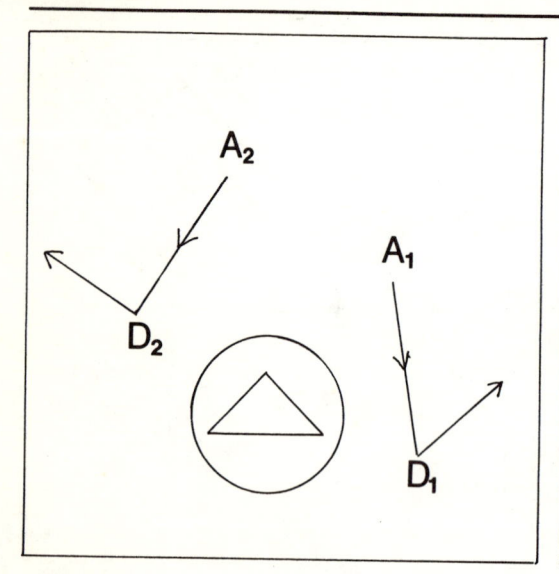

Diagram 6

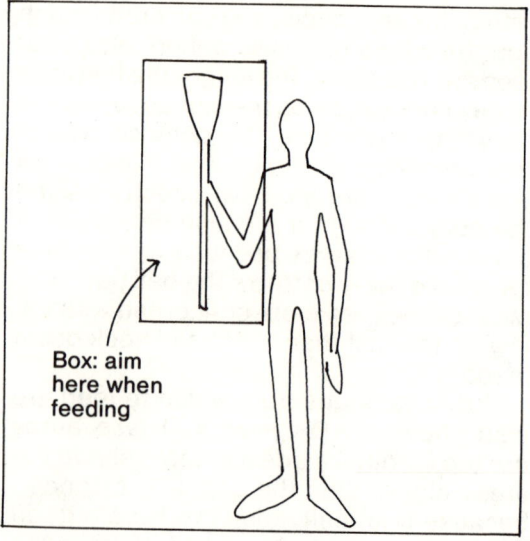

Diagram 8

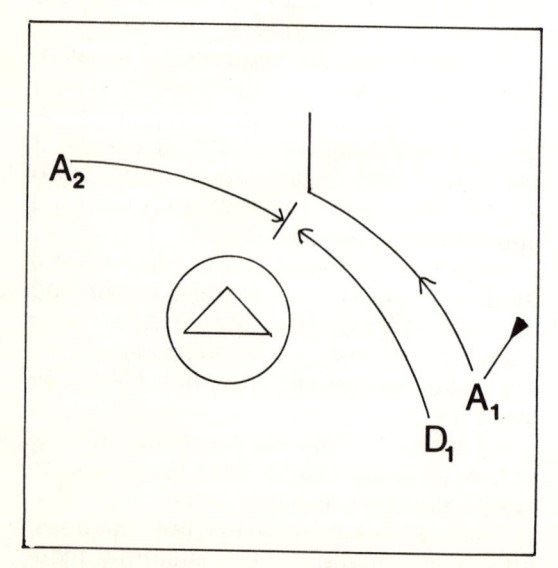

Box: aim here when feeding

Diagram 7

handle is the overhand throw. Feeding the ball accurately (into the cutter's box—stick side, shoulder high, as illustrated in Diagram 8) is essential. An overhand throw gives you this consistent accuracy.

At times, however, an overhand feed is impractical as well as ineffective, for example, when the feeder spots an open cutter but the defenseman has his stick on the attackman's glove or up into his chest. When this happens, the attackman cannot feed overhand so he must feed sidearm or underhand, preferably sidearm because underhand in most cases is the least accurate feed as well as the hardest for the receiver to handle. A sidearm or underhand feed also would be necessary if a feeder came off a pick and had to throw around the interference to hit his man. Another good time to use the sidearm or underhand feed is when the attackman has a step or two on his defenseman, is coming around the goal and draws a slide from the midfield.

Personally, I try to feed overhand as much as possible. However, if a feeder can put the ball in the cutter's pocket consistently using a one handed throw, then that is the way he should do it.

Generally, I try to establish eye contact with the man I am feeding. However, once I establish eye contact, I don't ignore him altogether but neither do I stare directly at him because I don't want the feed to be blocked nor do I want my cutter to get creamed.

A good feeder is like a good passer in football. When for an instant your man is open in a crowd, you have to rifle the ball to him hard. If, however, you have to lead your cutter, take something off the feed. Generally when I feed to the crease area, I'll feed harder because if a man is open in the crease, it's only for a short instant, and I want to get the ball to him as quickly as possible. If I have time, I'll just float the ball to my man, for example, if I beat my defenseman from behind and draw a defenseman from the wing as shown in Diagram 9.

Generally speaking, I do not spot feed to just anyone on the field. I will spot feed off a set play and if the cutter knows to look for a spot. When executed properly, it's a great play. However, if there's not some form of communication between me and the receiver, I will not spot feed.

Playing Off the Ball

When you don't have the ball, don't just stand around. Give your other attackman a pick, pick for the creaseman, or swing out in front for the ball. Be dangerous; be around the ball or the goal area—don't take yourself out of the action.

When a middie has the ball, I hang on the pipes. If my wing middie has the ball and

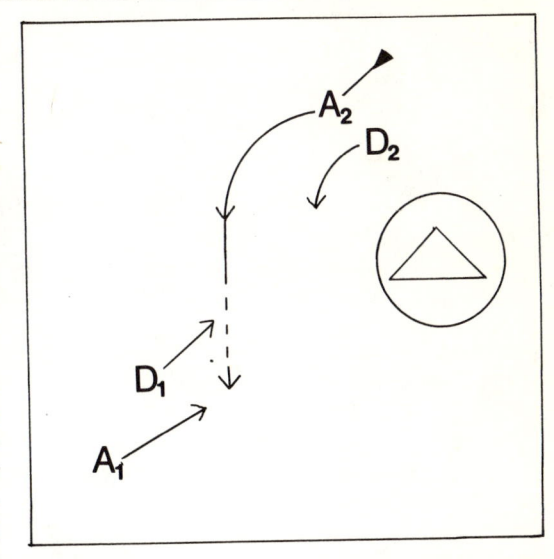

Diagram 9

dodges his man, I want to be there to help him out if there's a slide. Nine times out of ten, this is exactly what happens. (See Diagram 10.) If I hung in the back, behind the cage, my middie wouldn't have too many options.

When the other attackman has the ball behind, I generally move to get myself or one of my teammates open. I can give my other behind attackman a pick. I can pick the crease attackman's man. I can swing out front, using the crease attackman as a pick. Or, I can go back door if my defenseman turns his head to look at the ball. If he does, I cut right behind him.

[Take Mike's advice. I can't stress enough the importance of always moving if you don't have the ball to a position where you are making yourself or one of your teammates dangerous to the defense.—G.F.]

If I have the ball and then pass off, there are several things I do right away, the least of which is stand still. I can use the moves

O'Neill

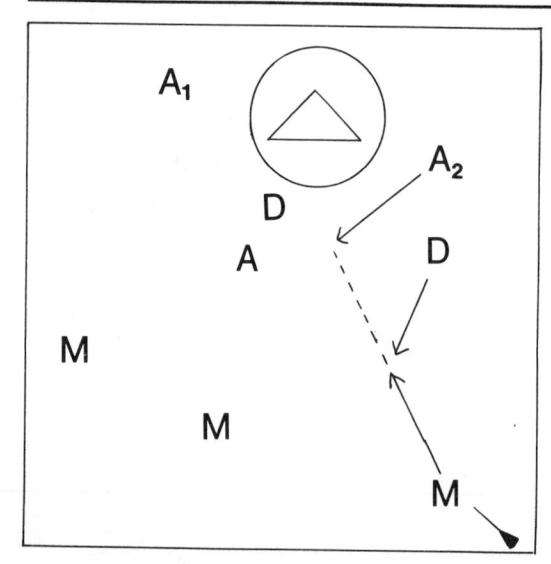

Diagram 10

I've already mentioned, plus another which can be used all over the field, the give and go. Instead of staying still after I pass, I go.

Give and go is my favorite play in any kind of unsettled running sport. It demonstrates teamwork and intelligence in playing the game. There are several reasons why it is so successful a play. First, once you release the ball to your teammate, your defenseman has a tendency to relax since his man no longer has the ball. Second, when you release the ball, your defenseman turns his head to follow the ball, and, as he does, you are past him and on your way.

Shooting

When I shoot at the goal, I shoot for an open area, pure and simple. I try to shoot on the cage where the goalie is not. As I said, I try to shoot for open area; but, at the same time, I usually have an idea where the goalie will be in the goal. As an example, when I am coming around the goal from behind, I know the goalie is probably going to be hanging on the pipe, so I try to predetermine where the opening is and, if it's there, shoot for it. If the opening is not where I thought, I quickly read the goalie and try to put the ball where he is not.

Although I do not usually fake with my stick, I also don't telegraph where I'm going to shoot by looking directly at my opening. I usually don't have enough time to use a stick fake. If I want to draw out the goalie to get a better angle, I'll use a head and shoulder fake instead of a real stick fake; I find that it accomplishes the same thing. The only time I really will use a stick fake on a goalie is when I'm one on one and have some time to fool around.

Ninety percent of the time, I shoot overhand. From the attack position, most shots are fairly close range. Because of this, a shot's accuracy is a lot more important than its velocity; and, as I mentioned when I was discussing feeding, overhand shooting is a lot more accurate than sidearm or underhand. Naturally, the farther from the goal you get, the more velocity you want so in such cases you might switch to sidearm or underhand.

I shoot when I have the best possible angle or the most goal to shoot at before I get hit. When I come around the cage from behind, I try to follow the arc of the crease as long as possible and hold the ball till the last possible second. A good attackman will take more lumps but get more goals this way. *[Remember this. If you got hit, you came around far enough. It's when you don't get hit that you've not come around far enough and end up shooting a step or two too early.— G.F.]*

Diagram 11 illustrates how the shooting angle improves as you move along the crease; with every step, you see more of

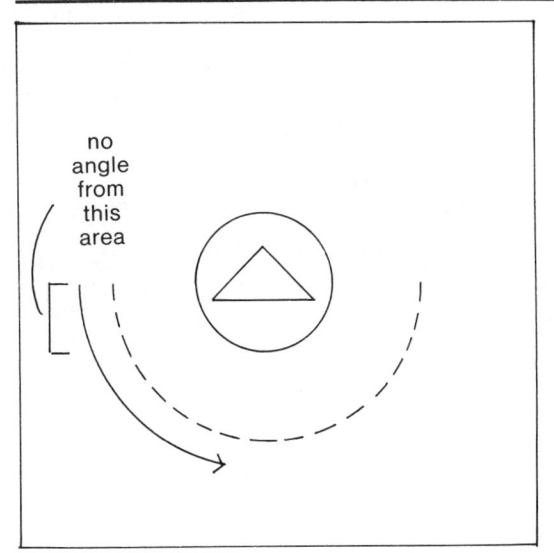

Diagram 11

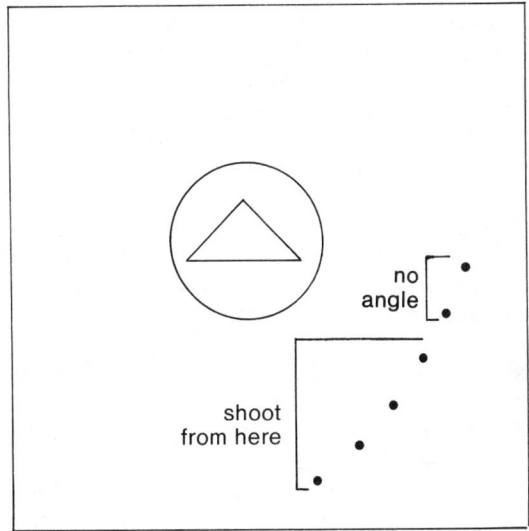

Diagram 12: There is no angle from the closer points, especially with the goalie hugging the pipes. The farther out you shoot, the better.

the goal. The same holds true when shooting out front. Players often make the mistake of overrunning their shooting angle. They feel the closer they are to the goal the better, but this is not always true as illustrated by Diagram 12.

Cutting

Cutting is a part of the game that demands a lot of skill. A player can be a less than adequate athlete and dodger but, through intelligent cutting, can score many goals. Here are a few rules I follow that have helped me as a cutter. (1) Before I cut, I try to establish eye contact with the feeder. This lets both of us know what is happening. (2) I will try to lull my defender to sleep before I make my cut. This is where some acting talent is needed. You might try to get him to look away by pretending that the ball is in a different part of the field. When he turns to look, cut to the ball. Or you can act as if you'll never get the ball in a million years. Let your defender relax; when he does, take off. (3) If covered, I never break straight to the ball. I run my defender one way and break the other. (4) If there is a pick set, I don't just run my man by the pick, I run him *into* the pick. It is the cutter's job to utilize the pick because the man setting the pick cannot move once the pick is set nor can he lean into or reach out and grab the defenseman. (5) The last rule I follow probably is the most important. If I am cutting off a pick and I don't receive the ball, I immediately stop and repick for the man who had picked for me. This play works very well because it happens so fast that the defense has a hard time communicating. A final note about cutting: while cutting, you should always keep your stick positioned where you want to receive the ball (right by your ear). This gives the feeder a good target; and, once you receive the ball, your stick and the ball are already tight to your body and well protected. *[Read Mike's rules over and over; memorize them. You have to know how to do each one to become a really good cutter.—G.F.]*

Picking

When I pick, I try to keep as wide a base to my stance as possible and almost flex my body when the defender runs into me. This serves to protect me from injury. When picking, I always have my stick in the box, right by my ear, so I'm ready to rebreak. After the cutter is past me, I read the situation to decide what to do. I may cut opposite. Or, I can wait for the cutter to repick for me. If a switch is called by the defense, I keep the defender on my back and cut to the goal. *[Here's another rule to follow. When you hear a switch called, go to the goal. Your man may be able to run his defenseman into you. Your defenseman feels that the only way to stop the cutter is to pick him up; this leaves the man playing you behind you.—G.F.]*

Playing Loose Balls

When I pick up a loose ball, I immediately bring the stick right to my chest for protection. As I am doing this, I'm also running for open field—get the ball and get out! As I'm running, my head is always up; I don't look down at the ground. I'm also looking for an open man I can move the ball to.

Attack

Dave Tickner

EDITOR'S INTRODUCTION

This three-time All-American is one of the greatest of Princeton's attackmen. Tic began playing when he entered high school and has been at it ever since. An All-American at both midfield and attack, he has a tremendous ability to score. Navy still remembers their loss to Princeton in 1975, a loss to which Tic contributed 6 goals and 2 assists.

After graduating and moving back to his home town, Baltimore, Tic starting playing with the Mt. Washington Lacrosse Club, where he won the award along with Bob Griebe as the Best Attackman of the Year. He works for IBM and has done some coaching at Gilman School. Dave takes a hard and close look at all the facets of offensive play, showing you step by step what's involved with the various moves.

PLAYER'S INTRODUCTION

The game has meant a great deal to me. It has helped me gain confidence in myself. Sports give you immediate gratification and positive reinforcement if you win, or a good chance for some self-evaluation and introspection if you lose. Both are essential to building your character. Also, lacrosse has given me the opportunity to meet a great many interesting people. It offers me the luxury of being part of a team while still being able to retain my individuality.

Because lacrosse helps you develop a competitive spirit, a healthy body, and a certain self-pride, I feel it can be beneficial to any type of business occupation you wish to pursue.

Philosophy of Attack

The primary function of an attackman is to make sure his team scores when the ball is down in the offensive end. This entails either scoring yourself, feeding someone, or getting the ball moving in such a way that it will be easier for your team to score. Since the ball is not down at your end of the field all the time, there is no sense in going half speed when it does come down. Make the most of the time when you have the ball. Always be thinking about scoring and always be prepared to move fast to score. It is good to be in a position where you can shoot and score.

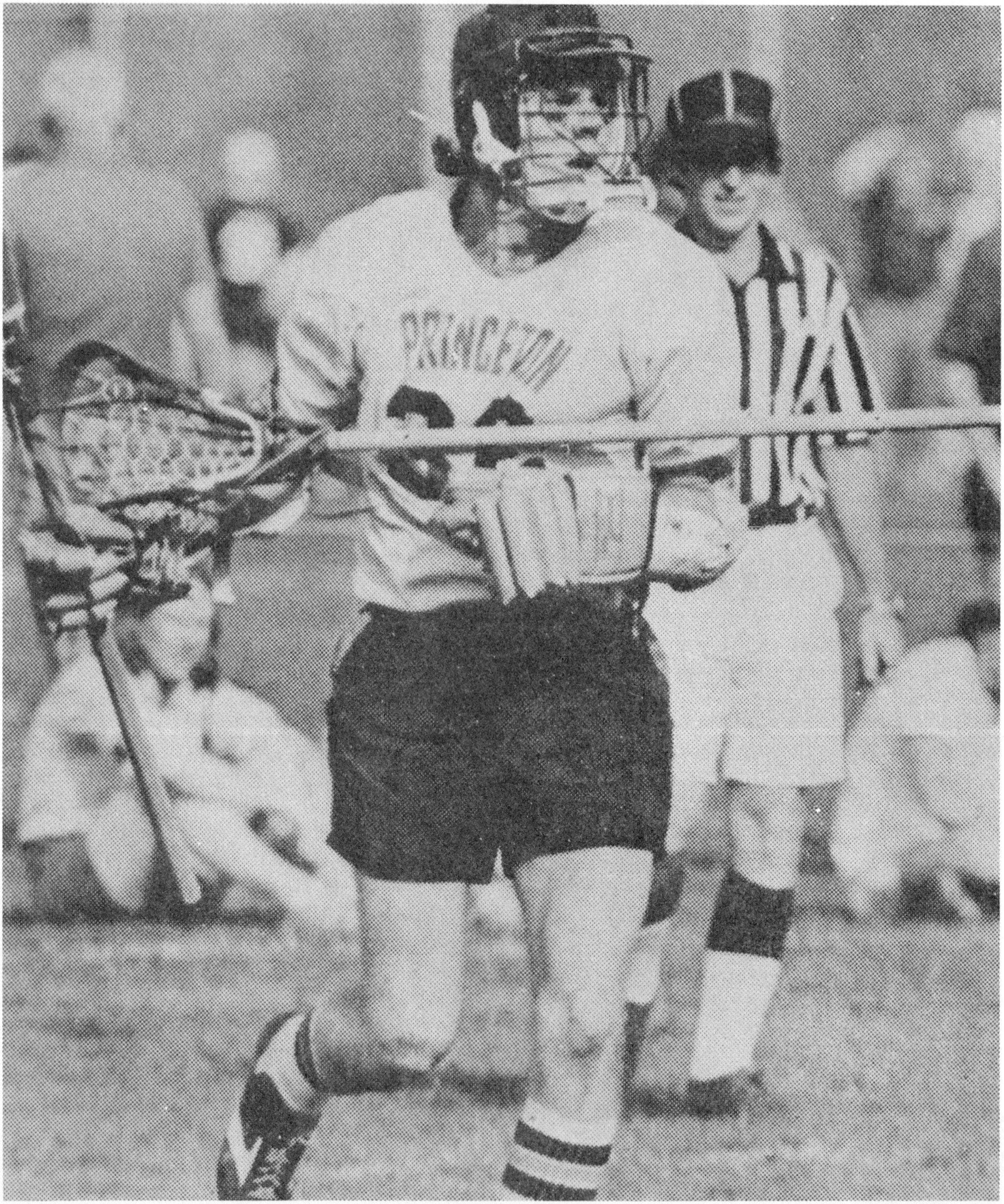
PRINCETON

Attack

Playing Behind

There are many things to consider when you are behind the goal. First, you should look to feed cutters or players breaking free on the crease. Second, you should find out how fast your defenseman is, how well he changes direction, and whether he plays position or goes after the ball. If he plays aggressively, go to the goal. Chances are he will have only one shot at you in trying to take away the ball. If he plays position, keep moving and concentrate on feeding. Third, when you are behind the goal, make sure that you are always in a position to beat the opposing team to the endline after a missed shot. Remember, make the most of the time when you have the ball.

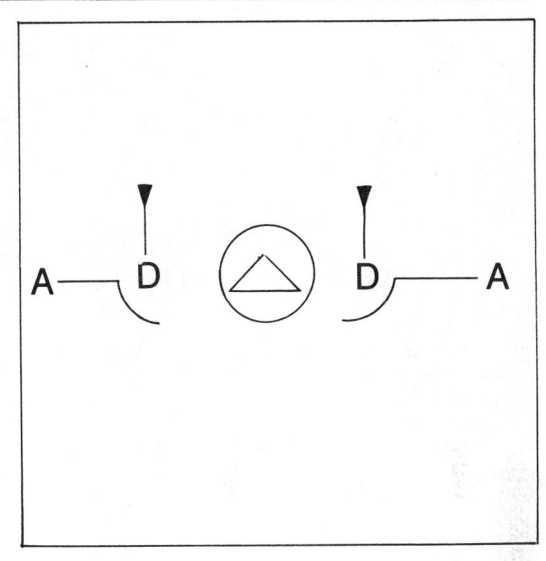

Diagram 1

Dodging

Dodging is a personal thing. Everybody is comfortable with his own style. I can only tell you what I feel comfortable with. If your defenseman is tired, go to the goal. If he is out of position, go to the goal. If he is playing overaggressively, go to the goal.

The most important thing to keep in mind is that you *dodge with your legs and not with your stick.* The faster you can run and the quicker you can change direction, the better you will be at dodging, regardless of your stickwork. If you are faster than your defenseman, take (dodge) your defenseman when he is playing you a good distance from the goal. If you can change directions faster than your defenseman, run him back and forth until you have a step on him, then go to the goal. If you are stronger than he is, protect your stick and run right through or over him.

Always try to get distance between you and your defenseman before starting your dodge. This enables you to get a running start on him.

Look to see if your defenseman holds his stick to one side or the other. If you are on the side of the goal and your defenseman is holding his stick to the back side of the goal, even as you get close to him, then you should be able to beat him by running straight at him and then breaking to the front side of the goal. There should be only a slim chance of his being able to pull his stick across his body to his other side fast enough to stop you. (See Diagram 1.)

Look to see if your defenseman changes hands with his stick. If he is playing with the opposite hand than the one you are driving to, you should be able to drive right through his stick. (See Diagram 2.) Unless he is much stronger than you, the only way he can stop you is to cross check or wrap you. [Do as Tic says. Just because a defenseman has his stick in front of you, doesn't mean you

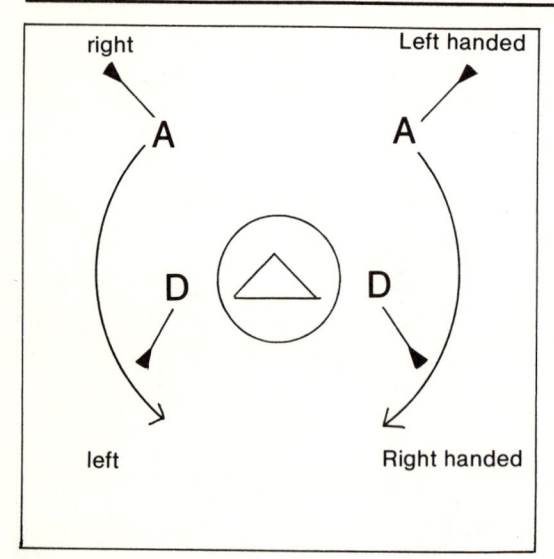

Tickner

Diagram 2

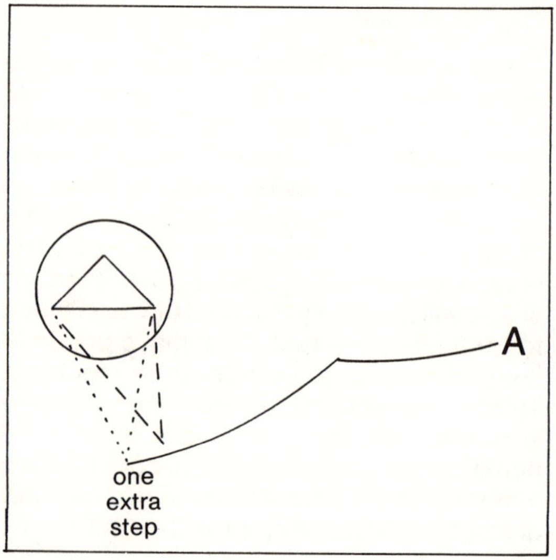

Diagram 3

can't go that way. Of course, he wants you to think that he's got you covered, but I think you'll be surprised at how easily you can go right through his stick most of the time.—G.F.]

Regarding dodging techniques in general, there are two important rules to remember. (1) *Protect your stick at all times.* Generally, this means carrying it straight up and down while dodging to avoid hanging it either in front or in back. Also, use your off arm and your body to help protect your stick. (2) *After you dodge, always take one extra step* to increase your angle on the goal and to draw the goalie off the pipe before you shoot. If dodging from behind the goal, bend around the crease when you come around to shoot and take that extra step. You might be hit, but, as shown in Diagrams 3 and 3a, your chances of scoring are greatly increased by taking that extra step.

Here are some specific pointers for the

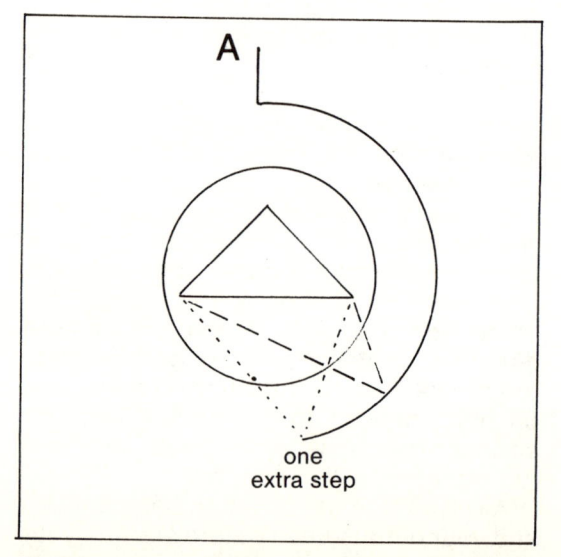

Diagram 3a

basic lacrosse dodges.

Bull Dodge: (1) Protect your stick. (2) Keep moving; don't stop. (3) Crouch lower than your defenseman and lean into him. (4) Use your off hand or arm as much as possible without actually warding off your defenseman. (5) Be prepared to take at least two hard bumps or checks (wrap, over the head, push). (6) Be prepared for someone sliding on you. The bull dodge is a good move if you are big and strong or if your defenseman is not playing you cross handed. It also sets up the inside roll dodge very well. Of the six points I mentioned above, making sure you keep moving is the most important because it's tougher to hit a moving target.

Face Dodge: (1) Get a running headstart at your defenseman. (2) Make your defenseman commit with his stick or body *before* you make your final move. (3) Fake with your head and shoulders as well as your stick. (4) When making your move, plant your foot hard and push off; pull your stick quickly and accelerate past your defenseman. (See Diagram 4.) From my own personal experience, I would say that it is harder to face dodge from directly behind or in front of the goal. However, this is a personal preference. Remember, there are benefits to dodging from directly behind or in front of the goal. From those two areas, there is not just *one* open side of the goal for the defenseman to protect. *Both* sides are open so you can dodge either way and still be in a position to shoot with a good angle.

Roll Dodge: (1) Get a running start at your defenseman. (2) Get him running hard in one direction. (3) Convince him that you want to keep going in that direction. (4) Let him get in front of you and close to you. (5) Plant hard and change directions. (6) Accelerate. (See Diagram 5.) There are sev-

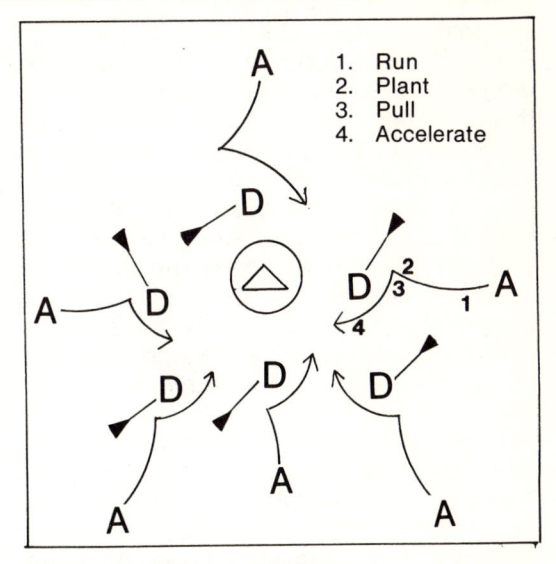

Diagram 4: The Face Dodge.

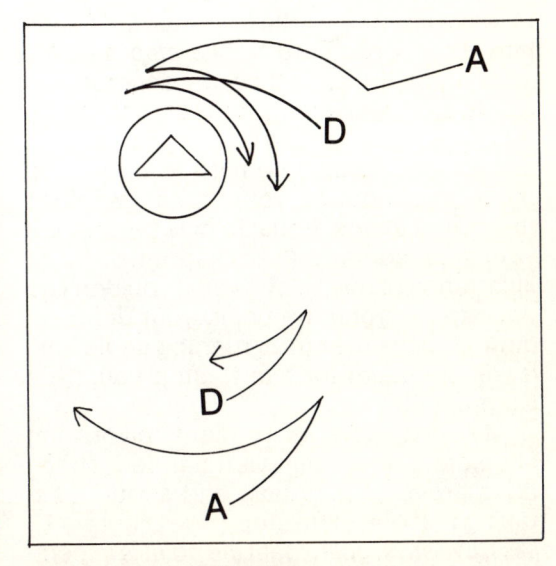

1. Run
2. Plant
3. Pull
4. Accelerate

Diagram 5: The Roll Dodge.

eral things to remember when roll dodging. First, do not be surprised if one change of direction fails. Generally, it takes two or three changes before you can beat your defenseman. Second, always accelerate and keep running after you change direction. Remember that even if the defenseman stops when you stop, he has not stopped your dodge because he still has to pull a much larger stick across his body and in front of you. He also has to start running with you again while he is doing this. And he must go through the same maneuver every time you change direction. This can get very tiring. *[Remember this point: your defenseman can't cover you every time you change direction.—G.F.]* Third, take at least five steps before changing directions for a second or third time so that your defenseman is running in one direction fast enough for you to make the dodge effective.

The roll dodge is my favorite move. Here's how I do it. First, I run hard right handed at my defenseman. (See Diagram 6.) I also try to leave my stick a little unprotected to bait him. Then I run hard to *one step past the point.* Usually by this time, my defenseman has to start respecting the fact that I might be going right handed to the goal, and he has to start coming up hard to try to stop me. At this moment, your running angle to the goal is almost equal to or is better than your defenseman's. (See Diagram 6a for an illustration of this.) However, if you don't go one step beyond the point, your defenseman will have the better running angle, and it will be easier for him to stop you. (See Diagram 6b.)

My next move is to plant, pivot, and accelerate after rolling left handed. Then I drive around the crease and shoot—*after* taking that one extra step. (See Diagram 7.) *[As Dave says, going* past *the point is imperative. Not only must your defenseman play you*

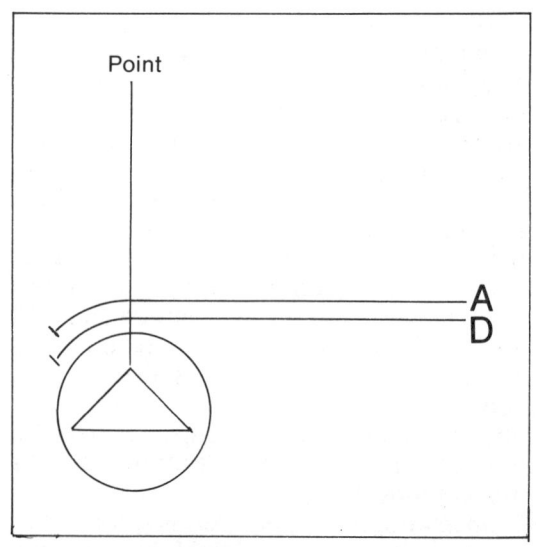

Diagram 6: The Roll Dodge.

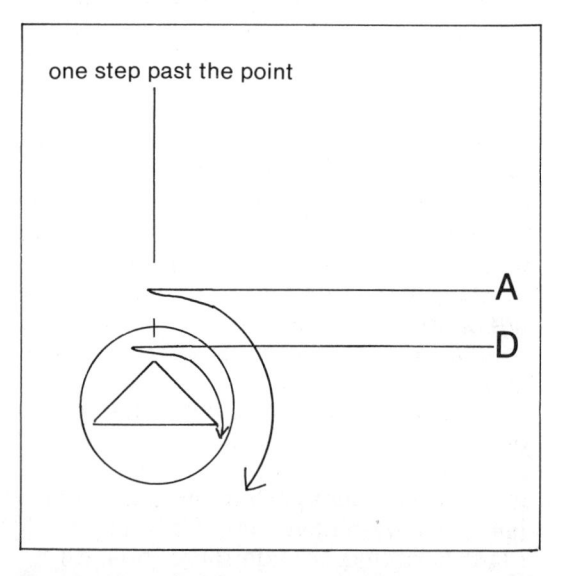

Diagram 6a

Attack

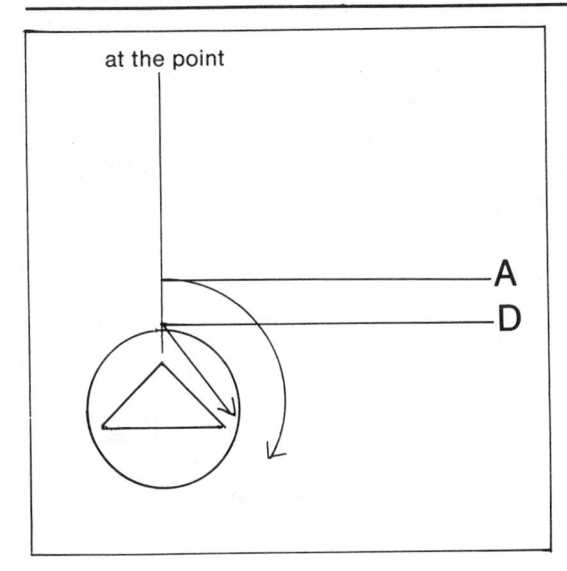

Diagram 6b

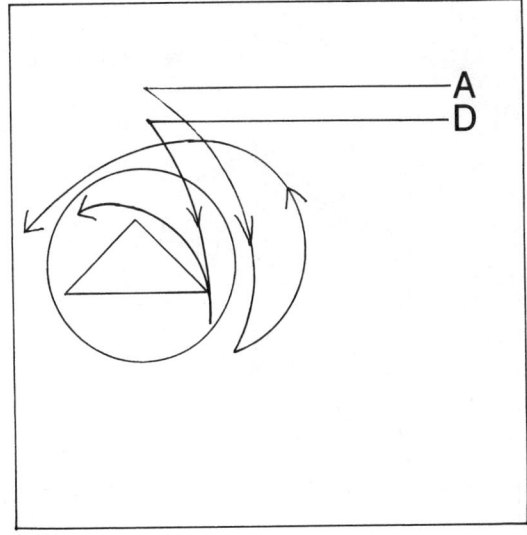

Diagram 8

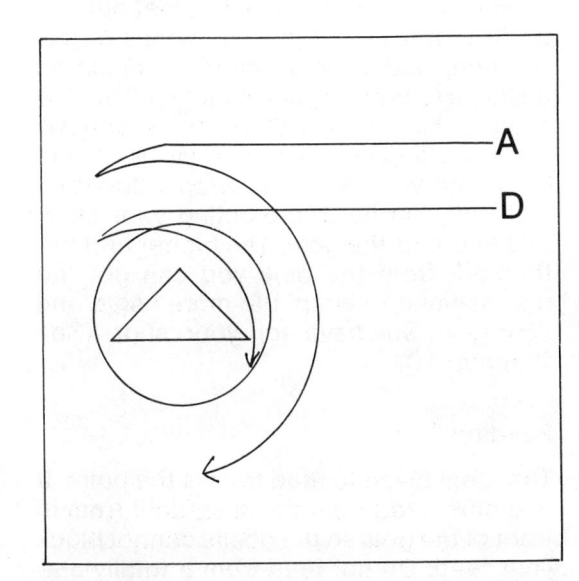

Diagram 7

as coming right handed, but he's been taught to check you because you're in feeding position. You must try to get him to that position in order to successfully complete the roll dodge. —G.F.]

If this move does not work for some reason, I change back right and drive up the right side of the goal even farther, as shown in Diagram 8. Again, the farther up the side of the goal you go, the closer your defenseman gets. When I feel the defenseman really coming up on my right side, I change (roll back) left and continue my drive around the *left* side of the goal and shoot, as shown in Diagram 9.

If, at this point, the dodge has not won me a step on my defenseman, I will try a bull dodge.

Checks

A defenseman who is going over my head is generally tall and fast. It is imperative to run

Tickner 72

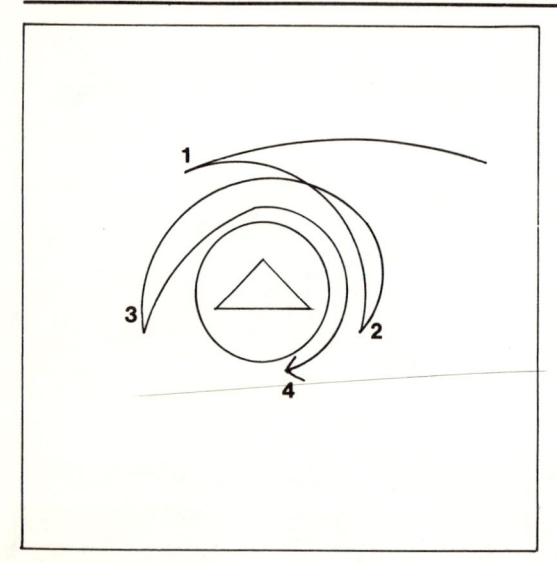

Diagram 9: (1) Roll left; (2) Roll right; (3) Roll left; (4) Shoot.

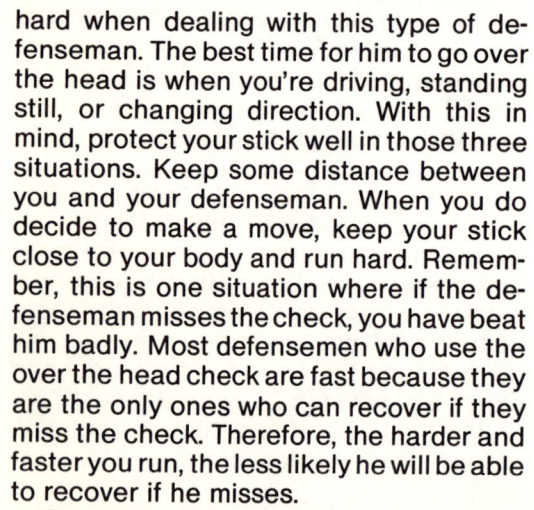

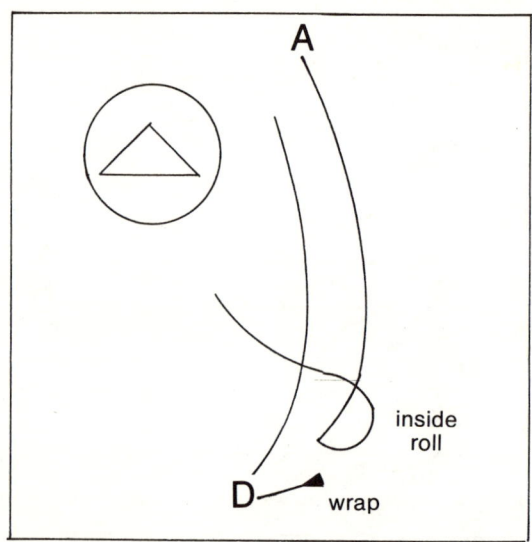

Diagram 10

hard when dealing with this type of defenseman. The best time for him to go over the head is when you're driving, standing still, or changing direction. With this in mind, protect your stick well in those three situations. Keep some distance between you and your defenseman. When you do decide to make a move, keep your stick close to your body and run hard. Remember, this is one situation where if the defenseman misses the check, you have beat him badly. Most defensemen who use the over the head check are fast because they are the only ones who can recover if they miss the check. Therefore, the harder and faster you run, the less likely he will be able to recover if he misses.

Generally, defensemen who use a wrap check are strong. Therefore, unless you are very strong yourself, do not try to dodge this type of defenseman. Keep your distance and run hard. Don't give him an opportunity to wrap. Pick a position where you want (and expect) him to use the check, for example five to ten feet out and up from the pipe. When he wraps in this position, use your off hand as much as possible to protect your stick. Don't get too close to him; if you get too close, you will end up rolling into him or he will be able to long john you. When he wraps, do an inside roll, run hard, protecting your stick, and shoot at the goal. The higher and further out from the pipe you can get the defenseman to wrap, the more angle and time you will have for your shot. (See Diagram 10.)

Feeding

The ideal place to feed from is the point. If you must feed from the side, do it from in front of the goal so the goalie cannot block your feed. Do not feed from a totally stationary position. (If your feet aren't moving,

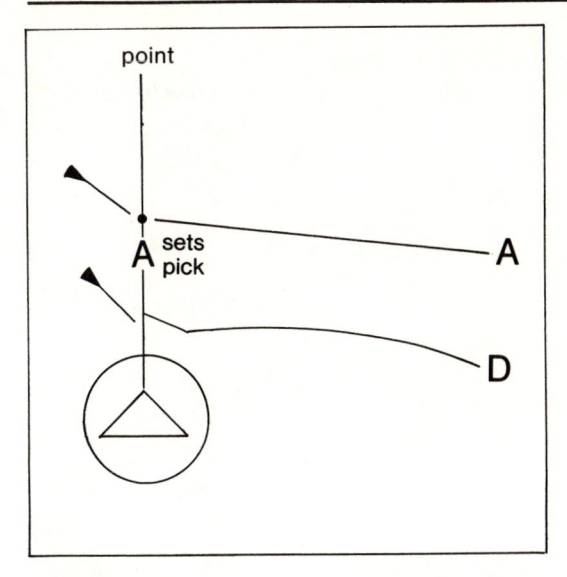

Diagram 11

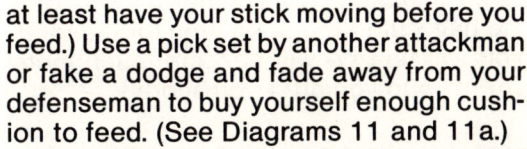

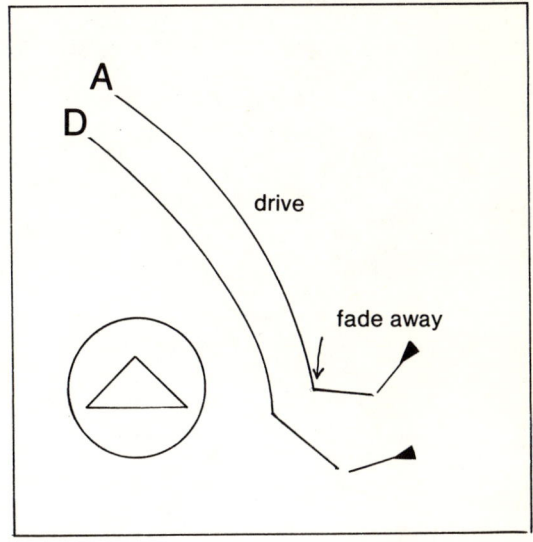

Diagram 11a

at least have your stick moving before you feed.) Use a pick set by another attackman or fake a dodge and fade away from your defenseman to buy yourself enough cushion to feed. (See Diagrams 11 and 11a.)

The easiest cutter to hit is the one who gives you a target. Similarly, the easiest feed to catch is one that is thrown overhand directly in the cutter's line of vision.

If the cutter is open, you should be looking right at him because (1) if you are in good position, the feed is in no danger of getting blocked; and (2) the cutter will be more aware that the feed is coming to him. However, in extra man offensive situations, you may want to fake the defenseman with your eyes so that he relaxes. This enables your feed to get through and the cutter to get off a shot without getting checked immediately.

How hard you feed depends on where the cutter is. If he is open and close to overrunning the goal, then the feed must be hard so that he receives it in time to take his

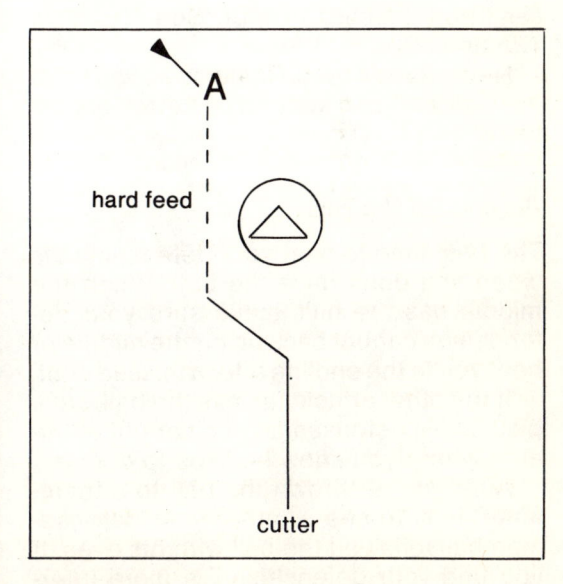

Diagram 12

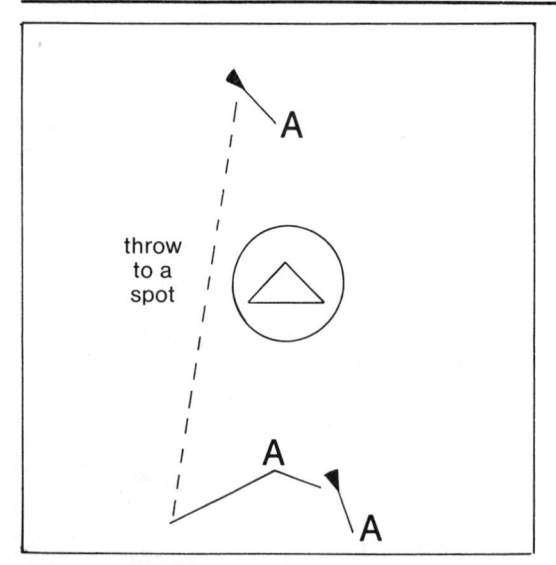

Diagram 12a

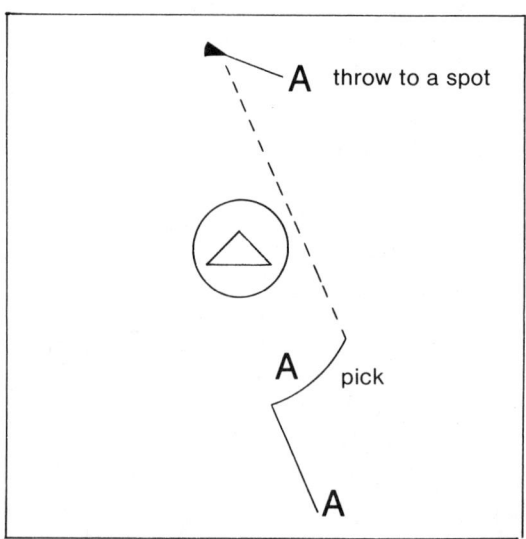

Diagram 12b

shot. (See Diagram 12.) If the cutter is coming off a pick, then you can anticiate when he will break free from his man and can throw the ball to a spot. (See Diagrams 12a and 12b.)

Never force a feed. Remember, you have the ball and can wait for a better opportunity.

Playing Off the Ball

The best time to beat your defenseman is when you don't have the ball. When the middie has the ball, make sure your defenseman cannot back up on the middie or beat you to the endline after a missed shot.

If the other attackman has the ball, set a pick on his defenseman or clear out of the area where you know he likes to dodge.

After you've thrown the ball to a teammate, look to see whether your defenseman has followed the ball with his eyes. If you find your defenseman is more interested in watching the other players with the ball, cut to the open area for the feed. You will find he will become much more attentive to you after you score!

Shooting

I try to shoot for the lower right part of the goal (playing left handed). Before I shoot, I check the goalie's movement. If he is moving toward one side, I should have a better chance of scoring by shooting to the other side. If you have the time, then faking before you shoot is a good idea. However, most of the time it is not possible. Generally, if your dodge has worked, you are close enough to the goal that a quick shot should be enough to get the ball by the goalie. A hard side shot that rises can be effective from a long distance, however, the best shot is an overhand bounce shot from five to ten yards out. *[Tic has scored many goals shooting sidearm. But, as he says,*

Attack

the ball tends to rise. To prevent the ball from rising so far that it sails over the goal, bring the hand that's on the butt end of the stick up 2 to 5 inches. This keeps the stick perpendicular to the ground and changes the trajectory of the ball so that it rises about 5½ or 6 feet off the ground—exactly where you want it.—G.F.]

If you have a screen out front, then shoot the ball. If you have dodged successfully, then shoot the ball. You can't score without shooting. But don't be reckless. Take good shots or you will find your teammates becoming reluctant to give you the ball.

A good shooting drill is to find a goal in an open field and bring two or three balls with you. Practice shooting from different places with both hands. Always try to shoot on the run. After missing the goal a lot, you will find that you will get in shape chasing all your missed shots, and the accuracy of your shots should increase as you become less and less enchanted with the prospect of chasing yet another missed shot!

Cutting and Picking

Cut when your defenseman is tired or when he is not watching you. Try to give the feeder a target to throw to and be prepared to take a check before you shoot.

I generally try to set a wide pick by spreading my legs so that I can help the cutter or attackman with the ball put some distance between himself and his defenseman.

After picking up a loose ball, always look for the open man. Preferably try to hit the man at the point. (In an unsettled situation, the man at the point has the best view of all cutters and the best place from which to feed.) *[First look to the crease area to see if there's an opening there. If not, do as Tic suggests and get the ball to the point.—G.F.]*

My Favorite Attack Plan

The attack plan I like to use the most is to move the ball quickly from the side to the point several times. This gets you running and the ball moving. If the ball keeps moving, then chances are someone will have the opportunity to get free on a cut. When the defenseman starts playing you tighter to cut down on the ball movement, it's time to try your dodges. The farther out the defense comes to play you, the better your chances are of dodging.

Future of Lacrosse

With the introduction and improvement of plastic sticks, the game has become much better because players can learn to play faster and throw and shoot more accurately. Once the catching skills reach the current level of shooting and throwing skills, offenses will become almost unstoppable. I believe this will cause more specialized types of defensive strategies and players (especially zone playing). This might be the downfall of the dodging, driving player. Yet, fast running, combined with fast ball movement, is a beautiful thing to watch, and I don't think the game ever will lose that.

Dave Warfield

EDITOR'S INTRODUCTION

Dave Warfield was the greatest attackman who ever played for Washington & Lee. This two-time All-American has the ability to break a game wide open. Towson State will long remember him because of their heartbreaking 15 to 14 loss during a game in which the Rave had 7 goals and dished out 4 assists. And he's just as dangerous in club lacrosse. The Rave was instrumental in helping the Chesapeake Club upset club champion Mt. Washington 10-9 in 1978. Dave contributed 5 of those 10 goals and assisted for another.

The Rave is 6' tall and weighs 165 lbs., but his speed and overall quickness make this attackman a powerful opponent and a real asset to his team. A member of the '78 U.S. National team, he's just finished three years of coaching lacrosse on a variety of levels to concentrate on his family insurance business, but he plans to referee and continue playing club ball.

PLAYER'S INTRODUCTION

In addition to the thrill of victory and team spirit that competition brings, I've enjoyed meeting the wide variety of people I've gotten to know through lacrosse. Lacrosse teaches you competitiveness as well as how not to give up or get discouraged when you suffer an initial loss or setback.

I've also found that attitude is extremely important to playing well, especially at the college level. Many times a college team will beat an opponent who has better players because of attitude and enthusiasm. Lacrosse teaches you the overall importance of a positive attitude in everything that you do.

Philosophy of Attack

The position of attackman is unique in its importance to a team. Not only does an attackman's stickwork and skill need to be superior, but he also has to have the presence of mind to control the ball while his team is playing offense.

Without detracting from the importance of the other positions in lacrosse, I believe that most championship teams have had at least one attackman on whom they relied for ball control and field leadership. To become an outstanding attackman requires not only years of practice and dedication but certain natural abilities such as speed and quickness.

As a totally offensive player, an attackman has to have outstanding stickwork. In addition to the shooting and dodging abilities required at other positions, the attackman has to be secure and confident in his ability to protect his stick. He must be able to control the ball without worrying about losing it to a defenseman. If an attackman is concerned with his defenseman, he will not be able to concentrate on feeding cutters or setting up dodges.

Equally important as the actual stick skills is having the presence of mind to control the game situation. A good attackman is also a good field leader. He has to gauge the momentum of the game and then either keep it going in his team's favor or shift it away from his opponents. Many teams lose momentum (and games) through forcing situations on offense; a good attackman will settle the rest of the team down and work to control both the ball and the game.

Technique

When I have the ball behind the goal, I try to control it offensively by settling it down and looking to feed. When I don't have the ball, I concentrate on backing up the goal and staying open for outlet passes if my man leaves to back up.

If I find my man overplaying me, I take him high then try to roll back inside. I try to get my defenseman to overcommit in some way.

I find that the best way to get free of my defenseman is to use an inside roll as shown in Diagram 1. Run your defenseman hard to the front of the goal. (Be sure to give yourself plenty of room—4 or 5 yards past the goal line extended.) Then plant your

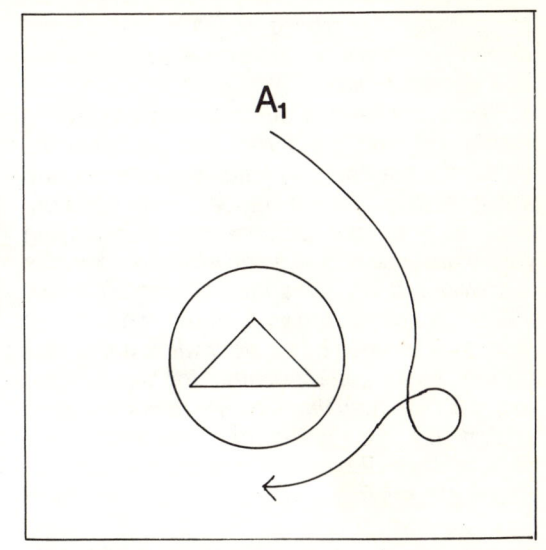

Diagram 1: Inside roll.

inside foot and pivot back. Hopefully, by the time your defenseman reacts to your move, you will have beat him and there will be a free lane open to the goal. Even if you don't completely beat your man, you'll be in a good position to muscle in and get off a shot. Remember to keep your stick tucked in close to your body. *When shooting do not bring your stick back behind your head.* Your defenseman is right behind you and will check your stick. You can set up a successful inside roll by running hard to the face of the goal several times *without* a roll back. Eventually, your defenseman will anticipate your move and try to stay in front of you. This is exactly where you want him for a successful roll. *[Rave has had success with this move for two sound reasons—he keeps his defenseman moving and, as he says, he gives himself enough room to be able to make his move. The latter point is important because, if you don't give yourself enough room, you'll find that as you roll back there will not be enough room to get off a shot. Then, you have

Warfield

to tight walk the crease or, if the defenseman doesn't push you in, the goalie will come out and get your stick.

There are several different ways to do the inside roll; one good way and probably the easiest to master is as follows: Come around the goal (assume left handed stick position) and, seeing your defenseman overplaying you, plant your right leg and swing backwards with your left leg, left shoulder and left elbow inside. By not moving your elbow and keeping it parallel to your body, your stick stays stationary, making it impossible for the defense to get it. (You may find it easier to control your stick if you put your thumb on the side of the stick instead of having it wrapped around it.) Some players move their bodies and sticks in two separate motions, but this approach makes it easier for your defenseman to wrap you. Using a single, integrated motion means that when your defenseman wraps he will hit your right arm which is out to take the blow. You actually want your defenseman to wrap you because, after he does and misses your stick, he'll pull back his stick in order to make another move or wrap. This will give you all the time you need to shoot.—G.F.]

If a defenseman goes over your head and misses, you have a free lane to the goal. If you think he's going to try a wrap, again keep moving, keep your off arm up for protection and your stick close to your body. When he wraps, try to change direction and beat him to the goal.

When I pick up a loose ball, the first place I look is to the crease. If no one on the crease is open, I look to see if anyone with a better position to continue moving the ball toward the crease is open. A drill that will help you here is to run alongside a brick wall. Pick out one brick and, while running, try to hit that brick with the ball. This drill will improve your overall shooting and feeding accuracy, and you can do it alone.

Feeding

It's too easy for the goalie to intercept a feed from directly behind the goal so I never feed from directly behind. When I feed, I do it while moving; never stand still to feed; you're too vulnerable. I buy myself room to feed by changing direction suddenly or by feeding off a pick. I usually feed overhand; but, if I'm trying to feed past a defenseman, I may feed sidearm. I always look at a cutter before feeding, but I try not to telegraph where I'll feed. I try to anticipate the cutter, waiting until he is just off a pick before feeding. For the most part, I do not feed to an area.

Playing Off the Ball

In general, make yourself available to help a teammate when you don't have the ball. Be open for an outlet pass or set a pick. If your man leaves to back up, move toward the goal and look for an outlet pass. Also be ready to receive an outlet pass if your wings or middies need a rest.

If the ball is behind, see if you can pick. Keep the play varied to make the opposition work hard. If you've just passed the ball to a teammate, wait to see what he's going to do. Sometimes, go right into a give and go play; again, this helps keep the defense off balance.

Shooting

When I shoot, I aim to the goalie's off side or near the pipes, but not necessarily at the corners. I always check the goalie's stick position before shooting. I let the ball go whenever I have a good angle on the goal.

I usually shoot overhand because shots are easier to control and more accurate when done overhand, although you do lose some speed. It's very important to keep

Attack

Bob Russell

Warfield

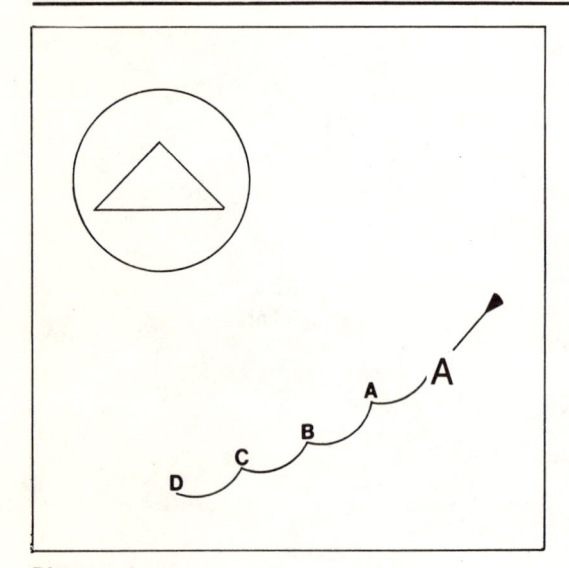

Diagram 2

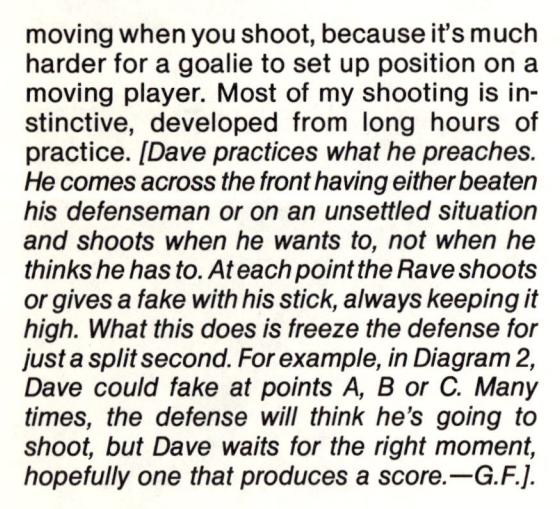

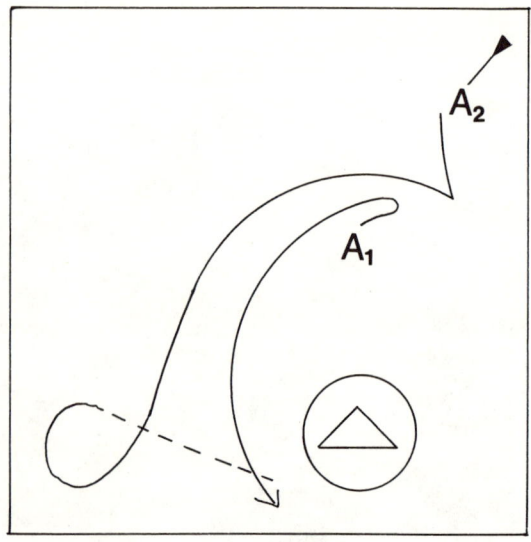

Diagram 3

moving when you shoot, because it's much harder for a goalie to set up position on a moving player. Most of my shooting is instinctive, developed from long hours of practice. *[Dave practices what he preaches. He comes across the front having either beaten his defenseman or on an unsettled situation and shoots when he wants to, not when he thinks he has to. At each point the Rave shoots or gives a fake with his stick, always keeping it high. What this does is freeze the defense for just a split second. For example, in Diagram 2, Dave could fake at points A, B or C. Many times, the defense will think he's going to shoot, but Dave waits for the right moment, hopefully one that produces a score.—G.F.]*

Favorite Play

My favorite play is a two man attack play from behind the goal, as shown in Diagram 3. A2 runs by the pick set by A1 and continues on to swing wide. As he begins to come back, A1 starts to break opposite, then changes direction and comes back. A2 feeds in front of A1 so that A1 can run into the feed and continue on around the goal without breaking stride and usually with several steps on his defenseman. The crease man clears the crease and moves to back up the goal.

Future of Lacrosse

I would like to see a move to more internationally-oriented rules—the running clock, ball in play immediately after an out of bounds, limited substitution, etc. From a spectator's point of view, the game is becoming too slow, largely due to more and more coaching with too many delays and timeouts to handle special situations.

I feel players are going to continue to improve at a rapid rate and the quality of play is going to exceed what we now have. More and more, a player's natural ability is going to be important—especially his *speed*. I see speed (both of individual players and teams as a whole) as one of the most important aspects of the game in the future.

Richard Scalera

2 Midfield

The greatest challenge that a good midfielder faces is learning how to play when he does not have the ball. This theme is hammered home again and again by each of the players who contributed to this section. The middie combines the highest skills of both the attack and the defense. In addition, he must be a superb athlete, able to run quickly from one end of the field to the other, arriving ready to play and with a plan of action already formulated.

Probably the most important technical skill that a middie must possess is the ability to cut. He has to know when, where and how to cut. He has to be able to cut to the ball for a feed and he has to know how to cut away from the ball so he can pull his defenseman out of the main action area.

The middies who are represented here all agree that the position is physically the most difficult and at the same time the most rewarding one in lacrosse. They all see the middie as the necessary link between the offense and the defense. If that link is weak, then the entire team effort fails.

I suggest that all attackmen read this section to better understand how their own middies see the game. Defensemen should read this section for its hints on how middies think and react both as an offensive threat to them and as a defensive counterpart.

Midfield 84

Richard Scalera

Bruce Arena

EDITOR'S INTRODUCTION

Bruce Arena played lacrosse in high school and at Nassau Community College on Long Island before joining one of the powerful Cornell teams. He was captain of the Cornell team and voted its most valuable player his senior year. Bruce played on both the 1974 and 1978 USA National Teams.

Since graduating, he's played club lacrosse for the Long Island, Brine and Central New York clubs. He's now head soccer and assistant lacrosse coach at the University of Virginia.

One of the quickest and ablest middies around, this former All-American sees his position as a vital link between defense and offense. His analysis of the way a good middie must play is useful to almost every position.

PLAYER'S INTRODUCTION

I have a very special feeling for the game of lacrosse. I have been fortunate to play not only high school, college and club lacrosse, but also professional box lacrosse. This experience has given me the opportunity to make money, travel all over the world, and form lasting friendships. My experiences while traveling with the 1974 and 1978 USA National teams were tremendous. The enjoyment, knowledge, and experiences I have had through lacrosse will affect me for the rest of my life. There is little doubt in my mind that, in one way or another, I will remain involved in the game for many years to come.

Playing under people such as Mike Candel, Richie Speckman and Richie Moran, greatly influenced me in other areas of my life. In particular, playing under Richie Moran, who is not only a great coach but also a true gentleman, taught me the value of discipline. I feel that the discipline I've learned on the field has enabled me to get the most out of myself off the field as well. The enjoyment and rewards that I have earned through hard work and discipline in lacrosse have made me a better and more productive person in the rest of my life's activities.

Philosophy

The function of a midfielder is to be able to compliment both the attack and defensive units. He is a vital link between both units. A midfielder who is capable of playing on both the offensive and defensive parts of

Arena

the field is greatly respected by his coaches, teammates, and opponents. Obviously, many players have limitations at midfield; some are better offensive players, and some are better defensive players. But a good midfielder must be capable of playing at both ends of the field.

On defense, a midfielder must be capable of playing good one on one defense as well as good team defense. Good team defense means having the ability to back up and slide when necessary. Another function of defense is picking up loose balls and clearing. And lastly, a midfielder should be capable of creating the fast break from his defensive end of the field.

On offense, a midfielder should be able to go one on one, be an excellent cutter, and have a good outside shot. Obviously, not every midfielder is capable of excelling in all three areas. Therefore, it is critical that a player (as well as his coach) know his limitations at the midfield. A good one on one ball player must have the ability to dodge his man and shoot or pass to a free teammate. A weaker one on one midfielder can learn the technique of becoming a good cutter, or how to play without the ball. By realizing his limitations, a midfielder can concentrate on excelling in one area so that he still can compliment the offensive unit. *[I totally agree with Bruce. Not only does it take time to learn everything, it's difficult to master all phases of the game. Don't let this lead to discouragement and disappointment. The key is to learn to do one thing well—G. F.]*

Playing Out Front

When I have the ball out front, I am looking for a couple of things. First of all, if it's a situation where one on one play is possible, I attempt to dodge my man and pass off to a teammate when the opposition slides on me. If I feel my opponent is really good at defense, I will not attempt to force dodge him one on one. I will either pass the ball to the attack and work a cut from the midfield, or pass to one of my fellow midfielders and move without the ball. When I have the ball out front, I like to do what I think is the easiest play in lacrosse—give the ball and go. Even though my opponent may be a good one on one defensive player, I generally feel that I can beat him on a cut.

Dodging

I feel dodging at the midfield is a spontaneous reaction to a certain defensive posture. As a rule of thumb, I will dodge an opponent when I notice that his defensive positioning is not ideal. I pay close attention to his feet, stick position, his size, and the defensive back-up. If I notice that my opponent is flat-footed, I will attempt to dodge him. Also, if I notice that he is carrying his stick across his body instead of out front, I will attempt to face dodge him. If my opponent is small or a scouting report indicates that he is slow, I will attempt to dodge him. There is no denying that lacrosse is an athlete's game and the one on one matchup at midfield many times boils down to certain physical attributes. Therefore, I do attempt to take advantage of my opponent's size or lack of quickness.

A particularly weak defensive midfielder is very often vulnerable behind the goal. In this type of situation I like to take him behind the goal and dodge him from his area.

Actually, the face dodge is my favorite move. I prefer to use it at the left side of the goal. I carry my stick in a three-quarter position in my right hand, accelerate quickly to my right, and use eye contact as if I am going right. I then quickly plant on my right foot, bring my stick across my body and drive hard to the left. It is important when face dodging to change your stick to your opposite hand. This prevents your opponent from recovering and checking the ball out of your stick. *[After you do face dodge and change hands with your stick, the closer you go by your man, the better because it makes it harder for your man to recover and it makes you go right at the goal, putting you in an excellent position to be an offensive threat either as the shooter or the feeder if the defense slides.—G. F.]*

Playing a Loose Ball

When I pick up a loose ball in the offensive end of the field, I immediately attempt to create an unsettled situation. After scooping up a loose ball, a midfielder can often create an unsettled situation by reacting quickly with either a dodge, pass or a quick burst of speed into the offensive end of the field.

When I pick up a loose ball in the defensive end of the field, I immediately attempt to run or pass the ball over midfield. If my opponents are able to react quickly and prevent me from running or passing the ball forward, I simply turn and pass the ball back to my defensive unit. We then are able to set up our clear.

Feeding

Ninety percent of my feeds are overhand and done with a flick of the wrist. The overhand pass is the simplest and most accurate form of feeding. As players become experienced and more adept at stick handling, the three-quarter feed or the underhand feed can become part of their repertoire. Generally speaking, midfielders feed off a dodge, as opposed to attackmen who are capable of feeding at any time.

I feel there are two different ways to get a defenseman in position so you can feed. One obvious way is to dodge your man, draw an opponent and then look to feed. By stepping away, you can avoid contact and can feed free of pressure.

The particular situation or flow of the game as well as the midfielder's experience, dictates whether a midfielder will be looking at the cutter while feeding. (Most of the time, I look at the cutter.) At the midfield position, you generally lead the cutter and throw stick high. This is particularly true when dodging and feeding to an attackman on a backdoor move.

Playing Without the Ball

I believe this is one area of play that many midfielders do not understand. A midfielder often can be much more effective offensively when he is moving without the ball. Bill Marino, former Cornell great, is a perfect example. Bill has scored perhaps 75% of his goals off feeds given him while he's moving without the ball. Bill has perfected the "give and go" play.

Movement varies with the set the team is in. If the set is a 3-1-2, one move that a midfielder without the ball can try is to set a pick for the teammate who is away from the ball. In a 2-2-2 set, the midfielder can try faking away from the ball and then cut back toward the ball to receive a pass back from his teammate. If the attackman has the ball, the midfielder should fake away from the ball. Head fakes and body fakes are important ingredients of being an effective cutter. Having the ability to disguise the direction in which you intend to cut is most important at the midfield because a straight 45° cut is usually ineffective.

Shooting

Ideally, a player should not decide too far in advance the part of the goal he will shoot for. Instead, he should react to where the goalie is positioned. In general, I look to shoot high hip side, or low opposite the goalie's strong side. When I have extra time before I shoot, I will fake with a flick of my wrists. In this way, I hope to get the goalie to commit himself. Then I shoot to the open side of the goal.

When shooting off a cut, I firmly believe a midfielder should shoot with a quick stick. Off a dodge, the decision to shoot is dictated by whether the defense slides quickly or whether I have time to shoot. Off a dodge, I like to shoot sidearm or underhand because after I dodge the positioning of my stick (toward the lower part of my body) often prevents my opponent from stick checking me.

Cutting

The correct way to cut is not to allow your opponent to know where you are going. Body fakes such as moving your head opposite the direction you want to go are often effective in getting open on the cut. Also, the ability to drive your man into a pick is helpful in attempting to free yourself.

The proper time to cut is when your teammate is in position to feed. Many players do not understand the importance of timing their cuts. I often see players making nice cuts but at the wrong time. Timing is the most important ingredient to successful cutting.

One last point. Being a good cutter not only compliments the offensive unit, but forces the opposing defensive unit to respect your movements which, in turn, helps cut down defensive back-ups on your teammates.

Picking

You should be in an erect, stationary position when setting a pick because you are better able to absorb any kind of blow. As a general rule, do not pick a teammate with the ball. Picking the ball creates a double team on your teammate. Most of the time, pick opposite the ball.

Midfielders generally pick opposite in a 3-1-2 set. When on the crease on a 2-2 set, they will pick with the crease attackman. Again, timing is critical. The pick should be timed so that your teammate can drive off the pick, free himself, and get open for a feed.

My favorite midfield play (and perhaps the most common midfield play) is a simple pick opposite. Generally, this type of play is set up off a 3-1-2 set as shown in Diagram 1. The ball can start with the center midfielder who passes to either wing. The center midfielder then picks at the opposite wing midfield position. The feeder has two options here. He can feed either the first midfielder coming through on the cut or the second midfielder following. Another option off the play is for the pick midfielder to hold and receive a pass for an outside shot or drive to the goal. (See Diagram 2.) A further option off this play is for the pick midfielder to clear through, which sets up a sweep for the ball handler as shown in Diagram 3.

Midfield Defense

There are certain keys to playing midfield

Arena

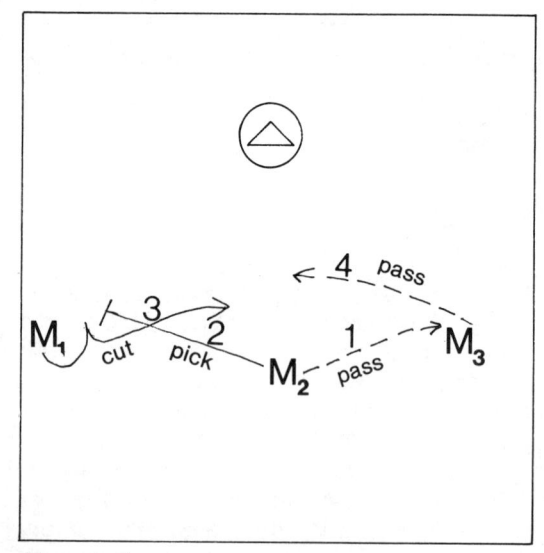

Diagram 1

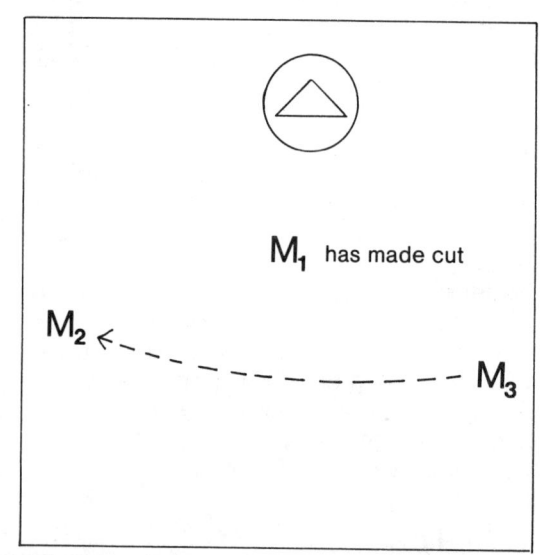

Diagram 2: After pick, M2 receives pass; he may shoot or drive to goal.

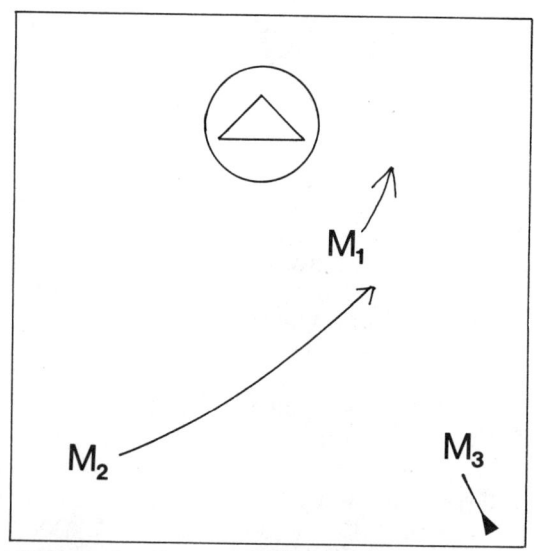

Diagram 3: Both middies clear through after pick, and open up a sweep for M3.

defense when my man has the ball. As I mentioned, I stand on my toes with one foot slightly ahead of the other. My feet are spread about shoulder width. My stick is directly in front of my body. This way if my opponent attempts to face dodge, my stick is in position to spear, and my body is in position to follow with my man. Holding your stick across your body prevents correct body balance; but, by holding the stick directly out in front, you maintain good body position and balance. As an opponent dodges on either side, I am able to step back with either foot and follow his movement. It is important that you never cross your feet when playing any type of defense.

When my opponent has the ball, I try to play good position defense. I attempt to play stick on stick and react to his movements. I am a firm believer in not overplaying at the midfield but reacting to what your opponent does. Therefore, if I notice my opponent is sweeping with his stick high, I may attempt to react by going over his head. Perhaps the simplest and safest check at the midfield is to check on the glove. This prevents my opponent from having free access in shooting or feeding the ball.

When my man doesn't have the ball, I must do two things. One is to be aware of the position of the ball on the field, and the other is to keep my eye on my man at the same time. Therefore, I must position my body so that I can see my man and the ball simultaneously.

Going Over the Head

Being tall for a midfielder, I find it relatively easy to go over the head. The key ingredients when going over the head are (1) keep your feet moving and (2) disguise the check. If the check is ineffective and doesn't work, I can recover quickly because I've kept moving with my man.

I find the wrap check very effective against a slow opponent. Before wrapping, I get myself strong side and come through with the wrap while keeping my feet moving.

Future of Lacrosse

Individual play and ability should improve greatly. We will notice stick work continuing to improve at all levels. But I think the greatest change will be in the area of coaching. The players of the last 10 to 15 years will be the coaches of the future. If there has been any area in the game that has been lacking in the last 10 years, I feel it has been in the coaching ranks. (I'm sure this will cause some debate!) Too few teams have dominated the game in the past eight years. As the players of the recent past go into the coaching ranks, the game will improve in all aspects: competitiveness, team offense, team defense, and, obviously, in the individual talents of players. Taking this one step further, I feel that as team concepts improve, domination by a few players will cease. Of course, superstars always will be around, but a coordinated offensive system will keep individual players from dominating the game as much as they can today.

Today's Middies

Let me close by saying that I think a better understanding of midfield play is important for younger players. As I have pointed out, the ability of a midfielder to play at both ends of the field is critical. The inability of today's crop of midfielders to play good defense has led coaches to install a six-man team defense whenever possibe. Too much emphasis is being put on teaching midfielders to score goals. I believe we must strive for a balance by teaching the defensive part of midfield play.

Offensively, I feel that today's midfielder is much better than those of the past. (This also is true of attackmen, defensemen and goalies.) Without doubt, the innovation of the modern lacrosse stick has drastically improved the game's offensive tactics. Perhaps the most potent weapon that the modern midfielder has in his arsenal, besides his ability to shoot better than the midfielders of the past, is his ability to create the unsettled situation. This is a direct result of improved stick work.

The unsettled situation has become a potent offensive weapon. The Cornell teams of the mid-'70's, as well as the

Maryland teams of the same era, excelled in this tactic. And it is the midfielders who many times initiate the unsettled situation. Therefore, from the coaching point of view I am a strong believer of instilling and encouraging this type of mentality in midfielders.

In terms of coaching stick work, we must continually stress the importance of concentration and repetition, as well as correct technique, in *all* stick work drills—including shooting.

I also think that we must stress the overhand style of feeding and in-close shooting. Although there's a real debate concerning the chances for success when shooting and feeding overhand as opposed to underhand, sidearm or three quarters, I feel that a player who masters overhand shooting and feeding has a real advantage over the opposition.

Jim Darcangelo

Midfield

Jeff Wagner

EDITOR'S INTRODUCTION

Jim Darcangelo is one of the most exciting midfielders who has ever played the game. Darky was a three-time All-American at Towson State University and his last two years there was voted the Outstanding Midfielder in the College Division. He played on the USA National team in 1978 and was voted Towson's Most Valuable Player in his Junior and Senior years.

Considered by many to be the best midfielder in Club lacrosse, Darky has continued his success, being named to the All-Club team each of the three years he has played for the Maryland Lacrosse Club. Jim is a salesman for Bacharach-Rasin so his job keeps him around the game and in touch with the rising stars of tomorrow.

He's a total team player and feels that mental preparedness is the most important aspect of the game. After making the Scholastic All-American team in high school as an attackman, he converted to midfield and here's his philosophy on how to play that position.

PLAYER'S INTRODUCTION

The game has meant personal satisfaction, excitement, joy, competitiveness, comradeship, agony, exercise and new experiences. It has helped me become trustworthy, mature, intense in what I do and dedicated. Throughout high school, college and at this point in my life, lacrosse is an important part of my life. I thoroughly enjoy playing because I think team sports develop character. They make you realize what it is to rely on others.

A lacrosse team is a group of individuals, all working toward the same goal—winning. But on the road to that objective many other things are accomplished as well. Unlike other team sports, lacrosse is one in which an individual can set his own goal and try to excel. I feel you can relate what you learn playing sports to your everyday life, for example, dedication to family, friends and occupation; competitiveness applies from something as simple as winning a game of checkers to being the best in your profession. The maturity that you gain on the playing field brings with it the ability to make decisions and take the consequences, to weigh things out beforehand.

I think having played lacrosse has helped me live life more easily and happily. I think it has helped me know myself and taught me that some things I may want changed are

Darcangelo

Russell Sport Photos

Midfield

uncontrollable; and, therefore, my beliefs or objectives may have to be re-evaluated and modified to make life easier on myself and the people around me.

Midfield Philosophy

Whoever coined the phrase, "The game is won or lost in the midfield" was generally correct. A midfielder should be thinking not only of offense but be ready to drop into the hole and assume his defensive responsibilities. Midfielders control the game, playing defense as a unit and moving the ball up field to the attack. They should know when the game has to be slowed down or speeded up. They should know their limitations—for example, if they are tired, they definitely slow down the play or change to more of a passing game until they recover.

When playing midfield, mental preparation is the most important key to success. You have to want to win and have confidence in yourself to be able to execute the plays properly. But don't get me wrong; you also have to have ability. (If I were a coach and found a good athlete who had lots of desire, it would be great because I could teach him the techniques of how to play. But a naturally great lacrosse player who lacks desire and motivation is awfully hard to convince that he should want it more and care more. You definitely need a combination of a good athlete and raw ability to make a successful middie.)

Confidence in yourself is very important to your attitude. Without confidence in yourself, your attitude won't be what it should. To develop confidence involves learning from your mistakes. Once you say to yourself, "I can whip this guy," and then go out and do it, you've developed confidence. Confidence *borders* on cockeyness. *[Many great lacrosse players seem to be very egotistical. The truth is that these players have built up a lot of confidence so when they walk on the field, they feel they are the best. Far from harmful, this is a positive attitude which you must cultivate in order to be a successful player.—G.F.]*

Positioning

Try to set up your man so that a pick can be effective. Don't waste your energy though. Only cut when you've made eye contact with the feeder or he is looking for someone to feed to. Too many players cut without paying any attention to what the feeder is doing. Also, cut to clear out for the man with the ball; take your defenseman away from the action. *[As Darky indicates, cut to the ball when the feeder is ready. Don't waste a cut or put the feeder in the position of having to force it to you. But this doesn't mean you have to stand still. You must keep moving to keep your defenseman from backing up.—G.F.]*

Learn your teammates' strengths and weaknesses; always take them into account when deciding on a particular option.

Dodging

As I work a man who is playing me, I am looking for a few keys that will let me know when I should make my move. Here is what I look for:

1. Is he coming out uncontrolled, with his stick high? If so I face dodge. If his stick is low, I may roll dodge.

2. If he's playing me tight and overcom-

Darcangelo

mits, I take him.

3. If he crosses his feet instead of shuffling, I take him.

4. I use the pick.

5. I like to talk to my teammates, telling them to flare out and take the ball. Often, an opponent will drop his guard just for a second and I'll be able to make my move.

Diagrams 1 and 2 illustrate my most typical dodge moves. In Diagram 1, I'm looking directly at the goal or possibly off to one side. I'm looking for the slide and dump. In Diagram 2, I'm moving across the front of the goal, sweeping from my left to my right, looking for a screen. (Sometimes I'll dodge the back-up and try to get too close to the goal.)

In general I like to carry my stick in my left hand and run directly at my man at first, then break to my left a little and look for his feet to cross. Then, I'll change direction when I think his feet are crossed and at the same time bring my stick out in front, switching it to my right hand and driving for the feed or right hand shot. Sometimes I set up my defenseman by faking a pass to my left while my stick is in my left hand. Hopefully, he'll play that fake, and then I pull my stick in front of me and switch it to my right hand for the drive. I like to talk. I'll call to the attackman and say, "Take the ball." I act like I don't want it. Ideally, this gets the defensive player to drop his guard and then I make my move. *[Notice the number of keys that Darky uses to see what his opponent is (or might be) doing. In addition, as he makes his move, he constantly looks for ways to create scoring opportunities.—G. F.]*

Playing the Loose Ball

If the loose ball is at the offensive end of the field, I scoop through it and look directly to

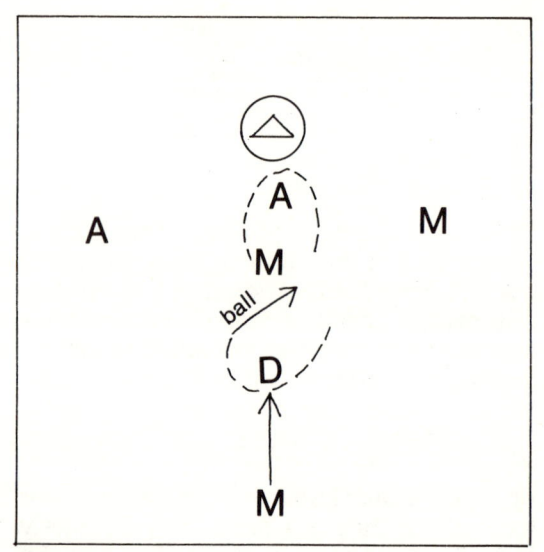

Diagram 1

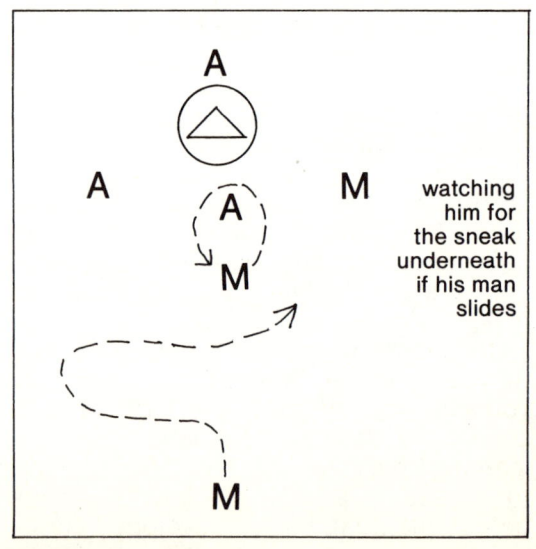

Diagram 2

watching him for the sneak underneath if his man slides

the crease area and then out, trying to find an open man. I love unsettled situations.

If the loose ball is in the defensive end, I scoop through it and usually run it out of trouble, then look up for a breaking teammate to create a fast break if possible. I almost never pass back to the goalie or back to a defenseman. It seems very silly to give up ground unless you are in big trouble. But I do sometimes lose the ball by playing this way.

Feeding

I'll feed overhand and underhand, anyway that is necessary—just as long as I feed to my teammate's stick. I usually feed out in front of my target. The best way to get a defenseman in position so you can feed is to keep running. When I feed it is usually off of a dodge and I'm on the run. I usually look in the general direction of my cutter. I try not to telegraph it, but I don't look away either. (I wish I could.) I also try to anticipate his movement, something that comes with time and playing together.

When I do feed, I place the ball so it leads the cutter just a little; usually I feed hard. I gamble a lot with my feeds and so have to feed hard and fast. To the spectator, it probably looks like I force the ball; but when a defenseman is right next to my teammate, it does not necessarily mean he is covered. I feel that if the defenseman is only looking at my teammate (face guarding), a feed can be successful a lot of the time, depending on (1) how the goalie talks, (2) how quick the defenseman is; and (3) the position of the defenseman's stick. *[This is one point of which very, very few players are aware. Many times your teammate is open; but, because he has someone next to him, you think he's covered. Learn to watch the defense. Many times they are so intent on backing up and sliding that they're not really guarding their man—it just looks like they are.—G. F.]*

Playing Off the Ball

When I'm playing off the ball, I have three basic options: (1) to pick away from the man with the ball; (2) to cut and (3) to pick opposite or for an attackman.

Picking Away: The objective here is to clear out the defense if you know one of your teammates is going to dodge. As he dodges, come off your teammate's pick looking for a feed. A lot depends on what the middie with the ball is doing, but I always keep myself in a position to be dangerous by forcing someone to play me. Then, if he leaves, I'll have a good percentage shot. Too many players don't make themselves dangerous; they stay way out, out of goal-shooting range and yell "Here is your help!" Who the hell wants to hit that guy? I want to hit someone with scoring potential. *[Defensive middies will play off you when you don't have the ball because they are trained to get into a back-up position. If you stand out front, not only do you allow your man to back up but, even if you get the ball, you are too far out to shoot. As Dark says, get into the action. Don't give up ground when you have the opportunity to penetrate.—G. F.]*

Cut: When I think my defenseman knows what I am up to, I cut. I believe in signals between middies and attackmen because when you both know what is going to happen, you're less likely not to waste your cut. I try to be aware when an attackman is driving to my side; I clear out, take my defenseman with me and think about whether to back up the cage. Sometimes too many teammates are watching the play

Darcangelo

instead of being involved, and so they forget about the back-up or clearing out.

Shooting

I myself like to shoot for the extreme high corners of the goal. I really try to shoot to where the goalie isn't. I like off hand high, but off hand hip is great too—at least that's what several goalies have told me. *[Note: a right handed goalie's offside is the left side of the goal and vice versa.—G. F.]* When shooting it's really important to take the time for a quick look at the goal to see if the goalie is out of position because when he is the shot is easy.

Quite often when within approximately eight yards, I will fake. But while I think it's great to do, it can be overdone. If you're on your fourth fake and the goalie is still on your second, he'll stuff you. Fake once, maybe twice, then shoot. I usually shoot overhand off a cut; off a dodge, I usually shoot sidearm. (I seem to be able to shoot sidearm better than overhand on the run.)

Cutting

I like to cut to my right. First, I try to set up my defenseman by driving him down the left side of where the pick is to be set. Then I cut off the pick, keeping very tight to the pick. I make sure I don't belly out; and, if the defenseman does sneak underneath the pick, I'll go down the back side on him.

I try to cut when an attackman or feeder sees what I am thinking or doing or when I can see what he is going to do. I don't cut unless there's some reason for it (for example, to take a shot or to clear out). I just don't like to run around for the fun of it!

The Pick

After I pass, I try to pick down low enough so that when a player pops out to take the pass, he can use me and the defense player as a screen. Usually this works best on a feed from your midfielder but can be used on a feed from an attackman. I like to start the play with a cut. Then, if I don't receive the feed, I pick for the creaseman or middie who is low. I set the pick facing the ball (leaving it up to the cutter to work his man into me) so that if the pass is bad I have a chance to grab it. Also, by facing the ball, I can see what is happening with the ball. Usually, after the cutter is by, I'll follow him, perhaps bowing out a bit; or, I'll cut down the opposite side. (It depends on how the feeder is moving.)

When I set the pick, I try to get as wide as I can, but I do like to face the action. *[I can say from my own personal experience that Darky, like the other middies in this book, are totally unselfish. They really believe that when they pick or clear out for the man with the ball, they are helping the team's offense. They don't need to have the ball all the time. If you watch these players, you'll notice that even though they move the ball, they still end up with 3, 4, or 5 points a game. For example, last year Darky had a phenomenal 9 points (5 goals, 4 assists) in a come-from-behind win over the highly touted Mt. Washington Club. The key is not always to hang onto the ball but to play every aspect of the game.—G. F.]*

Favorite Move

My favorite play (as shown in Diagram 3) is to swing to the left of the goal and then, making a quick move, come back across the front of the goal while my other middie out front (working a 2-2-2) curls around a

Midfield

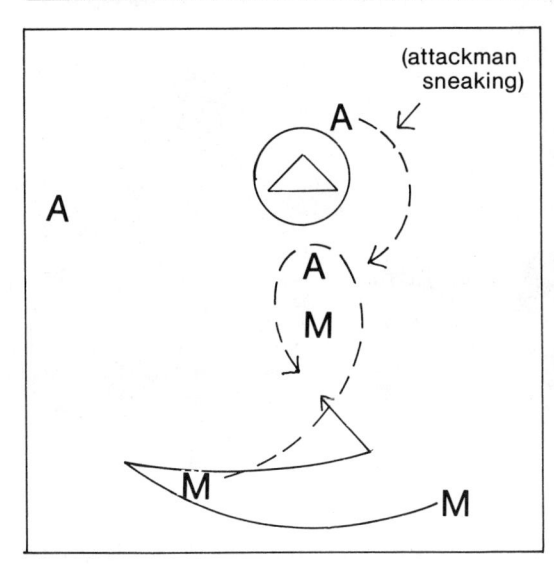

Diagram 3 (attackman sneaking)

double crease (stacked). I'll try to hit him as he comes up top. I also keep an eye on the sneaking attackman who's on the side I am driving into in case his defenseman decides to back up.

Defense

On defense, I try to get to know my opponent. Most players (including me) have maybe two moves that they like to use on offense. So, when watching the opposition in a game, pay attention to those you will be guarding. There is an excellent chance that these same moves will be used frequently against *you*. Here's what I watch for:

    1. Whether the bottom hand comes off the stick frequently and under what circumstances.

    2. The rhythm or cadence in the way the stick is cradled or carried.

    3. Whether his eyes light up when he is about to cut for the goal.

    4. Whether he usually carries his stick in one hand. If so I'll use a poke check behind his back when he brings his stick from front to back. I don't go over the head. I do wrap check one-handed, usually as the player is cradling from front to back.

Future of Lacrosse

The only thing I can say for sure about the future of the game is that there will be better players than any we've seen so far. I would hope that we would see better officiating. The sport should continue to grow in popularity, especially at the youth level. I also think the game will be speeded up in some manner, but I don't think the elimination of the faceoff after goals is the answer. I think we need to move more toward the international rules, substitutions on the fly, etc.

Bob Henrickson

Morris Peck Photographic Services

EDITOR'S INTRODUCTION

Bob Henrickson is one of the most dangerous middies to play the game. This three-time All-American has all the moves— both offensively and defensively. When called on, he's been able to make all the big plays necessary. He can explode as he did against against Cortland, scoring four goals and having 3 assists... and the next moment be all over the field.

Hondo was voted the best midfielder in the NCAA in 1978, an award that was well justified. He has played on a team that won 42 straight games and two championships. Hondo is now pursuing graduate work in animal science and serves as assistant JV lacrosse coach for Cornell, giving back to his alma mater some of the tricks and secrets he learned while on the team.

PLAYER'S INTRODUCTION

When I first took up lacrosse, I didn't realize what impact it would have on my life. I never thought it would make my transition from high school to college easier. Nor did I think it would get me into a good university; yet, it did both. I've met many of my best and closest friends through lacrosse. My coaches in both high school and college have left an imprint on me. Now that my college lacrosse days are over, I want to help the game of lacrosse. I want to see it expand into a national sport with more television and radio coverage. I feel lacrosse deserves such recognition because it is one of the most exciting spectator sports.

Philosophy

My philosophy on midfield is that the midfielder is the ball-hawk of the team. The midfielder should be the leading ground ball getter, and his main function is to get the offense moving. He should also play steady defense down at the other end of the field. Though the word "midfielder" itself implies the middle of the field, the middie has to be experienced at *both* ends of the field, and therefore he should be one of the best athletes on the team.

Offensive Play

When I have the ball out front, my first reaction is to analyze the man playing against me. Is he a defenseman that switched on

Midfield

David C. Kwan

me or is he a middie? After making this assessment, I decide whether to try a dodge. If the middie is weak in defensive play, I will try to dodge him. I don't try to dodge all my opponents. This is especially true if a defenseman is guarding me. The defensemen have longer sticks than I am used to on midfield, and my dodging ability will be hampered. If my opponent is a defenseman, I will look first for an open cutter and then for any attackman with a midfielder guarding him. This is a mismatch, and you should get the ball to him as quickly as possible so he can take advantage of his situation. Finally, my main objective is to draw a man so I can pass to the man who's left open.

When I do dodge, I try to get my opponent leaning in one direction; then I take a quick step right and go. Since I am right handed, I almost always will fake left and then cut back right. The key I am looking for is the position of the defenseman's feet. If I can get him to cross his feet when I fake left I will be able to get one or two steps on him before he will be able to adjust and recover.

As you can see in Diagram 1, I am going slightly away from the goal when I start my move. Then I cut towards it. I will line up on the left side of the field, get my man to move left, and then use my speed and a quick step and go to the cage. To do this, I put the stick in my left hand, get my man to cover me for three steps to the left as I am faking left. Then, when I see his feet are crossed, or that he is leaning to the left (expecting me to go left), I take a quick step right and go to the cage.

[Notice in Diagram 1 that Hondo started way over on the left side of the field, that he beat his man by making a quick step, driving right handed, and that when he shot he was in

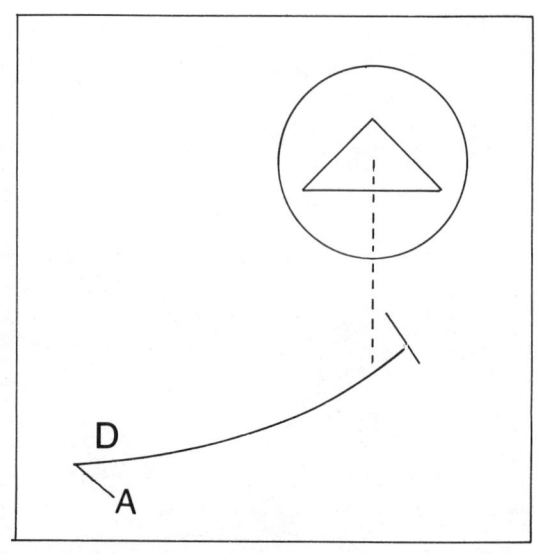

Diagram 1

front of the goal (his best angle). This is a much better technique than dodging and ending up reducing your angle because you're going away from the goal. (See Diagram 1a.) Ideally, when you get to the point, as shown in Diagram 1b, you should cut straight down to the goal. First of all, you will totally surprise your defenseman. He will be beating on your arm, but it will not have any effect on your move. The reason most middies keep moving away from the goal is that they think the defense has them covered. This is totally incorrect. All you need is that one step, protect your stick with your body, make your right-angle move, and then go to the cage.—G. F.]

Shooting

When I take a shot on the cage, I shoot for the largest open space. I prefer the bounce shot or the skim shot toward the lower extremities of the cage.

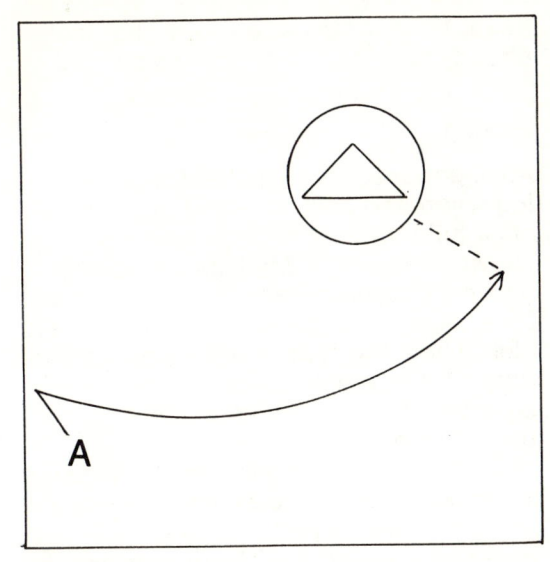

Diagram 1a

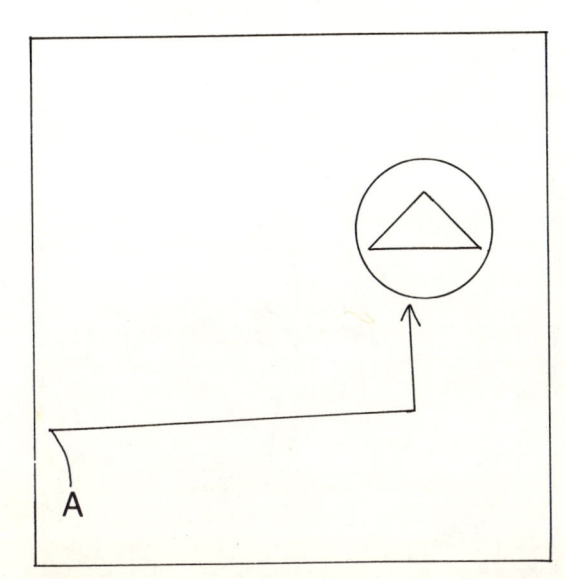

Diagram 1b

I try to shoot away from the goalie's stick. I have learned that many times the goalie is baiting me by setting up a large open area on one side of the cage. I don't shoot there if I feel I'm being baited. *[As Hondo does, watch the goalie when your teammates shoot. Does he try and make you shoot where he wants you to? Knowing what that goalie does many times will give you the advantage you need to score.—G. F.]*

Ideally, I fake before I shoot. I try to move the goalie and then shoot. So many times the goalie stops my shot because he can follow my stick and then react. If I fake one place and get the goalie to lunge that way and then shoot the other way, the goalie will have too much momentum to reach and make the save.

If I'm shooting off a cut, I look for the same things but I prefer a quick release shot instead of first throwing a fake.

Feeding

I feed overhand. The ball is easier to see and control this way. A side arm underhand pass is hard to pick up. With the overhand, you can see the ball from the start of the pass to when you catch the ball.

I feed when the defenseman doesn't expect me to pass. I set him up with my eyes. I will look one way and pass the other. When I want to feed, I will sight the man I want to hit. A split second later, I will look the opposite way. When the defenseman covering me reacts to seeing my eyes look the other way, I pass to my man who I've been watching out of the corner of my eye.

If the man I want to feed is guarded closely, I will throw the ball out in front of him so he can run and reach it with his body between the ball and his defenseman. I don't throw it too far out in front because I don't want to set up a "buddy" pass where my man will be reaching too far out for the ball and an opponent can get a good hit on him. I feed firmly but not too hard. I want him to catch the ball; I don't want to take a shot at him.

Playing Off the Ball

When another middie has the ball, I will do one of the following: (1) Cut through to give that middie room to dodge. (2) Fake my man down toward the cage, then cut towards my middie to get my opponent off me, thereby enabling my middie to make an easier pass to me. (3) Move, keeping my man on me so he can't double up on the middie with the ball.

When an attackman has the ball, my first thought is "Will the attackman try to dodge around my side of the cage?" If he is about to, I will cut through or hang outside so if my man goes and doubles on him, I can receive his pass and have a good shot at the cage. My next concern is to cut. I will cut only if the other middies haven't, and there is a chance for me to be open. I don't just cut for the sake of cutting.

If I'm throwing the ball to a teammate, I want to see if a "back door" play is possible. If so, I fake toward my teammate who has the ball and then I dart back behind my opponent and toward the cage. However, if the man with the ball is about to dodge, I clear out for him. He has priority because he has the ball!

Cutting

When I cut, I always fake first. I look at a cut as if it were a football pass pattern, that is, I am playing one on one.

I try to cut when the defenseman looks to see where the ball is. When he turns his head, I cut; then, when he turns back, I already have one or two steps on him.

Picking

An important part of midfield play is knowing when and how to pick. I pick with my stick held in two hands, across my body, shown in Figure 1. My legs are spread to give me maximum base, making it difficult for a player to get around my body. I like to pick when the man I am trying to pick doesn't see me and doesn't expect me. Diagram 2 shows an example of a play using some picks and cuts.

[This is an excellent play and Hondo does it to perfection. There are a number of reasons why this works so well. First of all, when M2 goes by M1 and picks off his defenseman, he will be open for the pass. But what usually happens is that M1's defenseman will switch and pick him up. M2 now stops and picks for M1.

Figure 1

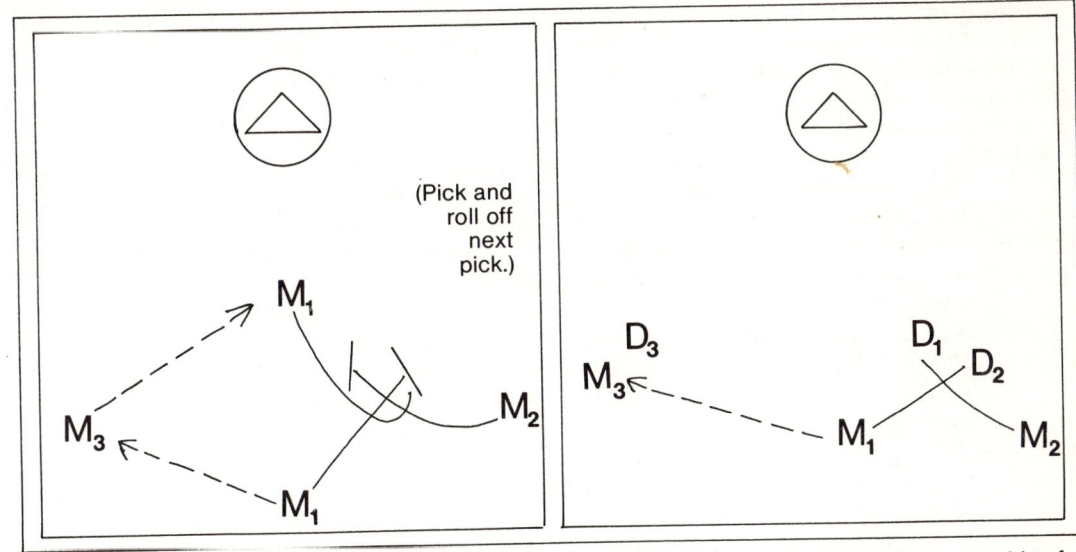

Diagram 2: M1 throws to M3 and picks for M2. M2 cuts and repicks for M1. M1 rolls off of M2 looking for feed from M3.

M2's stopping creates a tremendous screen because both M2 and D1 are screening D2 making it impossible for him to get through. Therefore, M1 will have a clear path.—G. F.]

Midfield Defense

Attitude has a lot to do with the game. One of the most important attitudes a midfielder can have is a positive defensive attitude. Many midfielders are great scorers but lack defensive skills. Their attitude is to let others play defense; all they want to do is score. This is totally wrong. A midfielder, more than any other player, must be able to play *both* ends of the field; his attitude must be, "I will and I want to play both offense and defense."

Personally, I get more satisfaction playing defense. I find it more of a challenge to take the ball away from my opponent than to score on him.

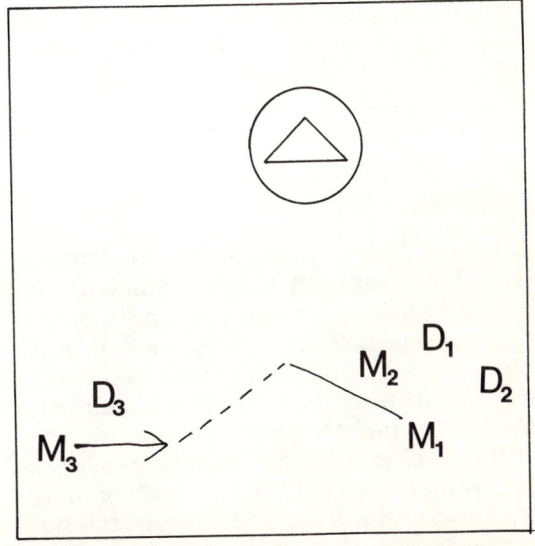

Diagram 2a: D1 will stop because M2 did. M2 now has picked D1 and M2 and D1 have picked off D2.

When my man has the ball, I just try to play good position defense. I don't try to take the ball away from him unless he is exposing a lot of his stick. I try to play good man on man defense. I call this a basketball type defense—keeping my man away from the cage with good, steady positioning.

In addition to positioning, the key to good defense is to watch your man's stick. I try to judge the frequency of his cradling. If he cradles with a big sweeping motion, I will anticipate the sweep and try a wrap check. (Someone once told me that I am the Doctor of Wrapology!) I have had good success with the wrap because I don't lunge so I don't get myself out of position when I do wrap. Therefore, I can take a chance with a wrap and still not be out of position if I fail. I use my strong hand when I wrap. I try to set it up to my right (strong hand) by faking my opponent (putting my stick on his left hoping that he will turn back right) and then beating him there with a wrap.

When my man doesn't have the ball, I try to split my responsibility, that is, I watch the man with the ball; and, with my peripheral vision, I watch my man. But I am always anticipating a cut by my man.

Loose Balls

When I pick up a loose ball in the offensive end of the field, I try to get the ball to the first open man I spot. So many times, offensive players pick up a loose ball in their offensive side of the field with the goalie way out of the cage, but they take their time moving the ball and lose a real opportunity.

If I can pick up the ball with the goalie out of position, I will not hold the ball for more than two or three seconds. I move the ball closer to the cage or to someone with a better angle for a shot! This is something that not many coaches stress, and taking advantage of this type of unsettled situation could lead to many quick goals.

If I pick up a ground ball on the defensive half of the field, I like to hit the first open man up field or use my speed and take off down field—out of trouble. I will not run toward the middle of the field but (if I can) toward the outside, away from the usually heavily-populated center.

As I mentioned, midfield is the position for the all-around athlete. It is a position for both the offensively and defensively minded lacrosse player. There is no place for the offensive or defensive midfield specialist. So many times I have seen a midfielder make a great dodge and score but then make a bad defensive play and allow a quick score down on the defensive end of the field. In summary, a midfielder has to be a smart, all-around, aggressive, ground-ball hungry, long distance running athlete.

Dave Huntley

EDITOR'S INTRODUCTION

The transition from Canadian box lacrosse to the American field game hasn't bothered this superstar at all. After playing 15 years in the box for the Rexdale Warriors, this hard-hitting Senior is one of the most prolific midfield scorers in Johns Hopkins' history. Dave was named All-American in '77 and '78 and played for the powerful Canadian team in the '78 World Championship (where the Canadians beat out the USA National team for the trophy).

Dave says his years of box lacrosse have made him particularly strong on midfield offense, but he also recognizes that to be a good middie, you have to be able to play well at both ends of the field. He also offers some solid advice on what to do without the ball.

Midfield Philosophy

Despite the game's increasing specialization, the midfielder still must be the most versatile player on the field. Although the majority of coaches seem to be more and more in favor of having both an offensive and a defensive midfield squad, each must be able to handle situations at *both* ends of the field. I suppose the one thing a midfielder should keep in mind is that he should try and play his role, whether offensive or defensive, to the best of his ability. At the same time, he should also realize that should the situation arise where he has to play in the other end of the field, he won't be excused from doing his job there just because his "specialty" lies at the other end.

In my three years at Johns Hopkins, I've been an offensive midfielder. Coming into the field game from box lacrosse as played in Canada, I was better adapted to the offensive rather than the defensive end of the field. And even though my defensive skills have improved over the past three years, the game itself has improved that much more. Thus, the best thing for our team is to use our seven best defensive players on defense and our six best offensive players on offense whenever we can.

Midfield Offense

Once the ball has settled down in the offensive end, I prefer to move it around so that everybody gets to handle it and so that the defense has to start moving out of position. If we have a particular play or system to run,

Huntley

then that is what I try to do rather than trying for the home run play or the big shot. Possession of the ball is important *offensively* because it puts pressure on the opposition's defense and tires them out mentally and physically, making it easier to score later in the game. It is also important *defensively* because (1) it gives your defense a break and (2) it makes the opposition's offense anxious which inevitably results in turnovers and, incidently, means less time I have to play defense. *[Remember what Dave says about moving the ball, especially when your team gets the ball after the opposition has had it for a long time. You don't have to go right to the goal; there is no reason to force it. More often than not, forcing results in one shot and a quick turnover.—G. F.]*

If you are going to contribute to the *team* offense, then you have to be able to generate some offense yourself. When your team is on offense, you are playing either on or off the ball. When I don't have the ball, there are three things I like to do. (1) I like to break for the ball which is one way of getting it back in your stick. Whenever I'm breaking for the ball, I try to get my man to move in the opposite direction from where I'm going to receive the ball. (See Diagrams 1 and 1a.)

There are two things I find helpful when I'm trying to get free for a pass. One is always making my initial move *toward* the goal. I do this because my defenseman is more likely to give ground and be conscious of me continuing toward the goal. If your move is out toward the sidelines, then he can stay closer to you, forcing you to receive the ball too far from the goal to be a scoring threat. The other move I try to use when breaking free helps me when my defenseman gets right up on me, making it difficult for me to move around. In this situ-

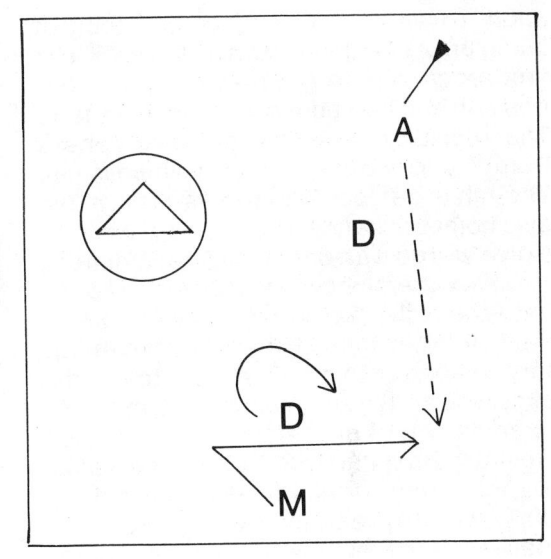

Diagram 1

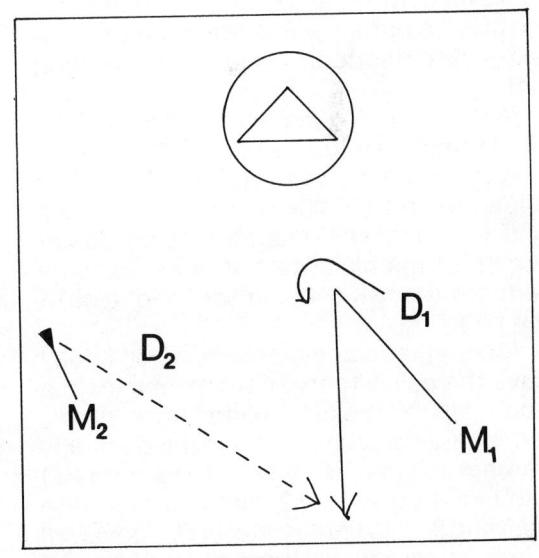

Diagram 1a

ation, I use an old box lacrosse trick of lifting up or checking down on his stick. His first reaction is to get his stick back into position and his second is to move his feet. The resulting delay gives me anywhere from one to two steps on him which is just enough to get loose for a pass. (This move also comes in handy when you are working a give and go with one of your teammates.)

(2) Another thing I like to do when I don't have the ball is pick and come off picks for the ball. When picking there are two things I try to keep in mind. First, I try to set the pick wide and position my feet so that they straddle one of my defenseman's feet, as illustrated in Diagram 2. This stance makes it a lot harder for him to slide around the pick, and it gives me a wider base that makes it a harder pick. The second thing I try to do is set the pick on the defenseman's blind side. This involves teamwork between me and the teammate I'm picking for but is well worth planning and practicing a few minutes before the game. The added element of surprise will often give you the extra step needed to get free for a good shot.

When I'm being picked for, I try to make my teammate's job easier by turning my defenseman's head away from him. This allows us to blindside him and, by getting him to stand still, makes him an easier target for the pick while at the same time reduces the risk of being called for a moving pick.

(3) Another maneuver I use when I don't have the ball is to try to set myself up in a good flip off position when one of my teammates is dodging. When the dodger is another middie, as shown in Diagram 3, I like to set up 10 or 12 yards out from the goal and 8 or 10 yards wide. In this position, I feel I'm giving my teammate plenty of

(Feet wide, straddling the defenseman.)

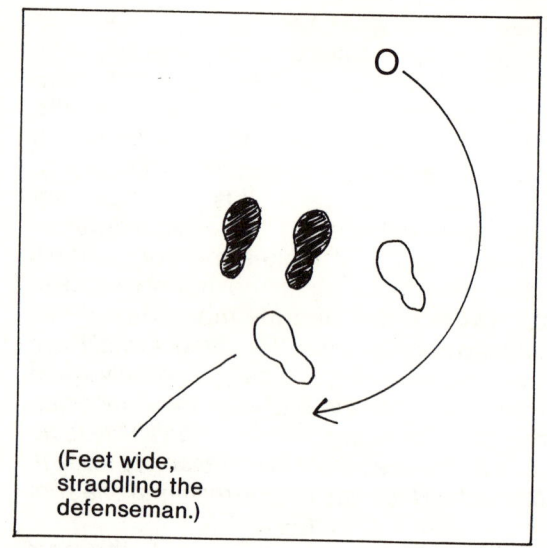

Diagram 2

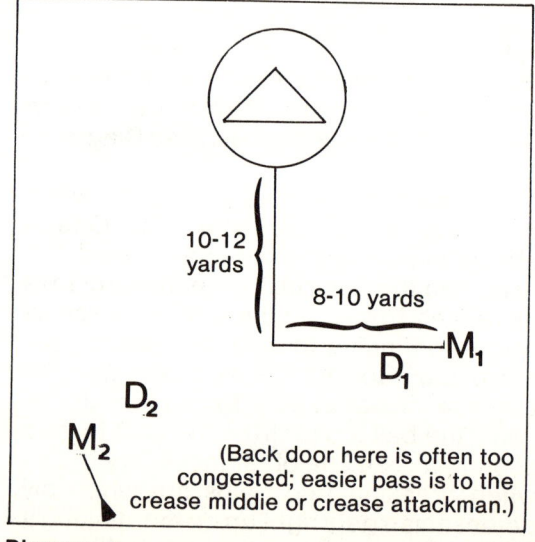

(Back door here is often too congested; easier pass is to the crease middie or crease attackman.)

Diagram 3

Midfield

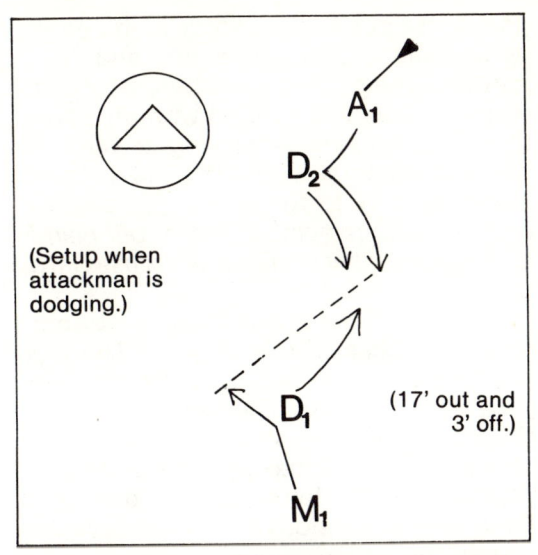

Diagram 4: [Note: a simple rule to remember—follow your defenseman. As D1 goes to back up, M1 cuts and finds the opening so A1 can see him and dump off an easy feed.—G.F.]

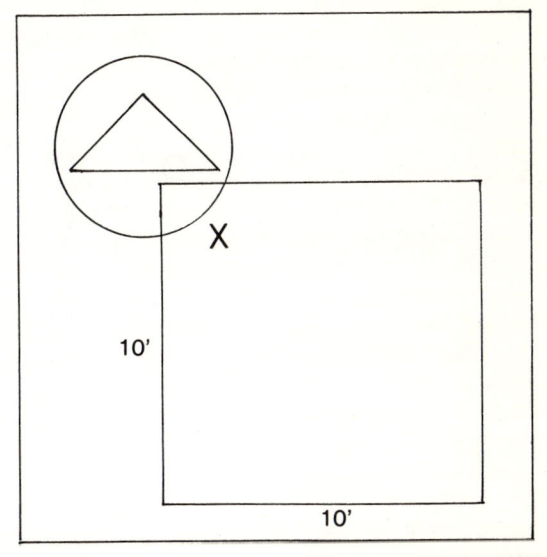

Diagram 5: [Dave plays primarily for the left hander. For the right hander, use the other side—G.F.]

room to dodge and yet remain a scoring threat which should delay my defenseman's slide. Should he slide anyway, I'll be far enough away from the slide to be able to read the situation and hit the open man or dodge the slider if he comes at me out of control. When an attackman has the ball, I try to set up 17 yards out and three yards off the pipe.

From this position, I can try to back door my man if he gets too close to the dodging attackman. (See Diagram 4.)

Since my favorite moves when I don't have the ball involve picks and flip off-type passes, it isn't surprising that my favorite midfield play incorporates both of these. I like to work my favorite play in the area 10 yards out from the left of the goal and 10 yards out front, as shown in Diagram 5. (This is generally my best playing area.)

The play involves a pick that occurs about 3 yards from the crease, at the point marked "x" in Diagram 5. I can be either the picker or the man who beats off the pick; in either case the end result is that I receive the ball in an area where I can make a shot with a good chance of scoring, or I can drive to the goal left handed if my defenseman overplays me when I'm about to shoot. (See Diagrams 6 and 6a.) *[In Diagram 6a, after M1 receives the ball, his first look should be to A1 because A1 has picked D1 and D1 will try to get through the pick. More importantly, D2, seeing M1 coming, will jump out or switch. A1, after making his pick, pops inside and looks for the feed. If he doesn't get the feed, he takes his man (D2) with him out of the back-up position.—G. F.]*

In both cases, the end result is the same. I have the ball about 8 or 10 yards from the

Huntley

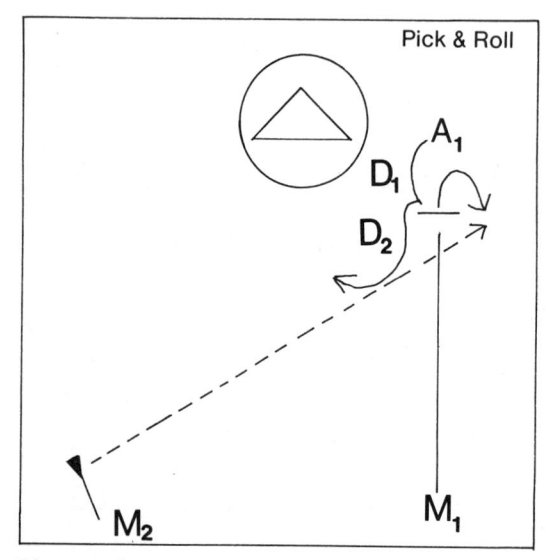

Diagram 6 — Pick & Roll

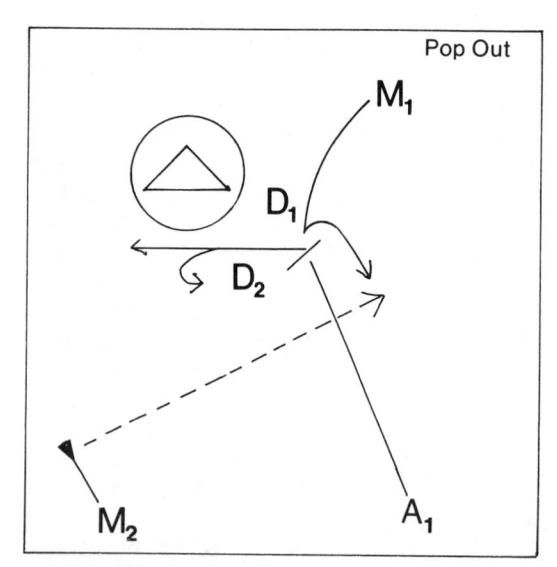

Diagram 6a — Pop Out

goal and have three or four steps on my defenseman. (See diagrams 7 and 7a.) If my defenseman gets to me before I shoot, I can still drive left handed with an advantage because he is moving toward me which considerably restricts his ability to move laterally to follow me. *[Do as Dave suggests and remember that if your man is rushing you, either side step him or use him as your screen.—G. F.]*

There are three things that are essential to the success of this play. (1) The pick must be set and used properly; (2) when you come off the pick, your feet must be moving to get away from any stick checks that might make you miss catching the pass; and (3) don't turn toward the goal for the shot or dodge until *after* you've caught the ball.

Offensive Fundamentals

There are three fundamentals that are essential to being a good offensive player: Passing, catching and shooting.

Passing: If you can't throw and catch with your stick, then you can't play offense, no matter how well you dodge or move without the ball. When passing the ball, I try to keep several things in mind:

I try to move my feet. This helps me throw a crisper and more accurate pass and prevents my defender from knocking it down. *[Don't overlook this point. Since the advent of the plastic stick, it is very easy to stand flat-footed and throw. But, if you don't move, you'll have the problems that Dave mentions.—G.F.]*

I throw the ball to a player who is moving unless when he is standing still he's already open. (Two examples are an attackman getting ready to dodge, behind the goal, and a middie preparing to dodge out front.)

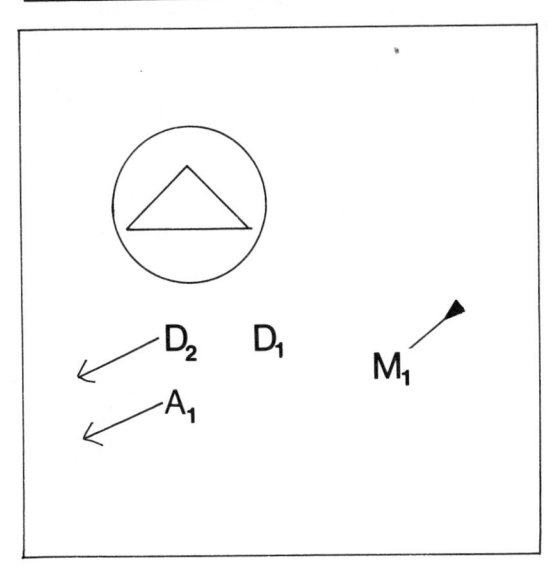

Diagram 7

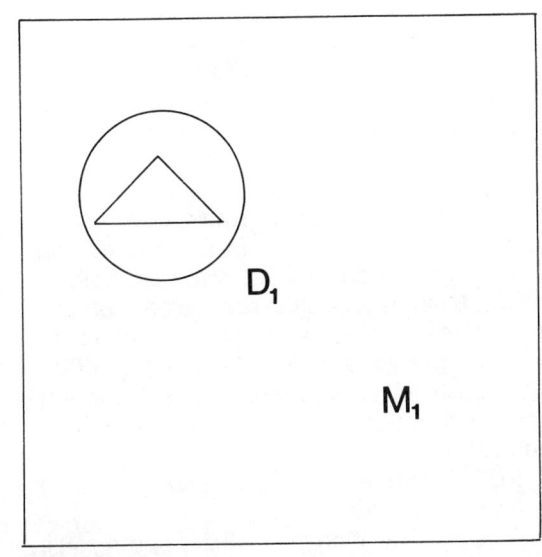

Diagram 7a

Whenever I try to thread the needle with a pass, I like to throw it to a guy who is breaking, aiming at his hip or well over the defenseman's head. This way the defenseman can't just hold his stick at the normal height to knock down the pass; he has to work for it.

For basic passes, I try and throw the pass crisply, three quarter arm, and at head level to the outside of the defenseman so that my teammate receives the ball in a position where he can make another pass without having to move his stick too far.

Catching: When catching the ball, you have the opportunity to make a good pass look bad or a bad pass look good. Here are a few things I keep in the back of my mind when I'm catching a pass:

I try to give the passer a good target by keeping my stick where I want the ball; I don't wave it around a lot.

I try to get in front of my defender and step to the ball (unless it's a timing play or a lob pass where we are trying to make the defenseman overcommit and go for the interception). The proper and improper positions for receiving a pass are shown in Diagrams 8, 8a and 8b.

I relax my top hand but keep a firm grip on the bottom of the stick with my bottom hand. This way I can better handle hard passes because of the extra give provided by my looser grip.

I constantly remind myself not to shoot until I've seen the ball go into my stick. (I suppose no matter how much you remind yourself of this, you're bound to shoot before you have the ball a few times each season.)

Shooting to score goals is the raison d'etre of all offensive plays. If the ball doesn't go in, then the play has failed. How you shoot the ball is a very individual thing,

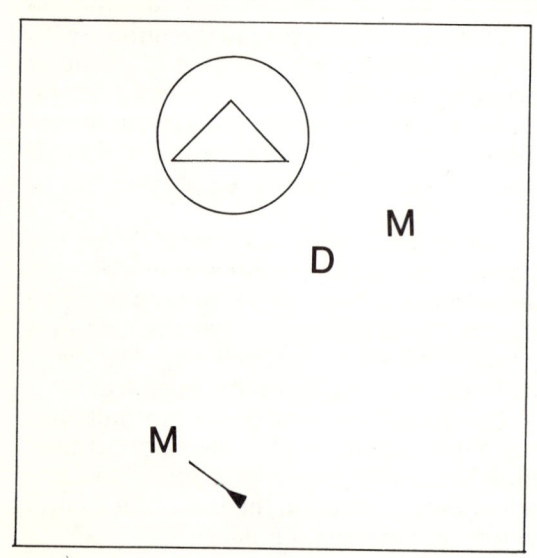

Diagram 8: Poor position to receive pass.

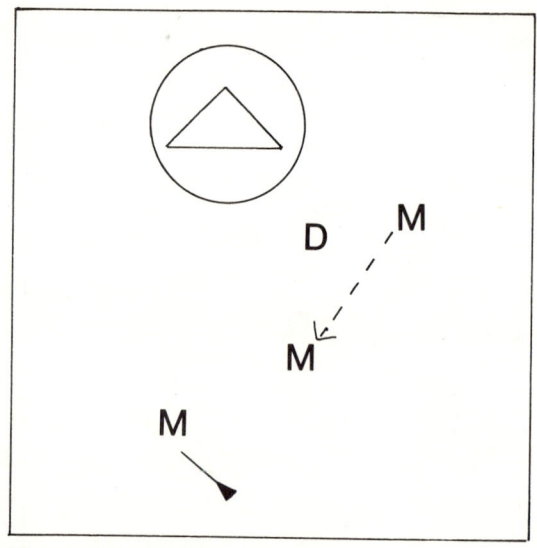

Diagram 8b: Moving to the ball.

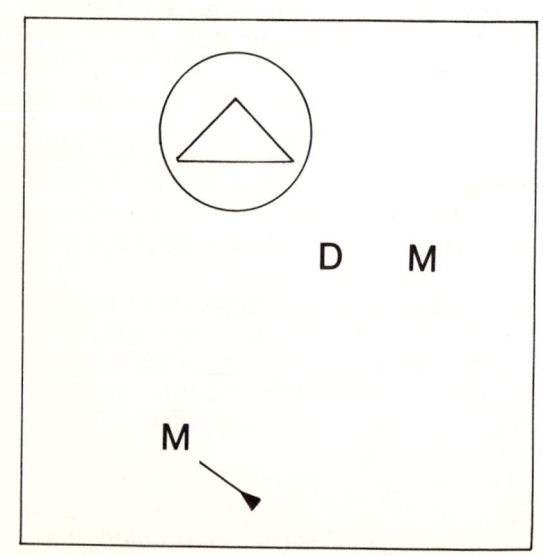

Diagram 8a: Better but still not right.

so I can only give you a few suggestions:

Keep you hands fairly close together at the bottom of your stick. By doing this you let the stick do some of the work for you.

Always snap your wrists and follow through. Your wrists give your stick whip and put English on the ball. The follow-through adds velocity and directs the ball to the target.

Develop a large repertoire of shots. If you can master a lot of different shots, you will be a more dangerous shooter, able to shoot from many different areas of the field. The way to develop your arsenal is to watch a player who excells at a particular shot; then copy his technique. Practice and improvise on that shot till it fits your game and abilities.

Put the ball on the goal; it won't go in if you miss the net.

Practice shooting from all the spots you'll shoot from in the game. Use all the shots you can from each area and practice them constantly.

Some players are natural shooters; but, even if you aren't gifted in this way, the more you practice your shots, the more success you'll have. During the game I don't know *exactly* where a shot is going, but I am confident it will go somewhere within six to twelve inches up, down, left or right of where I've aimed. This confidence comes only as a result of practice and knowing where the goal is.

Skip Lichtfuss

EDITOR'S INTRODUCTION

At 6'4" and 220 lbs., Skip Lichtfuss is our biggest midfielder. This three-time All-American takes great pride in his defensive abilities and many consider him the best there is at this. But don't think for a second that this All-Club performer can't score. In his college days at Washington & Lee, he beat a tough Towson State team in overtime, ending with a total of four goals and two assists. His overall play has been a key factor in helping the Mt. Washington Club win three straight championships.

Skip started playing while attending Towson High School in suburban Baltimore. Now a stockbroker with Merrill Lynch Pierce Fenner & Smith, he intends to keep playing for the Mt. Washington Club.

Philosophy

Today's lacrosse players are bigger, stronger, and faster than ever before. Gone is the "pure lacrosse player" and ushered in is the "pure athlete." This suggests to me that the basic requirement for being a successful lacrosse player today is to be as finely tuned as is physically possible.

It's not possible for every athlete to be the biggest, strongest, or fastest, nor is there any one formula for how to prepare yourself most efficiently. However, I cannot put enough emphasis upon taking utmost advantage of whatever attributes you might possess.

The position of midfielder can only be referred to as the backbone of any particular lacrosse team. I hate to refer to an old cliche, but how often is it said, "That game was won in the midfield"? Because the overall game and particularly the midfield position require more stamina today, you must strive at all times to be as physically fit as your own capabilities will allow.

Along these same lines, although it merits mentioning on its own strengths, is something which is as much a mental process as a physical one—thinking you can do something (a check, feed, shot, etc.) is the first step in really being able to do it. At the same time, it is equally important to exploit an opponent's apparent deficiencies.

Midfield Offense

My strongest attributes through the years have been my size and my speed. Accordingly, I have emphasized these qualities

Midfield

Lichtfuss

in my playing and exploited those who could not compete in these areas.

As a result, my strongest move always has been from the front of the goal, beginning a little outside of the restraining line and a few yards to the right of the goal as I face it. From here, I move directly toward the defender's left hip, but straight in rather than at a sideways angle. Once I get the defender to turn his hips to his left, I quickly cross-face and drive hard to the goal with the stick now in my left hand. I usually take the shot as soon as possible while there still is considerable angle. I prefer to shoot back to the goaltender's off side, high or low, overhand or sidearm, depending on the goaltender's positioning, angle, etc. (See Diagram 1, 1a, and 1b.)

On this play always be aware of double teaming. Alert your fellow middies to move without the ball and make themselves available while at the same time keeping their defensive middies out of your way.

Should my defender not turn his hips and attempt to poke check or play my body, I lower my leading shoulder and try to power through the check. This is an example of exploiting a defensive situation by utilizing my size.

[It's important to do as Skip suggests when he says drive through the check. Most players feel that as long as someone is checking them, they are covered. This isn't true. As long as you are moving and are protecting your stick, the man playing you is in trouble. You'll find that most of his aggressive checks are thrown to make you feel as if you are being guarded.

Note in Diagram 1b that when Skip goes through the check, he goes straight to the goal. He does this for two reasons. First, he gets a better shot because, if he went away from the goal, he'd lose his angle. Second,

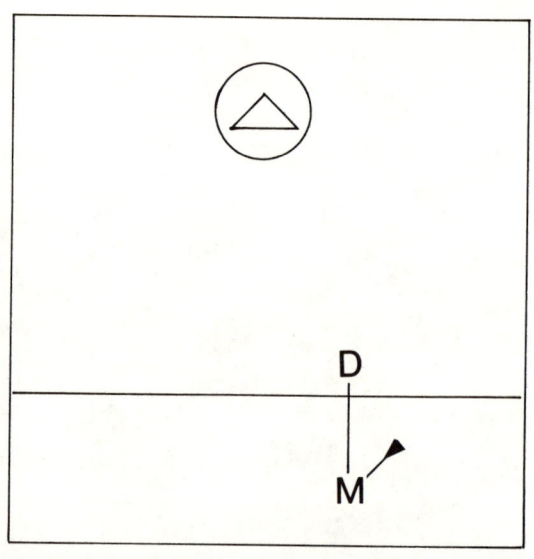

Diagram 1: From 7 to 10 yards from the defensive middie, run at his outside hip and cross-face to your left hand when his left leg drops behind his right leg.

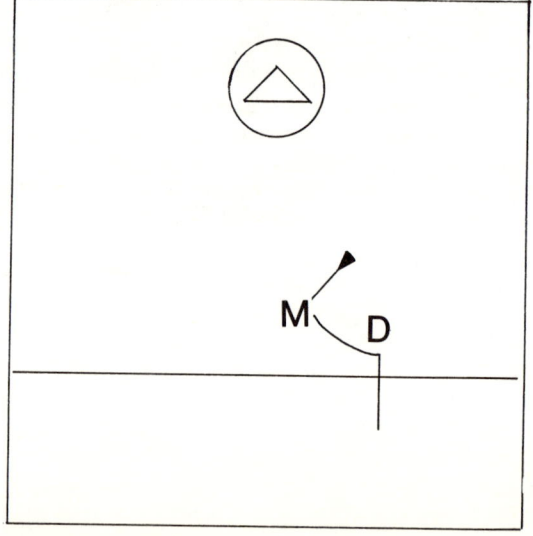

Diagram 1a: Angle as much toward the goal as possible. Shoot to the goalie's off side.

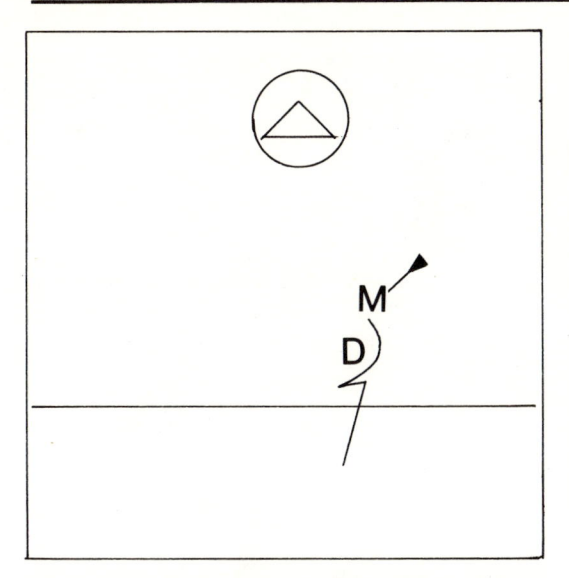

Diagram 1b: Should the defender take away your face dodge, quick step back to your right, lower your shoulder, and drive through the check.

and more importantly, by going straight to the goal, he's created a situation which forces one of the defensive players to slide. This in turn can lead to a flip off to a man inside who is now open for a shot because his defenseman has slid.—G. F.]

Other offensive tips of use to a middie are:

Work hard to move without the ball. By participating in other sports (for example, basketball or soccer), you become acutely aware of how important this skill can be in lacrosse.

Believe it or not, fundamentals are probably more important than ever, but there is less time spent on them. With the increased speed, agility, quickness, and strength of today's athletes, the demands on fundamental stickwork, talking, etc. is necessary if for no other purpose than to reduce the rapidly accelerating injury rate.

Again, learn to exploit your opponent. Be a student of the game. Learn, through experience, to react to (rather that think through) all possible situations. This, in my mind, is the difference between the mediocre and the truly exceptional lacrosse player.

Midfield Defense

I'm deeply concerned about the developing attitude of midfielders today that their primary function is to score goals. I couldn't disagree more! Despite the introduction of the plastic stick, higher scores, and better athletes, I maintain that good defense still wins games. And, more importantly, it is just as rewarding to be able to hold down a leading scorer as it is to be one yourself.

Personally, I usually try to play my opponent as close as possible. (Don't, if you can avoid it, allow your opponent to get a running start directly at you.) I *always* try to take away something from the offensive player. By being a student of the game, I am usually well prepared to anticipate my opponent's moves and react to them.

Checking

My favorite check is the poke check. It is also, for my money, the most effective since you never commit yourself. There is always time to recover as long as you keep your feet moving. The wrap check, over the head check, and others inevitably leave you out of position should they fail. A good poke check is always effective when it hits the lower hand (which must be placed on the stick when feeding, shooting, or face-dodging).

Some Defensive Tips

(1) Learn, before anything else, to talk. Talking is extremely important not only to team defense but to individual defense.

(2) Move your feet. Don't be lazy. Don't rely on just your arms and your stick.

(3) Prevent your opponent from doing what *he* wants. Overplay strong hands and obvious tendencies.

(4) Be convinced that turning a defensive situation into an offensive situation wins games (not to mention personal recognition).

(5) Stay close to your opponent without sacrificing good team defense. Utilize the poke check.

(6) Be as finely a tuned overall athlete as you possibly can. Work as hard, if not harder, on the defensive end of the field as on the offensive end. Exploit your opponent's deficiencies and your attributes. Study your opponents and learn from them both what to do and what not to do.

Bill Marino

EDITOR'S INTRODUCTION

This topflight player was one of the most dangerous middies to ever play at Cornell. A three time All-American, Bill received the 1976 Peter Banker Memorial Award from Johns Hopkins as JHU's Best Opponent. He began playing while in high school and now plays ball for the Upstate New York Lacrosse Club while he works on an MBA from Cornell.

One of the all time great cutters, Bill feels that a good midfield play begins with good defense—first man to man and, once you've mastered that, good team defense. This All-Club performer is truly an outstanding star.

PLAYER'S INTRODUCTION

Lacrosse has meant a number of different things to me during my experience with it, but most of all it always has been something I thoroughly enjoy. For me, lacrosse is a means of escape from the everyday activities of life—something to look forward to. It is a chance to compete and prove my athletic ability, mostly to myself but also to others. I enjoy the competition. I also have enjoyed the comraderie associated with participating in a team sport. I have developed many lasting friendships through lacrosse and have had many rewarding and memorable experiences on the field.

Lacrosse also has taught me things that I would not have been able to learn anywhere else. I have learned how to win graciously and to accept defeat honorably. I have learned to work closely with others toward a common goal, to rely on and trust other individuals' abilities. Many of the things lacrosse has taught me have been or will be useful in other areas of my life.

Participating in lacrosse has taught me to believe in myself. It has helped me develop an ability to formulate and maintain goals or aspirations and work towards them without being fearful of falling short. I learned what it means to commit myself to develop an ability by working long and hard to see it to fruition. Through this, I have learned discipline and sacrifice; and how to set priorities and follow them.

Midfield Philosophy

Anyone who wants to play lacrosse properly has to be in top physical condition, especially midfielders. The midfielder must be a very versatile athlete. He must master

Marino

all aspects of the game. He must be an offensive threat as well as play sound defense. The midfielder also needs to be totally aware of everything that is happening on the field.

The midfielder's most important job is to play sound defense. Before stepping on the field, he must fully develop this skill. (This may change with the new rule eliminating faceoffs after a goal because a whole "defensive" midfield can be substituted after a goal.)

The second key middie quality is running ability. Good speed is a desirable quality for all lacrosse players but it is an exceptionally valuable asset for midfielders. Speed can help a middie get to a ground ball first, get back in the hole for defense, or gain an extra step when dodging, clearing or fastbreaking.

Defensively, a middie should first learn good, solid man to man defense. Having mastered the one on one technique, he then should develop his ability to play team defense. He has to learn to slide when backing up a teammate, to slough in on the weak side, to talk and coordinate with his teammates, and to cover cutters. The best team defense in my opinion is a loose man to man, where the ball and the two opponents adjacent to the ball are played tight while the other defensive players cover their men loosely and are ready to back up when necessary. As the ball moves closer to each defender's man, he should be covered more tightly.

Offensively, a middie should play an active role. He should not always give the ball to the attack and content himself with just being a cutter. A totally attack-oriented offense is easier to defend against than one that can strike from out front or behind. On the other hand, the middies should not always keep the ball. There should be a balance between attack-oriented and midfield-oriented offense. Basically, both middies and attackmen should be involved in a team offensive. *[If the opposition knows the attack is going to get the ball, they simply will drop their defense in toward the crease. This makes it easier to back up on the attack and will prevent the offensive middies from cutting to the ball. Do as Bill does and keep the total offense involved. Make the defense move.—G. F.]*

Playing Out Front

When in possession of the ball in front of the goal, I first look for an open man whom I can feed. If no one is open for a feed, I look for some other advantage that might exist due to an opponent being out of position. Should I see no advantage, I react to what my defender and teammates are doing. If I am being covered very tightly (overplayed), I will either dodge or pass to a teammate and cut to the cage, looking for a return pass (give and go). When my defender is playing me loosely or normally, I work with my teammates to create some type of advantage by getting the defense out of position.

Dodging

When overplayed, I will dodge or give and go, regardless of what anyone else is doing. When being covered normally, there are certain conditions that I consider prerequisite to dodging. First, there should not be a second defender in a ready back-up position. For example, in an unsettled situation or when my teammates are moving enough to occupy their men, I would tend to dodge. I also find it advantageous to dodge off of some team movement that results in a defender coming out of the hole toward me. *[Bill's first reaction is to see what his teammates are doing. If he sees them keeping their men occupied, he dodges because he knows he won't be double teamed. If a defenseman does slide, he looks to find the open man to flip off the ball.—G. F.]*

When dodging, my technique depends upon the situation and my defender. If I have a running start, I like to face dodge and attempt to get the defender to commit himself or sit back on his heels. If he commits himself, I break the other way. If he is sitting back, I usually break away from his stick or the back-up defender. I also use a face dodge when someone is coming toward me. If I'm close enough to the cage, I like to fake a shot and then face dodge.

In fact, one of my favorite moves is to drive straight at a defensive player and then use a face dodge. Often times I don't even use a full face dodge, because I've found that I only need to dip and break. Basically, what I attempt to do is to get the defensive player to move with my fake and thus commit himself. Once he does, I drive in the opposite direction, pulling my stick to the side of my body away from him and in front of me to protect it from a desperation check from behind. My dodge depends totally upon the action of the defensive player. My fake is simply a stutter step or hip and head fake coordinated with the stick fake.

Occasionally, I will use a roll dodge, particularly when dodging a defenseman. Sometimes it is not desirable to face dodge a defenseman due to his greater reach when checking. When using a face dodge against a defenseman, I like to hold my stick back, farther from the defender than my body is. That way, I can get closer to my defenseman without giving him the opportunity to check my stick. One critical aspect of the dodge is the distance from the defender upon execution. If I am too close, the defender can push me off stride; if too far away, the defender has too much time to react. Thus the dodge must be executed at just the right distance.

I will dodge from out in front of the goal, behind it, or to the side. (I have a slight preference for the side or front.) In most cases, from all three areas, I am moving straight to the cage after my initial move. Occasionally, I will sweep out front in which case I move on an angle to the cage.

Ground Balls

Upon gaining possession of a ground ball in the offensive or defensive end of the field, I always look for open men and unsettled situations. If someone is open up field or towards the cage, I immediately throw it to them. If no one I can see is open but I sense an unsettled situation, I attempt to force my way to the cage. When in the defensive end and no one is free, I attempt to outrun the opponents up field to create a fast break. If I am closed off or surrounded by opposing players, I redirect.

Feeding

Most of the feeding I do is overhand, although occasionally I will use a flick of the wrist when being covered tight or feeding in a hurry. In the course of a game, I will feed from out front, the side, and behind if the offense allows such freedom. Otherwise, I do the majority of my feeding from out front. In order to free myself of my defensemen when feeding, I keep moving. I will change pace, roll back, or fade away to lose a defender.

Once I have determined that a cutter is

open and I know where he is cutting, I try to look away while feeding him. The type of feed I throw depends on the situation. I prefer to throw a firm, direct pass, but I have found feeding to a spot very effective when I know the moves of my teammate well enough to anticipate his actions. Generally, I feel it is not a good idea to always feed the same way because it becomes easier for my defenseman to anticipate my action and stuff the feed. *[If you only remember one thing from Bill's article this is what it should be. Every time you get the ball think, what is my defenseman thinking? What is the total defense doing? If they have scouted me, what does my man think I'm going to do?—G. F.]*

Playing Off the Ball

When another middie has the ball, I do a number of things that accomplish one of three objectives: to get myself open, to entertain my defender so he can't back up well, or to get a teammate open. To get myself open, I might cut through, looking for a feed over my shoulder, or I might cut off a pick. In order to occupy my defender, I will keep cutting. If I am trying to free one of my teammates, I will pick for them; or, in the case of the one with the ball, I will look for a give and go or cut through to remove the back-up and give my teammate some room to dodge.

When the attack has the ball, basically I try to free myself, another middie, or the crease attackman. I will free another middie or the crease attackman by picking for them or by driving off their pick and getting their man and mine to cover me. I free myself by cutting either with or without a pick.

My favorite move in this situation is a give and go. Often times I will find my defender flat footed or just not ready to move. If my defender is alert and reacts well to my cut, I abandon it and go pick for someone away from the ball. *[You can see there is always something to do when you don't have the ball. His last point is very important. If you find that the defenseman has you covered pretty well, don't keep trying to get open. Go pick for a teammate to create a scoring opportunity for your team.—G. F.]*

Shooting

I am, for the most part, a pure overhand shooter. I seldom shoot sidearm from the outside; but, when I do, I almost always bounce it low, aiming for the low corners. The vast majority of the time, I shoot from within ten yards of the cage, and I aim for the high corners about 90% of the time. When in close, I will use a low shot only when I feel a goalie is exceptionally poor low, exceptionally good high, has stopped me high a few times, or has come out high on me which forces me low.

When it comes right down to it, I shoot for the area of the cage that looks uncovered, although there are a few spots I will shoot to just because a goalie least expects it. These areas are the near pipe, the near high corner, hip level opposite stick side, and just over the goalie's shoulders.

I feel that the most important aspects of shooting are faking and accurate placement. Speed becomes critical only as you move away from the cage. I will fake when a goalie is ready for me to shoot; but, if I can catch him off guard, I just shoot away (for example, after receiving a weak side feed or a feed from behind when out front). When cutting, I often use a quick stick technique, and I aim for the high corner opposite the goalie's stick side. I will fake off a cut when the goalie seems ready for my shot. Following a dodge, I shoot over-

Marino

hand; whether the shot is low or high depends upon the situation and the goalie's actions and abilities. I don't predetermine where I will shoot or even whether I will shoot when dodging. I simply react to the situation and the goalie.

Cutting

I don't attempt to cut unless certain conditions exist. I first check to make sure that there is someone else backing up in case of a fast break. Second, I look to see if the crease is open or congested. If it is open and I have a back-up, I follow the man with the ball to time my cut so that he will be able to feed me. Once he is ready or I anticipate his being ready by the time I am open, I look for a lane through which he can feed me. I start my cut when my defender turns his head to look at the ball. If I get a step on my defender on my initial move, I continue at full speed into the feeding lane. When my defender is playing me loosely in anticipation of a cut, I will move at half speed until he's either in a position where a teammate can sneak behind him and pick him off or until he's on the opposite side of the crease attackman from the ball. (See Diagram 1.) [Note that in Diagram 1, Bill first wants to make sure that his attackman is ready to feed. He then must get his defenseman in a position to be picked off. He moves to his right; and, after he gets his man in position, he cuts hard to his left, running as close to his man (M2) as possible.—G. F.]

Picking

I will pick opposite immediately following a pass. I also will pick for another middie when the ball is out front or on the side using one of two techniques. The one is to

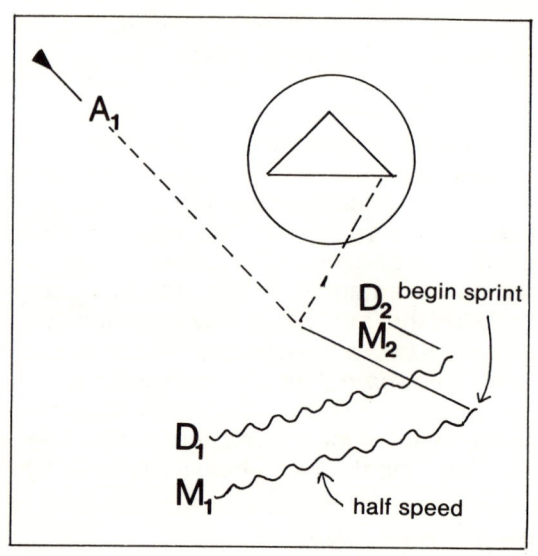

Diagram 1

sneak up from behind and set a pick very close to the defender. The other is to set a pick five or eight yards from the defender and allow my teammate to run the defender into me.

My favorite midfield play from a basic 3-1-2 offense is a simple pick opposite, where the man cutting off the pick has three options, as shown in Diagram 2. These options are to catch a feed off the pick and shoot; to catch a feed off the pick and drive to the cage; or not to receive the feed but to pick for the initial pick man. The man with the ball has the option of feeding or dodging.

Defensive Play

When the opponents are in possession of the ball, I determine first the offensive set they are in and second what they are attempting to accomplish. I am aware of who the dodgers are, who the shooters are and

Midfield

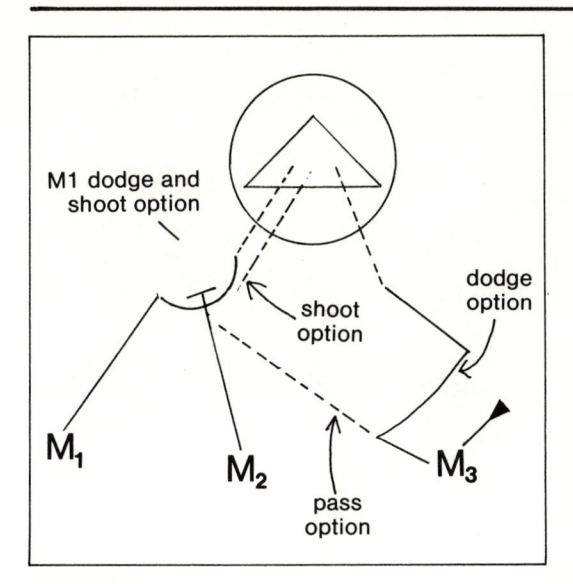

Diagram 2

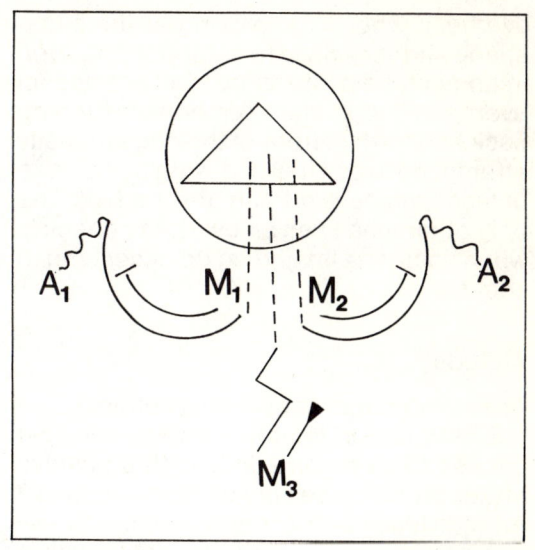

Diagram 2b

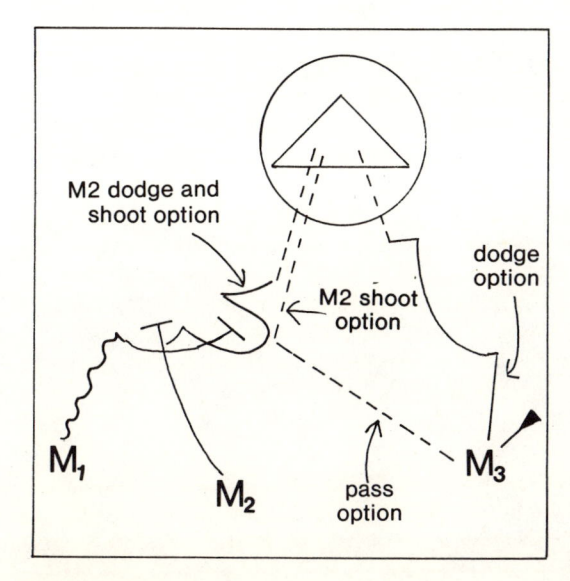

Diagram 2a

who the cutters are. I look for any opportunity to double team.

When the opponent I am covering has the ball I look for a chance to check his stick and steal the ball. When my man has the ball, I like to play tight, aggressive defense and attempt to force him into an error. When my man doesn't have the ball, I play loose looking for him to cut; I stay ready to back up.

Checking

The are certain times when I always use a wrap or overhead check. One is when my opponent is standing still or changing direction with a slow roll because, if I miss the check, there is minimal chance of his beating me. If the opponent is hanging his stick, I go over his head; if it is well protected, I use a wrap. (This is the only situation in which I will use a wrap check.) I also go overhead when I am moving at the same speed and very close to my opponent, even in an open field situation. I will not use an overhead check when someone is running back and forth in front of the cage (usually attempting to bait me) or driving to the cage unless I am *certain* I can get the ball. The only other time I use an overhead check is when someone is winding up or cocking to shoot.

Attitude

As in any endeavor attitude is critical. The only way for me to approach any activity I choose to participate in is with a positive attitude; otherwise why be involved at all? An individual with a positive attitude will learn more quickly than he would with a negative one and have more fun doing it. A negative attitude is counterproductive and results in an unenjoyable experience. I play lacrosse for pleasure; and, since I feel having pleasure and having a positive attitude are complementary, the only conceivable way for me to play is with a positive attitude. Why play at all if you don't have a positive attitude?

Future of Lacrosse

I expect that lacrosse will move into a rapid expansion stage within ten years. Presently, the foundations for this expansion are being laid. All over the U.S., people are becoming more aware of and interested in lacrosse. Each year, more athletes are getting involved with lacrosse. It is on an upswing in popularity on those campuses where it already exists and new lacrosse teams and clubs are being started in many parts of the country. All these things point to a very optimistic future for lacrosse.

Midfield

Mike Page

EDITOR'S INTRODUCTION

Mike Page is one of the all-time great middies. He was All-American and All-Ivy three times, and co-captain of the University of Pennsylvania's team in 1977. That same year he was awarded the Lt. Donald C. MacLaughlin, Jr. Memorial Award as the best midfielder in the country and the Jason Stranahan Award as Most Valuable Player in the North-South Game. Currently, Mike is teaching at the Delbarton School in Morristown, New Jersey where he also coaches lacrosse. He plays club lacrosse for the powerful Long Island Athletic Club.

Mike believes in being what he calls the "complete middie," that is, one who is equally at home playing both offense and defense. But he feels that midfield defense is a dying art and so has gone to great lengths to pass on some of his secrets for successful midfield defense.

PLAYER'S INTRODUCTION

I would never want to say that lacrosse was the greatest influence on my life, but it did determine many of my early years. The game helped me tremendously. Besides the pleasure it afforded me (and always will), lacrosse enabled me to attend an Ivy League school, my proudest accomplishment to date. The game has taught me that hard work and persistence still can pay off. But probably the most subtle and most important attributes of lacrosse, or any team sport, are those intangibles that one gains from the game. It would be impossible to determine which traits in my make-up would be different if I had never played, but I know for sure that lacrosse has made me a better person.

Midfield Philosophy

Midfield is a three-man position. You, as an individual, are only as good as your two midfield partners. You must develop as a unit.

The basic purpose of the position as I see and play it is to support *both* the offensive and defensive efforts of your team. You have to maintain control of the midfield, especially when a mistake occurs. You have to see yourself as both a scorer and defender. However, defense is almost a non-existent part of midfield play these days. Yet, to my mind, a good defensive middie is worth his weight in gold.

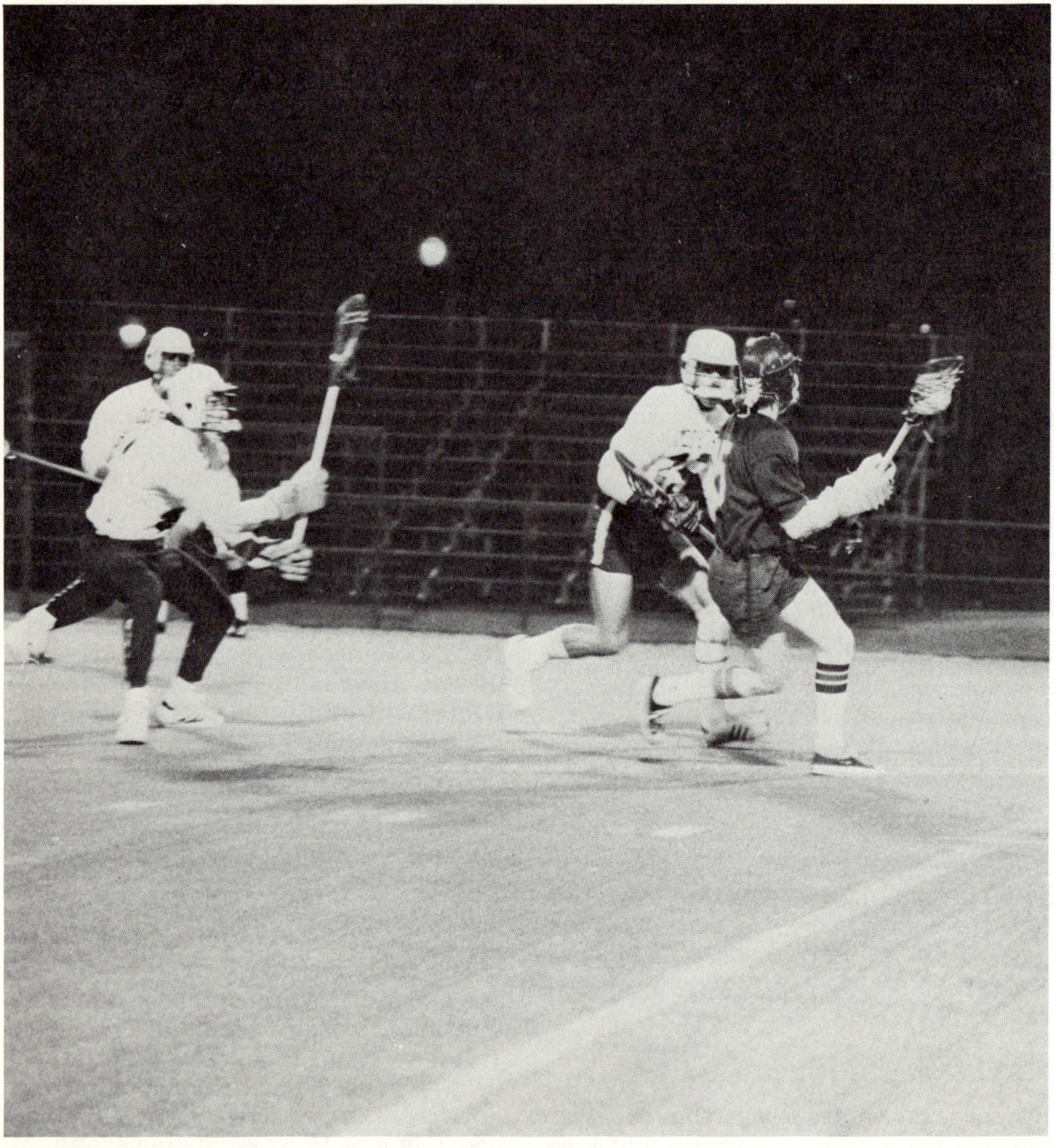

Midfield

When playing midfield defense, confidence is the key to success. You must remember that your job is to protect the goal, not get the ball. Be patient. Don't worry all the time about making the big play. Also, don't get involved in personal conflicts. Talk a lot. Defense is a team effort.

Offense

I think that to be a really good midfielder on offense, you first have to master playing defense, because even on offense you should always be defense conscious. If you haven't mastered good defensive play and your team loses the ball out front, you'll find it almost impossible to stop your opponents or regain possession while the ball is still in midfield.

When playing offense, always try to be a threat to your opponents. Develop one dodge that you can count on to work and be able to cut, feed, and shoot. If you can't do all of these (and few of us can) master one of them, and you'll be a useful member of the offensive team.

You also need a good attitude. There always will be room for the player with a great attitude, no matter what his level of talent. Attitude is a multiplier of total performance. You can add good shooting to good field moves, but when you factor in attitude you get a multiplier effect. Good attitude always produces an increasing return; bad attitude will inversely diminish returns. And attitude goes hand in hand with the most important ingredient in making a great middie—discipline.

Position

As a rule, always try to keep the ball in front of you (except when it's behind on defense). Exact position will depend on your midfield partners because you have to learn how to react as a *unit* to developing situations. So, talk to each other. Talking is important in determining your correct position in relation to your fellow midfielders. While there are no hard and fast rules about positioning, there are some general guidelines for how and where to play depending on where the ball is.

When the *ball* is *out front*, being a midfielder is like being a guard in basketball. The objectives are (1) to move the ball (and your body) and (2) to penetrate.

If you are not a penetrating type player, you can become good at moving the ball and your body. Too few players today really know how to move when they don't have the ball; it's a lost art.

The key to being a good penetration type middie is learning how to dodge. The dodge's basic purpose is to create a man-advantage situation. You beat your man one on one and use the advantage to score.

When I find myself with the ball out front, my first reaction is to look for a teammate who is open and has a good chance at making a goal shot. If no one is open, I will either dodge or move the ball to a teammate depending on how good my defenseman is. What I do also depends on the game situation. I'll make different decisions depending on whether my team is winning or losing, how much time is left, etc.

I'm most likely to try to dodge my man if I feel the defense isn't completely set up because then I have more space in which to maneuver and my man doesn't have any practiced back-up. Also, on an all even situation I'll set up an offensive set of 1-4-1 and go. In such cases, if you're the dodge, go with the idea of moving right to the goal. *[Mike has certainly patented this move; but, as* he says, he does it only when the defense is not ready to back up. Keep in mind if you are one of the middies without the ball, it is your job to keep your man occupied. If your man does slide, get yourself into a position to receive the pass.—G. F.]

Before dodging, position your defenseman. *Run straight at him* so you have the option of dodging him either left or right. Also, stay near the center of the field so you can dodge either way and end up in front of the goal. Diagram 1 shows what I consider prime dodging territory. Here, there's plenty of time to see a back-up man coming, and there's no angle to deal with when making your shot.

I'm basically a right handed player, so I almost always dodge from left to right. First, whether I have the ball or not, I draw my defenseman to the part of the field where I want him to be. Then I run straight at him to put extra pressure on him. I carry my stick at my side, slightly in front. My grip is as if I were holding the lower part of a rake. (See Figure 1.)

Proper body position makes or breaks a dodge. A good defenseman won't be beat with a simple stick fake. Instead, I attack my man with short steps, moving about one-quarter or half speed. About 5 feet from my man, I head fake left and then jab step off my left foot and accelerate to the right. This is a move that depends on quickness; it requires a lot of practice to develop the correct timing. Once I've dodged, I change my grip to a regular right handed grip (two hands on). I don't have to move my stick very far if I've kept my body moving correctly.

Confidence in yourself is the key here. You can't be watching your stick to make sure you still have the ball. You have to practice until you *know* you can do it without losing the ball.

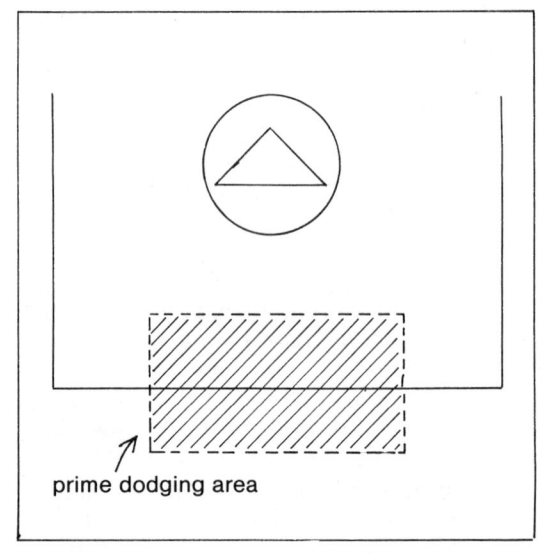

Diagram 1

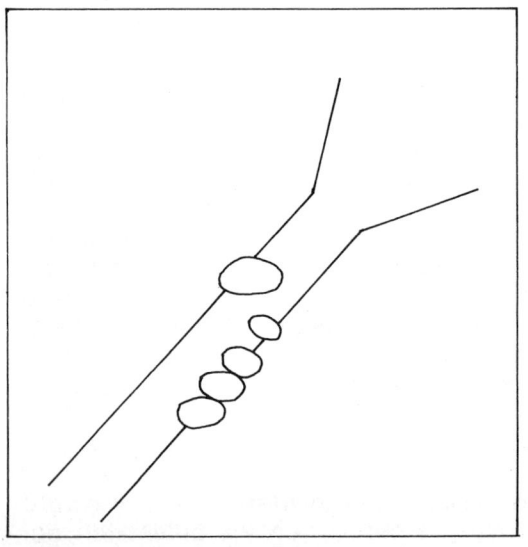

Figure 1: Dodging Grip

Midfield

Playing the Loose Ball

When the ball is loose in the offensive end of the field, you've got a critical situation, since 70% of all goals are scored on unsettled situations. You must try to convert as many of these as possible. Here are my techniques for dealing with this situation:

Put pressure on the unorganized defense by: (1) Taking a shot. (2) Passing to assist on a goal. (3) Passing to a non-scoring, open man. (4) Dodging to the goal. The key here is how to decide which option is the correct one. This decision requires a good game sense and the tools to execute your option. Close behind these two requirements come *experience*. Quick recognition is so hard to teach and learn; it takes time. And, since no two game situations are ever exactly the same, there are very few, if any, set rules. My basic rule is: *Move bodies and the ball to capitalize on any incorrect defensive alignment*—and *anticipate* these situations.

When the ball is loose in the defensive end of the field, quickness, cool, and team talk are very important. Assuming that the player with the ball is not scott free of riders, here are some ideas of what to do when you pick up a loose ball in the defensive end: (1) Keep control of the ball to avoid an unsettled situation. (2) Look to the head man upfield. (3) If this isn't possible, get the ball away from riding pressure by passing or running. (4) Keep cool; even though you're in your defensive end. (Remember that you can always kill the play by throwing the ball up the length of the field to your offensive end—what is called a Gilman clear.) *[This clear takes its name from Gilman School in Baltimore. Gilman once had a goalie, named Cy Horaine, who whenever he was in trouble simply threw the ball the length of the field.—G.F.]*

Feeding

I prefer to feed overhand or three quarters because they're the types of pass that are easiest to pick up when cutting. Remember that you are always a feeder when you have the ball. This may sound very ideal, but a good offensive player constantly tries to put pressure on the defense.

However, you must be a dodging threat before you can be a great feeder. Then, when you feed, you have the defensive player back on his heels, worried about getting beat. He'll give you room! A nondodger is going to get pushed out of feeding position if he hasn't gained the respect of his defenseman. He will be overplayed and so dominated that he won't be able to really contribute to offensive play.

In tight situations, you must try to hit a spot, not a man, with a hard feed. But, off the dodge, you can lay in a feed to your cutter since it is probably a slide that has left him open.

In conclusion, remember that the best feed is the one that leads to a goal!

Playing Without the Ball

Probably every coach has told his players, "Move when you don't have the ball." I feel this advice is too general and does nothing to coordinate a team offense. I also feel that there is a difference between "moving without the ball" and "keeping your defenseman occupied." I'd like to define each term.

Moving without the ball is setting yourself or a teammate up for a goal. That's its purpose, pure and simple.

Occupying your defenseman means trying to eliminate your man from whatever back-up system the defense is using. This includes setting yourself up for a scoring chance off a back-up to a dodge (1-4-1).

I find myself moving without the ball when my attackman has the ball or when the ball is in the attack area. I find myself occupying my defenseman when another middie has the ball.

I feel that playing basketball is a better way to learn how to move without the ball than playing lacrosse and should be encouraged by every coach.

Shooting

Personally, I tend to shoot high. Because a goaltender's body can block more net down low than up high, there is usually a lot more unprotected net up high.

Coming off a cut, your shot must be quick, hard and accurate. You should have an idea of where you are going with your shot before you shoot during the cut. Coming off a dodge, the quicker the shot, the better. Come out of the dodge ready to move the ball; shoot or pass right away.

I only pay attention to the goalie when shooting from outside because, if he's high in the crease, this negates the bounce shot. All goalies leave the same parts of the net open; experience tells you where they are. The only difference between goalies is that a left handed goalie can protect the left side better than a right handed one and vice versa.

Remember: A big shot is just a little shot that kept shooting!

Cutting

Like dodging, cutting has only one real purpose—to let you score or assist in scoring. Cutting is predicated solely on having an open feeder or open cutter in a position to score. You must work extensively with your feeder. It may take years to get in the position where you and your attackman working together can *force* a cutting or scoring opportunity.

Diagram 2 illustrates the drill I like to use to help my sense of timing.

I personally like my attackman to go to the point and come back. Peter Hollis, who played with me at Penn, was a tremendous "point and back" feeder; the best I've ever seen.

Picking

Here is my golden rule on picking: *Pick off the ball only!* Never set a pick for the man who has the ball. Personally, I don't like picks; they are very dangerous. *[Even though some teams feel that it's advantageous to pick for the man with the ball—usually behind the goal or on the side—it does limit the ball carrier's options because he now has an additional defenseman to contend with.—G. F.]*

My Favorite Play

My favorite play is the quick 1-4-1 or 1-3-1 off the clear in an all-even or slow break situation. (See Diagram 3.) It is designed to get to the defense before they can set up. The better the dodger can read when the defense *thinks* they are set up, the more successful this play will be. (As a guide, wait for the lull, then execute.) The offense sees the development since the dodger gets the ball with "unsettled room." This play is very creative since the ball penetrates from various areas, depending on the situation. The actual play consists of

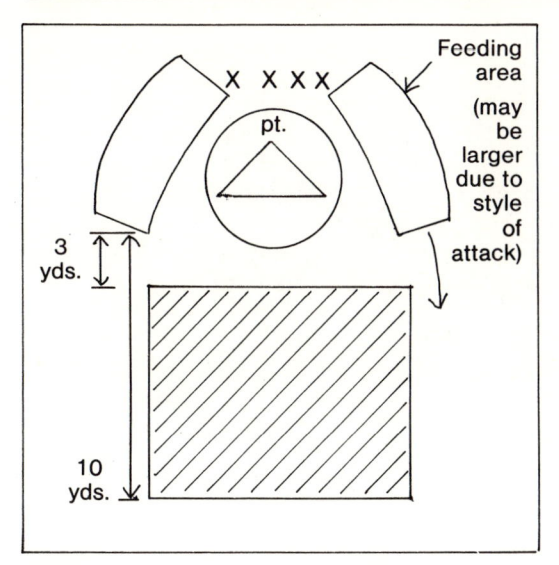

Diagram 2

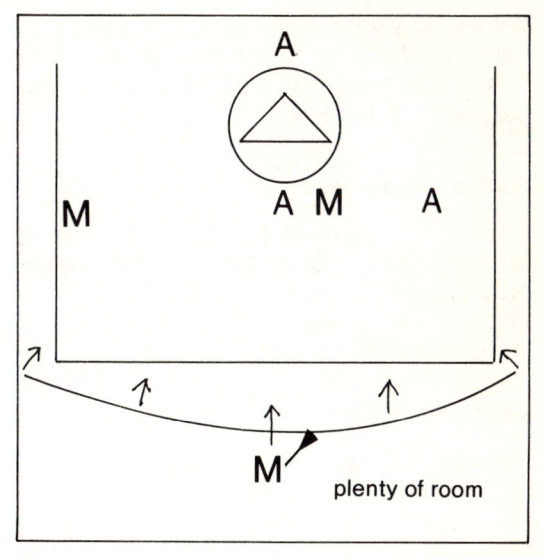

Diagram 3

beating one man and dumping off. The last resort is a second dodge.

Defensive Midfield Play

Middie defense is a dying art. The complete middie takes pride in his personal efforts on defense. It is really just a very aggressive form of basketball defense, with plenty of fouling.

When playing the man with the ball: (1) Do not cross your feet. (2) Be prepared to give ground but stay between your man and the goal. (3) Be a pest; give that man plenty to think about. (4) Always be a half step ahead of your man. (5) Save your checks until the last second because then there's a better chance of disrupting a pass or shot. Remember that you aren't required to take the ball away. Don't overcommit yourself trying to steal the ball. Just use good defensive posture—legs spread, body balanced, ready to hold off your man. And never go over the head from midfield; it's too dangerous. *[Patience is very hard to learn, especially with the lightness of today's sticks. It is very tempting to want to take away the ball; but take Mike's advice—play position. Remember that the offensive player wants you to overcommit. Isn't that what you wait for when you have the ball?—G.F.]*

When playing off the ball divide your attention; give 60% of it to your man and 40% to the ball. Also, listen to your teammates. Defense talk is the main key in being effective off the ball.

You have two responsibilities on off-ball defense—to stop your man and to help a teammate who has been beat. If you're not on the crease, play your man 60% and the ball 40%. Never turn your back on the ball. If you're on the crease and the ball is behind play your man eye to eye. (You can have your back to the ball in this situation.) If the set is 1-4-1, use a 60/40 position and get ready to back-up.

Future of Lacrosse

I think the future of the game has been complicated by the no faceoff rule. In general though, I see higher scoring games and the total disappearance of the complete middie. The game will continue to pick up pace and will truly be the fastest game on two feet.

Doug Radebaugh

Midfield

EDITOR'S INTRODUCTION

Doug Radebaugh is not only one of the premier faceoff men of all time, but a player who can meet every challenge on the field. This University of Maryland graduate has played extra man offense, extra man defense, played the opposing team's top offensive threat, taken every faceoff, and more. A three-time All-American, he was captain of his team and Most Valuable Player in '74 and '75. After receiving the award as the Outstanding Midfielder in the country, Duke put in one of the most outstanding offensive exhibitions that has ever been seen in the North-South All-Star game of 1975. Not only did he take the majority of the faceoffs, but he also scored 6 goals and had 2 assists.

Duke currently is working in his family's greenhouse business in suburban Baltimore and will continue to play club lacrosse. Duke's section on faceoff techniques should be read again and again by every offensive player.

PLAYER'S INTRODUCTION

Lacrosse has meant not only fun and good times but has given me exposure to an endless number of people, many of whom are now fast friends. The game has fascinated me since I first picked up a stick and started to play at age 15 for Calvert Hall School. Though it's now a smaller part of my life than it was while I was in college, it still provides me with rest, relaxation, and a healthy outlet for frustration and tension.

The game has helped me most in learning to get along with people. It's helped me deal with both the defeats and victories that come in all areas of life.

Midfield Philosophy

Whether you're playing midfield or any other position, I feel it's important to realize your full potential as a player and to do what you can do best so that the entire team benefits. Every successful team is just a collection of individual talents who are content to do best what they know they can do. A team of grandstanders, of players who are always playing beyond their abilities, isn't going to make it. Unselfishness, teamwork and knowing your strengths and weaknesses are what make a championship team.

Radebaugh

Jeff Wagner

Midfield

The basic function of a midfielder is to play strong and hard to help his team control the ball when it is in midfield. This includes riding, clearing and controlling ground balls.

Offensive Play

If the ball is out front, you first must check the position of your teammates and then the defensive players. Look for any obvious defensive flaws, for example, premature slides or poor positioning. Then make something happen. Dodge, draw a man and drop off the ball or pass it and set a pick. I dodge whenever I feel that my defenseman is incompetent or uneasy or when he is over-aggressive or impatient. But I won't dodge unless I know my teammates are set up or have cleared out because it's wasted effort. Some players are better depending on whether the situation is settled or unsettled. If this is the case with you, limit your dodging to the situation you can best handle. Play your strengths, not your weaknesses.

Because of the skills I've picked up on the faceoff, I'm particularly good at scooping up loose balls. Whenever I do capture a loose ball, I immediately look to pass to an open man, even if it seems senseless. (But I don't stop to do it; I pass with my feet moving.) A ball moves faster in the air than in a stick and each pass causes the defense to shift. If you do enough passing, eventually the defense will break down and your team will find itself in a good scoring situation.

If, after picking up a loose ball, I find myself in a tight situation with no time to look around for an open man, I wheel to an open area of the field and listen for the voices of my teammates to tell me where to feed.

Feeding

When I do feed, I aim in front of where my teammate is heading. I also never like to feed when standing still because there is too much chance that the defenseman will knock down the pass or check my stick.

Playing Off the Ball

Knowing how to move when you don't have the ball is the key to successful offense. Your aim is to keep your man busy so it is hard for him to participate in a back-up. I'm constantly setting picks and posting, cutting and recutting. But I don't move about senselessly or randomly. I try to back up feeds, back up the goal, be in position to get in the hole for defense, receive a feed, etc. One sure sign of too much individual play or lack of good ball movement is that this kind of off-ball movement stops. *[As Duke suggests, you must have a purpose in mind when you move. You can't just run around.—G.F.]*

Cutting

Cutting must be coordinated with the offensive unit, or, at least with the post (or pick), the feeder and the cutter. Otherwise the cutter may not be open when the feeder is able to pass the ball. Use eye fakes to throw off your defenseman. Also, manipulate your man so that he can't see the pick coming, as shown in Diagram 1. *[Notice that Duke has his man moving first to the right and then straight down. He knows that D3 is taught to play between his man and the goal, and he takes full advantage of this by running his man right into the pick and, at the last second, breaks right for the ball.—G. F.]*

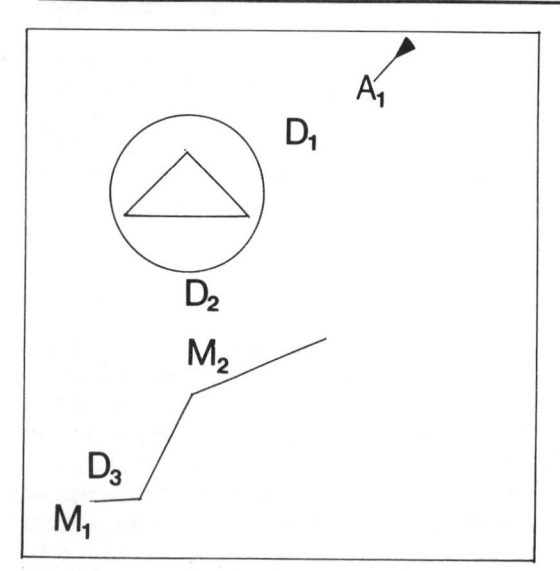

Diagram 1

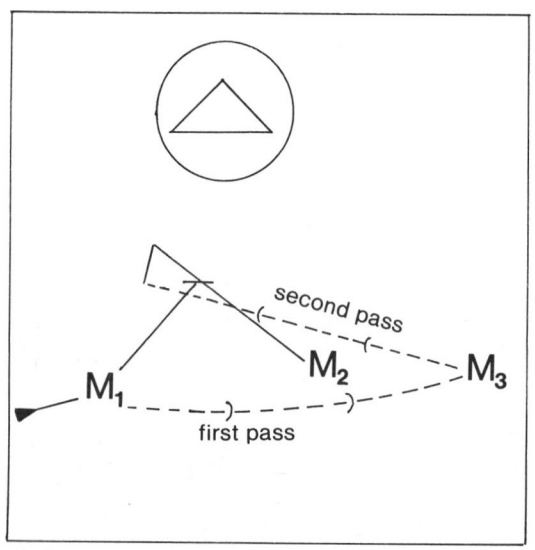

Diagram 2

Constant picking or fake picking upsets the defense, keeps them busy and wears them out. My favorite play involves a cut and fake out pass. It's shown in Diagram 2. Here M1 has the ball; M2 cuts down for a pass and acts real let down when he doesn't receive the feed. M1 passes to M3, and then sneaks down to set a pick for M2's defenseman, allowing M2 to receive a pass from M3 and shoot.

Shooting

Unfortunately, I don't consider myself a very good model for learning good shooting technique. I've always felt that sheer power is more important than precision. While at times this is true, I wish I were more of a precision shooter. Timing and quick release are the most important elements in being a successful shooter.

When I shoot I try to use either my own body or my opponent's body as a screen. I try to hide the *head* of my stick when I release the shot so the goalie can't tell where it will go.

Faceoffs

In a faceoff situation, initial body position is vital to your effectiveness in executing a quick movement after the whistle blows. Your ability to make a quick initial movement against an opponent will give you an overwhelming advantage in gaining possession of the ball.

Many coaches advocate one particular stance; however, I believe players should be allowed to adjust and develop their own faceoff position. The beginning faceoff player should develop and refine the most comfortable stance for a quick and explosive movement at the whistle. I, personally, prefer a staggered stance with the left foot forward and the right back. From this stance, I can make the quickest initial movement, and quickness is *the* most important element in subduing a stronger and more powerful opponent.

The position of your hands and wrists will vary according to individual preference and the technique being used. Generally, the left hand is placed in a comfortable position a distance of at least 18" from the right hand. From this position, considerable pressure is created on the right arm and hand. I like to think of the right arm and hand as a fulcrum with the left arm acting as the levering force, allowing you to exert a maximum force on the head of the stick.

Intense concentration is an integral part of a good faceoff man. You should know exactly what technique you are going to use against a particular opponent. Last minute changes as the referee backs away usually cause you to hesitate and lose the advantage. Don't concern yourself with how the wing midfielders are aligned or any other distracting element. Concentrate on the technique you are going to execute and the whistle. If you've studied the techniques of your opponents, you should know what technique to use to counteract your opponent *before* lining up. Watch and study your teammates as they faceoff against various opponents. Remember your opponents' numbers and their respective techniques.

Keeping your eyes on the ball as the whistle blows can be extremely difficult even for a veteran faceoff man. I believe that an alternative to watching the ball is to develop a sixth sense so you can *feel* the direction of the ball as it comes out of the stick. The development of this sixth sense will help you find the ball in the confusion which follows the whistle.

Although there are numerous methods of facing off, I will touch on the two most basic—the clamp and the rake.

The clamp is the safest and most neutralizing type of faceoff. After the whistle sounds, it is vital that you drive the ball into the ground with a quick rotation of *both* wrists. Simultaneously, your right leg and foot should be stepping into your opponent to gain an advantageous body position and subsequent ball control.

Stepping and placing your foot quickly at the head of your stick will provide you with the insurance of having an ace in the hole in case your move is unsuccessful. The foot is the neutralizing factor which slows down ball control, thus allowing the faceoff to become a 3 on 3 ground ball battle. Once you've attained proper body position, the ball may be flipped or kicked to an open area. It is important to keep your body between the opponent and the ball at all times.

Against an opponent who can be overpowered, it is better to use a delaying tactic in which the clamp is held for a longer period of time to insure proper body position and subsequent control of the ball.

In the rake technique, there are three different stick maneuvers: (1) half clamp and rake; (2) perpendicular rake, and (3) the under rake. Unlike the defensive or neutralizing clamp, the rake is an offensively oriented faceoff technique, ideally used to begin a fast break.

Generally, in all three variations of the rake, pressure should be applied forward as well as to the side in one motion. To insure good body position in case the rake is unsuccessful, it is important to step with the right foot. The same techniques are used on all three variations of the rake, the only difference is the angle at which the head of the stick is held in relation to the ground. Hand and foot movement remains the same as with the clamp.

In general, the faceoff is basically a controlled ground ball situation which puts the ball up for grabs. The intensity of the face-off situation depends upon the tempo of the game. The effectiveness of a faceoff man depends much on his determination and desire for ball control.

Playing Defense

Some middies don't enjoy defensive play, but I enjoy the challenge. I play my man heads up and wait for the opposing offensive team to make the mistake. I play an aggressive defense with numerous slides to try and force the offense into making an error. To play this way, you need an extremely tight defensive unit that's had plenty of practice together.

When I'm playing one on one defense, I hold out my stick to force the offensive man to go where I want him to go. Most players favor one side and usually dodge that way. You must anticipate this move and either encourage it or work harder and discourage it, depending on where you want your man to go. [When the ball is out front, Duke plays with only one hand on his stick. (Inside, he uses both hands.) Out front, it's easier to run and play position on your man with one hand because you don't have to play him as close.—G.F.]

When my man doesn't have the ball, I form a triangle like you would in basketball (ball-me-man) with myself between my man and the goal as shown in Diagram 3. As for checking, I only go over the head as a last resort when my man has beaten me. The wrap check is excellent, especially with the new, lighter sticks. But you must do it quickly and not stay in tight. Move back in position as soon as you can.

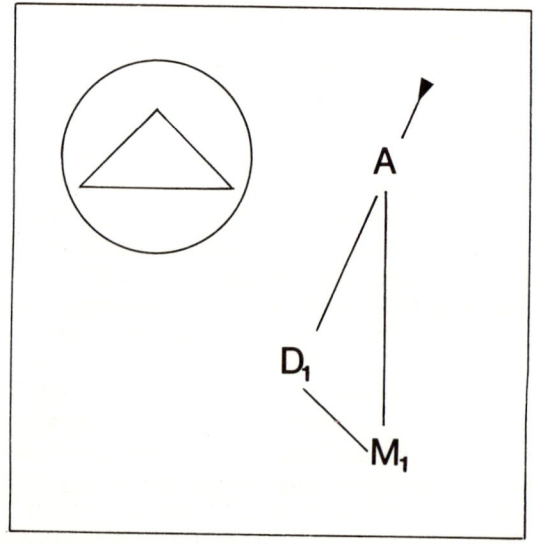

Diagram 3

Future of Lacrosse

Unfortunately, due to rule changes, the function of the midfielder has changed. Coaches are now almost forced to put in strong offensive middies or six defensemen in controlled situations. The play between restraining lines has been much reduced and unsettled situations will become less prevalent. There will be gradual growth in the game's popularity in the United States. The introduction of professional level lacrosse would be a major change—whether for the better or for the worse I really don't know.

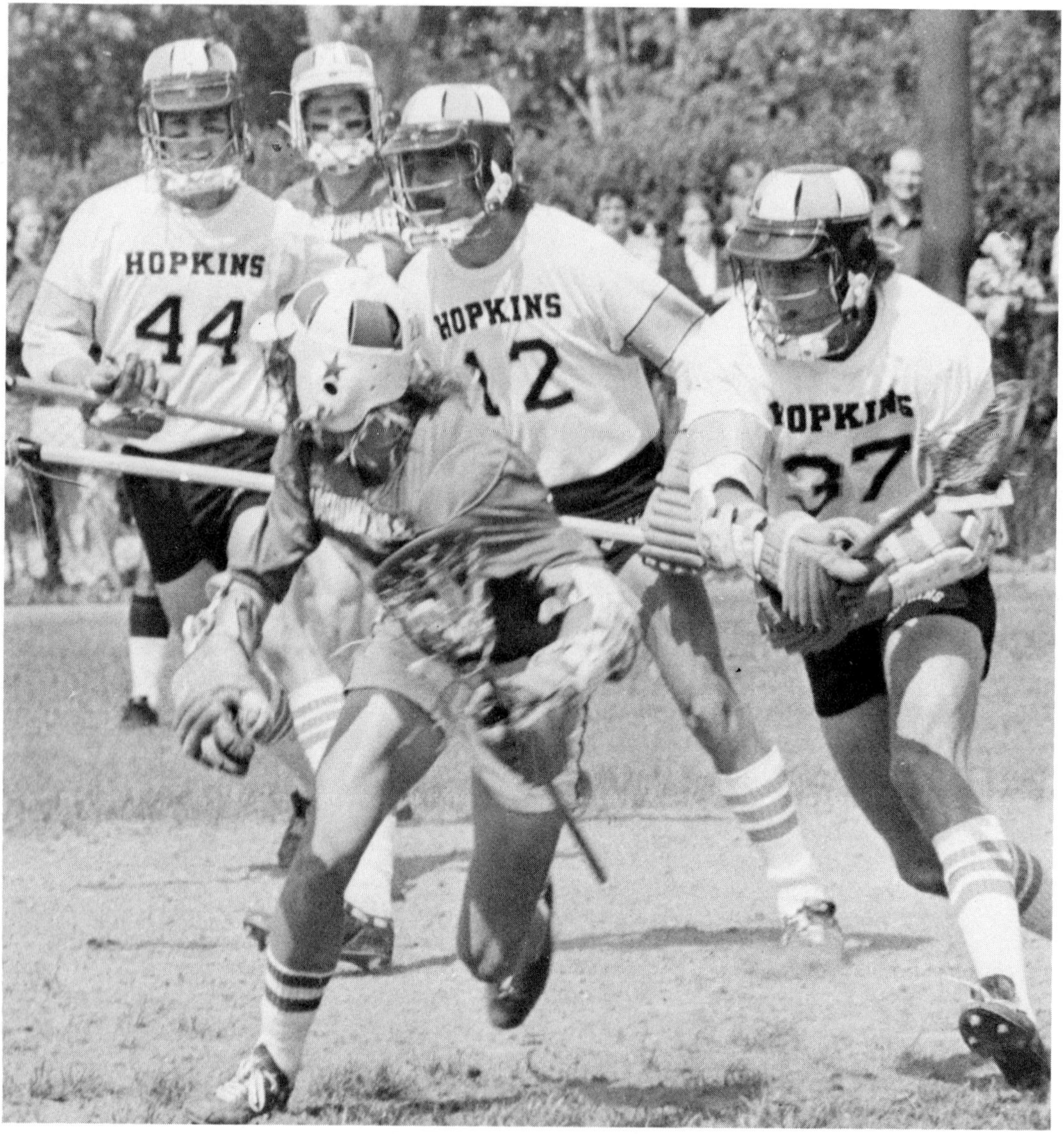
HOPKINS
44
HOPKINS
12
HOPKINS
37

Defense

Defense has to be one of the toughest positions on the field. The offense knows where it's going—at least that's what most players think. But in this section, you'll see that the great defenseman not only tries to stop the offense but succeeds in forcing the offensive players to play where and how he wants by taking away the offensive options in advance.

Defense is one position that has totally changed over the last 10 years. Today's defenseman needs to be an excellent athlete capable not only of taking the ball away from his opponent but of playing all over both ends of the field. During rides he functions as an attackman, and he replaces the wing middie on the faceoff.

The defensemen in this section are quick, aggressive, have excellent speed and can play from sideline to sideline without hesitation. They know they're part of a team and that they have a job to do which contributes to the team's success. They also know that because the offensive players are getting better every year, they have to drill and experiment continuously in order to improve their own defensive skills.

There are two basic types of defensive style represented in this book. The difference springs from a difference in objective. For those players who see the defenseman's primary role to obtain possession of the ball, play is more aggressive. For those who see their job as holding off the offense until it makes a mistake, the style of play is more or less conservative. Each type handles the various techniques of defensive play slightly differently.

Defense is a much-neglected aspect of lacrosse. As you'll learn by reading what our stars have to say, it's as exciting and challenging a position as attack or midfield.

Jeff Wagner

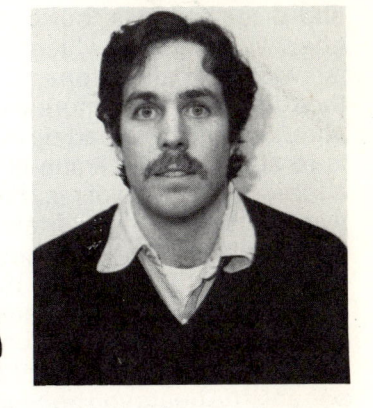

Bing Devine

EDITOR'S INTRODUCTION

After a successful two years playing for Nassau Community College, Bing Devine moved on to Cornell University where he became a two-time All-American.

Known for his quickness, agility and aggressiveness, Bing always covered the opposing team's top attackman. He has proved himself a top defenseman, serving as Co-captain on the North-South game, playing on the '78 USA team, and being named to the Club All Star team.

Bing is presently coaching at Nassau Community College while pursuing a career in the film industry. No doubt he's passing on to a new generation of lacrosse All Stars his concept of "offensive" defense and the particular plays that make his own defensive play so hard to beat.

PLAYER'S INTRODUCTION

Lacrosse has always been a free spirited game. Not quite as regimented as other sports, it has more room for freedom and change. But the freedom the game offers should not be confused with loss of discipline. Just as with any other sport, lacrosse requires a strong mental conditioning, as well as a physical one if a player wishes to attain proficiency and complete enjoyment of the sport.

The current 1978 World Lacrosse Championship in England, in which I participated, will exemplify the disappointment a team and individual face when a let down in attitude occurs inopportunely. The opening rounds permitted us to catch the Canadian team sleeping and defeat them 28-4. This was less of a blessing than it seemed, since our over-confidence and a fine Canadian team able to rebound after defeat beat us in overtime of the championship game.

I believe in well balanced playing, that is, play with intensity, never over confident and never bitter afterwards. Because of its current small range, lacrosse has created enormous friendships, even among rivals on the field. I enjoy the fierce competition, but also I revel in the warm atmosphere at the completion of the contest.

The Devine Defense

Reviewing my lacrosse experience as a player, coach, and spectator, I have concluded that there are two basic concepts of individual defense. Both have advantages and disadvantages, but both are equally effective. The first, which I'm more familiar with, I'll call "offensive" defense. Although it exhibits a more exciting style of play, it does lack steadiness. The purpose is to strip the attackman of the ball. This aggressive method of play has as its objective to cause an important turnover, to weaken the opponent's confidence, and generally to try to change the momentum of the game. Its disadvantages include the frequent development of unsettled situations, unnecessary goals made by your opponent if he beats you because you've overcommitted, and frequent fouling due to the closeness with which you play your man.

"Offensive" defense demands excellent control of the long stick and a refined ability to retrieve loose balls once they're jarred from the attacker. It should be mentioned that in addition to just stopping an attempt at scoring, gaining possession and moving the ball up the field quickly are major overall objectives.

Not every coach agrees with my preference for playing offensive defense. It is risky. Plus it demands certain abilities and drills not every defenseman may have developed. The alternative philosophy of defense I'll call "shadow" defense. Often, when an attackman has scored or assisted due to my over playing, I've wished that I played the more conservative shadow method. It tends to be less embarassing!

The theory behind shadow defense is that inevitably any offense will lose possession when up against a frustrating, impregnable defense, a defense that never permits mistakes that the attackmen can take advantage of.

For a defenseman, playing shadow defense means that he personifies his attackman's shadow. It requires much patience, tenacity, and concentration. You have to allow your opponent possession of the ball, but this is all you allow. Some of the game's greatest defensemen rarely steal the ball from their opponents; but, and this is what counts, they contained their attackmen's scoring.

Both of these philosophies of defense contain their own faults and merits. One relies on consistency and subtle mechanics; the other, while a bit more sublime, is unsteady. Each practitioner of each method has his own style which best utilizes individual abilities (lateral quickness, stick control, concentration, judgment, etc.) to prevent the exultation and cheers of the rival fans. I could say a lot more about each of the two basic styles of defensive play, but I'll stick to elaborating on my own style of offensive defense.

Playing the Ball

I'll start by drawing attention to one important point—learn as much about your opponent as you can, especially during the first few minutes of play when he is just becoming accustomed to the game. Be aware of his physical abilities (speed, agility, etc.) and get to know his method of play (favorite dodge, direction of movement, right and left hand strengths, etc.) This idea may sound hackneyed, but it will help you better predict your opponent's motion, thereby reducing the attackman's advantage of being able to initiate a play before you can react properly.

[Reading your attackman's body language is a real defensive advantage. I can always tell when I'm up against a defense that has practiced what Bing is suggesting. —G.F.]

Now to some specific techniques. As

Defense

Jeff Wagner

your attacker receives the ball, you should be moving toward him and arrive as he catches the ball. This forces him to react to you and move away from the goal. It also may provide a vulnerable moment in which you can check his stick while he's attempting to catch the ball. Once he has secured the ball, you should relax, take an even stance, and prepare to move with him. Keep no more than a stick's length away. It's important to be within reach of a check. This closeness puts some pressure on your attackman's ability to feed. Also, since it is very difficult to cover cutters in front of the goal, keeping close to your attackman will augment your team's overall coverage.

Your stick should *not* be in constant checking motion (slapping, poking, etc.) because you tend to develop a pattern that the attackman can work to his advantage. Be unpredictable with your checks. Always aim for the bottom glove once it is placed on the stick.

Watch for him to bring his stick in front of his body. Since you're only a stick length away, it's easy for you to poke a face dodge or any type of dodge when he does bring his stick around.

Stick and body must work together. While your opponent is behind the cage, place more emphasis on the stick use. But as he approaches the pipes, use your upper body to drive him away to the side. (See Diagram 1.) Such driving is done by continuously pushing with your feet, using your arms, not your shoulders, to push him away. When driving, always remain stick to stick to prevent him from shooting or feeding over your shoulder. Too much use of your shoulders and head makes you vulnerable by overcommitting your body; your attackman can then roll in the opposite direction and beat you to the goal.

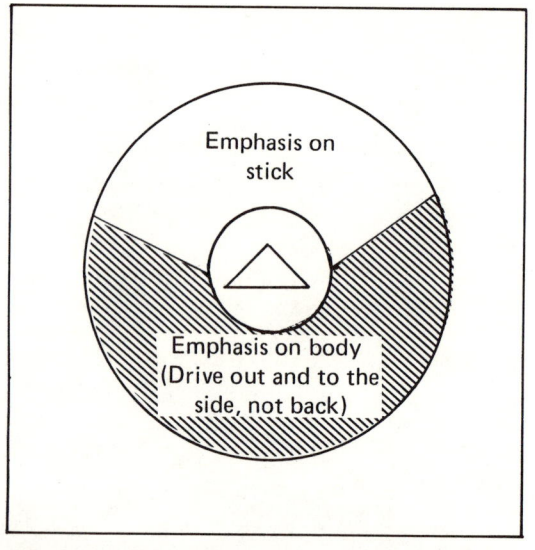

Diagram 1 [*Bing hit it on the head here. It's very difficult to dodge when you play off of the attackman. Most attackmen wait for the defenseman to overcommit before making a move.—G.F.*]

Playing the Dodger

When it comes to playing the dodge, be aware that the attackman has the distinct advantage. He will know where he is going much sooner than you will be able to respond. So, it's important to respect your attackman's abilities. He will, naturally, gain the step in his assault on the goal. The best defense is just to run, stick to stick with him, until you can come abreast of him. Then use checks or body pressure. Being overly aggressive while your attackman is dodging his way to the goal often results in decreasing your chances of recovering and controlling his movements.

[*Remembers, as Bing hints here, that the goal of a good defenseman is to be able to control his attacker's every movement; the more you can control your attackman, the easier it is for you to prevent him from scoring. Here are some specifics on how Bing gains this control over his attackmen.—G. F.]*

One technique that will come with experience deals with setting up your attackman or forcing him to react to you. As an example, during the crucial time just before your attacker is planning the direction to dodge, a sudden thrust of your stick in front of him may make the decision for him. Now, *you* know which way he will dodge before he has even become aware of his decision. The technique for setting up your attackman is similar to the principle of restraining him by forcing him to change direction, whether behind the goal or at the critical point—the pipes.

If you try one of these moves and fail, it is important not to become desperate or give up. Just keep up the pressure by pursuing him until a teammate can come to help. You may even create a double team situation thereby placing even more pressure on the offense.

Playing the Feeder

It's very difficult to decipher whether your attackman intends to dodge or feed. Although you must be cautious and respect the dodger first, you cannot ignore the feeder. The feeder must be watched constantly, because of the difficulty of covering cutters to the goal. During the time between checks, hold your stick up in the imaginary path of a feed and move continually to distract potential feeders. By playing this way, it's not too unusual to knock down feeds or, with a little luck, catch them. (A real crowd pleaser.)

It should become clear that your attackman is ready to feed when he moves laterally, looks to the crease, and places two hands on his stick. Now is the time when being only one stick's length away is vital. Attempt to anticipate the passing motion. Use a poke—your stick on his bottom hand or across his chest. This should jam or misdirect the feed enough to prevent its completion. This timing, along with the ability to read the attackman's intentions, can only come from experience and practice. The goalie can help enormously in such situations by calling the impending play as it develops. He can usually tell from the motion in front of the cage what the attackman is thinking.

Playing the Crease

Crease defense play requires a different outlook, one that depends on mind reading and understanding facial expressions. Because the crease attackman has the ball for only a split second before he shoots, you have very little time to react. Most good creasemen will have the goalie raking the ball out of the cage while the crease defenseman is still checking him. Thus it is essential for the crease defenseman to watch for certain clues and concentrate on the goalie's voice. Reacting must take place before the ball reaches the creaseman, not after.

When playing crease defense, your position should be between the ball (feeder) and the crease attackman, matching the head of your stick with the height of the creaseman's stick. This helps to hinder feeding the ball inside. Practice being aware of the ball's location using a combination of quick scans, the goalie's voice, and a sense of the overall offensive flow.

Strict eye guarding is not advisable since there are many other duties for the crease defenseman, such as helping out with cutters, backing up other members of the defense, and picking up loose balls in front of the cage. *Resting your stick on the attackman is a good method to use while looking around.* It maintains your awareness of the location of your attackman. When you can't locate the ball or the attackman is moving quickly, watching the overall action or even facial expressions can be helpful. Many times the attackman's eyes will light up with visions of glory moments before the ball reaches his stick. This is an excellent clue because it comes before the attackman actually gets the ball. You can time a check for the second before he catches the feed.

These principles are fundamental to playing crease defense and don't alter even when there are two men on the crease. But *when you're playing two men on the crease,* the problem is compounded by their motion and interplay—such as picking for each other. Your positioning should undergo only minor adjustments. Keep your stick between your man and the ball, even if you can't possibly maneuver your body to this position.

Communication is the single element that will make or break the multiple crease defense. Talk between the two players is a necessity. Although the type of defense played here is actually a zone arrangement, I prefer to call it a "switching man to man." This may sound like a semantic nicety, but my term conveys the idea of communication more effectively than does the word "zone." "Switching man to man" means a tight man to man defense, unless a pick upsets the coverage and the picked-off defenseman loses his attackman. Now the defenseman or middie who is off will call for a switch and jump out to cover the loose attackman while the picked-off defenseman covers the off-man's attackman.

Timing is crucial on the crease because events occur so quickly. The defenseman also should be alert if the attackman steps back from the pick instead of moving laterally. Standing beside the pick may facilitate a quick jump to pop a pick on this open man.

Knowing when to slide while playing the crease is also very important. Slides have become longer so that the multiple crease defense must be aware of when to slide either by communication or watching the play carefully.

Team Defense

[Even though Bing plays a very rugged, individualistic game, his insistence on constant communication indicates the importance of a total team effort. I asked him how he felt a player should approach team defense; here's his answer.—G. F.]

Team defense is difficult to talk about since today many teams play a combination of zone and man to man defense. But there are two fundamentals that don't appear to vary—communication between players and positioning. Communication begins with the goalie and spreads throughout the rest of the defense. From my own experience, I firmly believe that complete team talk will make it very difficult for any offense to penetrate to the goal. This principle must be constantly re-enforced because breakdowns occur frequently in the heat of the game. It's a skill that should be developed until it's second nature, but coaches often ease up on it as the season goes on.

Positioning varies with each team, so I'll only discuss *sloughing* and *backing up.*

Sloughing means that the further you are from the ball on the perimeter of the of-

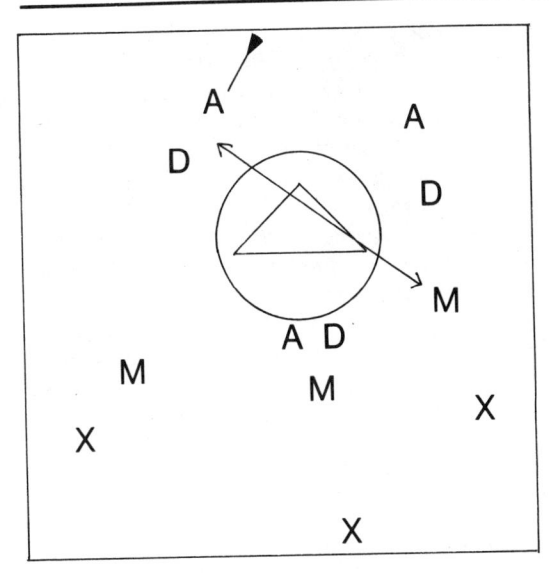

Diagram 2

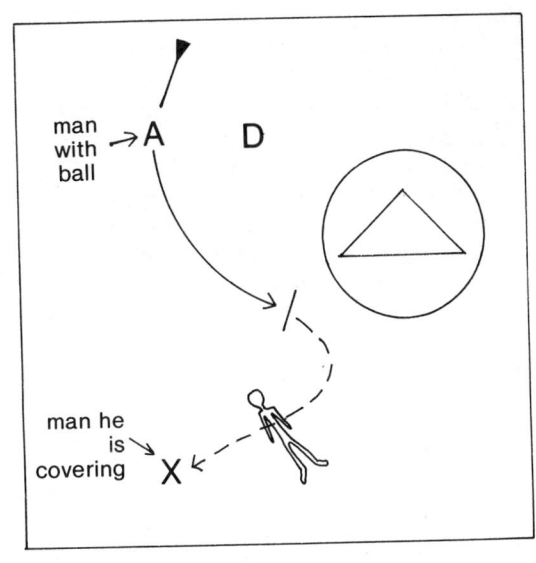

Diagram 3

fense, the closer you should be to the crease area. Hence, the man opposite the ball is closest to the crease (aside from the crease defenseman). (See Diagram 2.)

Being in position to *back-up* requires the man playing defense to be in a comfortable range between his own offensive man and the ball and at an angle that will permit him to turn and force the man with the ball if he has successfully dodged his defenseman. This can be made easier by turning your body so only your head must turn to watch both the man with the ball and the man you are covering. (See Diagram 3.)

Over the Head Checks

Probably my favorite defensive maneuver is the over the head check. It's flashy yet effective if it's not considered an all or nothing check. It can be a legitimate way of taking the ball away without being beaten by your attackman as he moves. The easi- est way of being beaten is to overcommit. To prevent this, use only your stick; don't overcommit your whole body to the check. Also be prepared to recover quickly in case the check fails.

Moving with the attackman should be automatic, regardless of the type of check. But too often defensemen stop their feet while checking. This creates a make or break situation if the check is unsuccessful because the attackman has not stopped moving his feet. By the time you recover, he's away.

Only the stick should be involved in the check. Keep your hands down toward the butt end and use the head to go over the attackman's head. This helps prevent lunging at the attackman and getting out of position. Control of the stick is important so you don't foul your attackman. A good way of preventing losing position is to bring the stick back over the attackman's head after having gone over the first time. This will help you regain your momentum and may provide a second chance at the attackman's stick since his first reaction to an overhead check is to drop his stick in front for protection. As he does so, he may overreact and expose too much of his stick.

Not expecting to accomplish the check successfully will provide a contingency for recovering steps lost while attempting the check. So, by planning ahead, you can be aware of the direction you must go in order to intercept your attackman if he has gained a step on you.

Wrap Checks

Another check that is effective in taking the ball away from your opponent is the *wrap check*. The wrap check can be done with one or two hands on your stick. A one-handed hold may provide more reach and less chance for overcommitting yourself, but there is less strength and control. Hold the stick just up from the butt with the hand that coincides with the direction of your attackman's movement. Next, get close to your attackman and wrap your stick around his body level with the head of the attackman's stick. You must unwrap your stick immediately to prevent being called for a holding foul.

A *two-handed wrap* provides more leverage but requires more caution. Assume your attackman has his stick in his right hand. Hold your stick in your right hand. Your hands should be roughly a foot apart and close to the butt end of the stick. Place your right hand as far across the attackman's chest as you can. Your left hand then moves outward, pivoting off the right hand and wrapping the head of your stick around the attackman.

Both types of wrap necessitate getting close to the attackman, so I recommend that you be prepared to drop step back with the foot that's opposite the attackman's stick. Remember that the only direction the attackman is free to move is opposite his original direction. This drop step will help your recovery by getting you close to the attackman.

One warning: *Never throw an over the head or wrap check anywhere except behind the goal,* where there is room to recover from an unsuccessful check. Never throw these checks near the pipes. If you miss one of these checks at the pipes, there is no room for recovery or for anyone else to back up. The result too often is a goal for the opposition.

Future of Lacrosse

The game will constantly change in the next five to ten years. But these changes will never match those caused by the introduction of the plastic stick. Future changes will come about because of the game's growth nationally and internationally in the form of field rule changes. The most noteworthy rule change (which occurred just recently) is the removal of the faceoff after a goal. Although this is a step backwards, it represents the type of experimentation that we're likely to see in the future.

After playing international rules, I believe the adoption of some of them would certainly improve the game's excitement and pace without creating new specializations, which I think the no faceoff rule might do.

Some rule changes that I suggest are:

No horns; substituting only on the fly except for penalties. Penalties should not start until the penalized is seated in the box, although the referee may start play before he gets off the field. The result will be that the guilty party must sprint off the field to serve his penalty time.

Require that a new ball always be ready so play can start immediately when the ball goes out of bounds. This will greatly reduce dead time.

Have 30 seconds for faceoff. If only one man is ready on the field, he gets the ball and play begins. If no one is ready I think the official should blow the whistle and start the clock. This would definitely encourage teams to prepare right away for a faceoff.

These are a few of the rules I think will show up in the future. It may only be my opinion, but I believe lacrosse can go the route of some pro sports and lose its spirit to an overemphasis on what appeals to the fans. The game is best, the more rudimentary and original it remains. I would hate to see it head toward specialization like football did or out and out boredom like basketball did. Right now lacrosse has the exciting elements of hockey with more goal scoring. Let's keep lacrosse pure and unpredictable; don't be afraid to leave the variables in the game.

Chris Kane

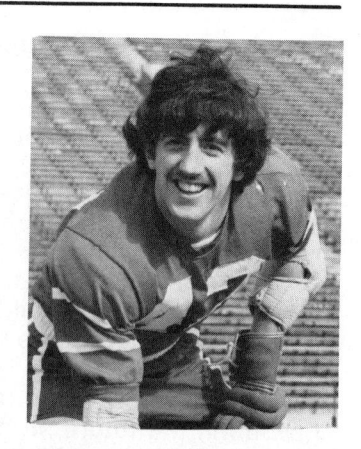

EDITOR'S INTRODUCTION

Chris has been called by many "the best defenseman to ever have played college lacrosse." He actually started out playing midfield for Cornell, but coach Ritchie Moran moved him to defense. Chris responded with a level of play that led to his being named Outstanding Defenseman in the Country, not once but twice. This plus his award as the Hero's best defenseman makes him only the second defenseman to accomplish this feat.

Chris also was named to the First Team All Ivy and All-American in both his Junior and Senior years and played on the USA team in 1978.

His eventual goal is to become a defensive coach for a college team so that he can share what he's learned "by being coached by the best coaches ever and playing with the best lacrosse players in the history of the game" as he himself puts it.

PLAYER'S INTRODUCTION

The game of lacrosse means a great deal to me. When you can put a team of non-scholarship athletes on a lacrosse field with the goal of winning a national championship and do it, there is a great feeling of accomplishment and satisfaction in doing what you set out to do. The pressure times I've had on a lacrosse field will surely help later in life when I have to make quick, pressure situation responses.

I suggest you play lacrosse with extreme confidence at all times. One thing I've always enjoyed about lacrosse is that you can make a mistake and come right back with a super play. So take the cocky attitude—you are the best and no one can beat you. When you believe you are the best, you play like the best. But you cannot have this attitude unless you're working very hard all the time to improve your game.

Chris Kane on Defense

My philosophy of defense is to be well rounded in every skill, from setting a pick to picking up a ground ball, at the same time realizing what your strong points are as a lacrosse player and using them wisely and expertly. For example, time and time again fans say to me, "You're Chris Kane? I thought you were a lot bigger." It's a justified statement because while I'm 6'2", I weigh only 175 lbs. (I don't look at it as being skinny, just lean and mean.) But I

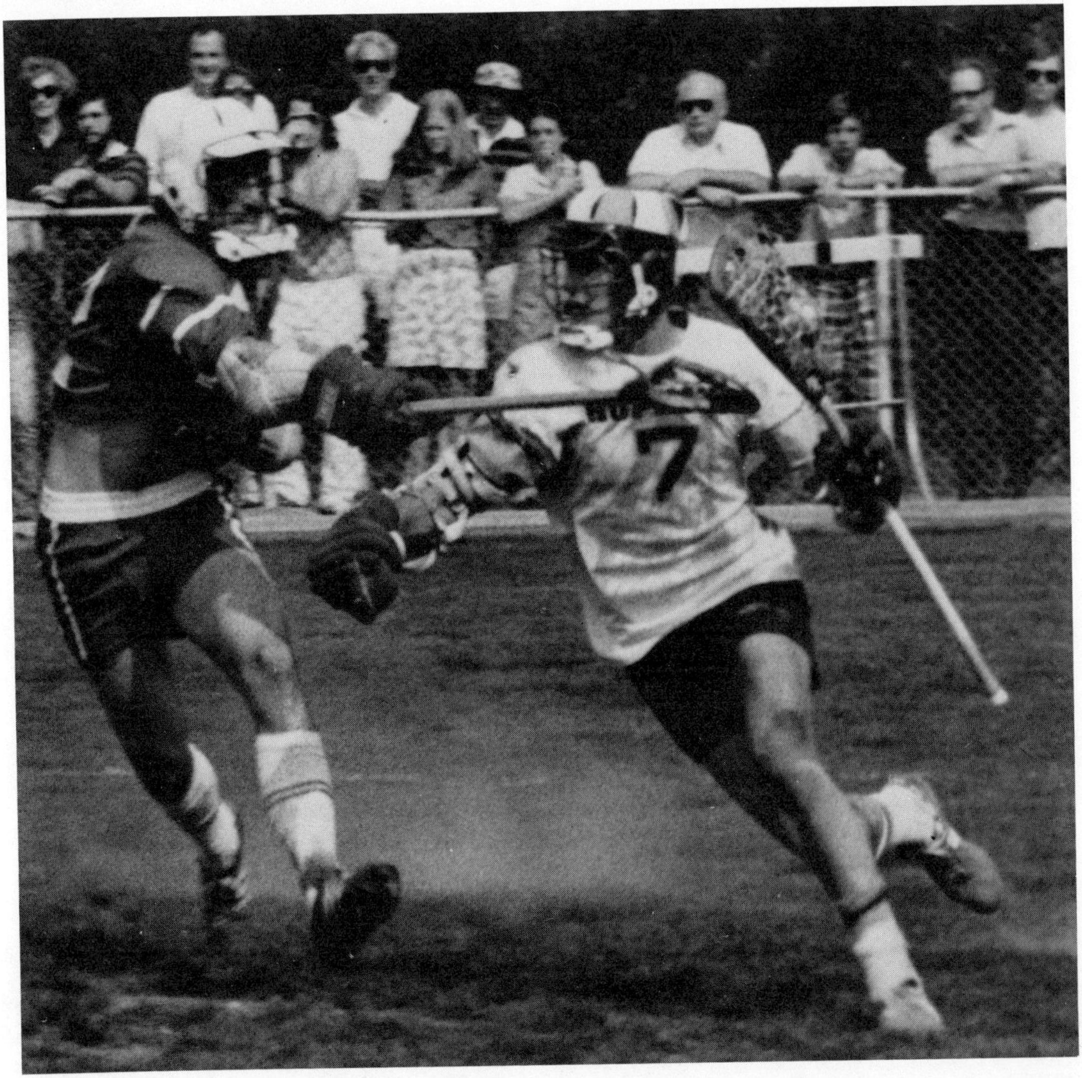

Kane

know I'm not going to be muscling the big guys around so I rely on quick lateral movement, a squared up defense, and persistent poke checks on the attackman's bottom hand. Always the bottom hand! I never look at an attackman's upper body because you fake with your upper body. I believe that where your waist goes, you go. I also believe in making every check count, so I don't check a man much unless he has two hands on his stick. You cannot pass, shoot or pick up a ground ball with one hand. The only time it's good to have one hand on your stick is when someone's taking your picture!

When an attackman has one hand off to protect his stick, be patient. Use a squared up defense and wait until he puts his other hand on his stick. Then start poke checking.

Despite what I look like when I play, I am an extreme conservative. The only times I'd ever take a gamble are when I knew I had someone backing me up or if my man beat me. Knowing you have back-up to your right and left should you miss or overcommit yourself on a check is truly a great feeling for a defenseman.

Playing Behind the Goal

I play a man behind the goal with lateral movement, never crossing legs, using constant poke checks to keep pressure on my opponent, and close enough so that I can always reach his bottom hand with the head of my stick. (This is easier said than done.)

I try to set my man up with various checks, trying to get him to expose his stick. For example, if I poke checked my opponent three times, he would pull his stick back. I would then fake an overhead check, causing him to bring his stick directly in front of him. This exposes his stick and I can come straight down and check his stick. A complicated set up, but this is one check which works very well for me. I think it's very important to be able to use your stick to set up your man to make him expose his stick. That's one of the best techniques a defenseman can use.

Playing a Dodger

A defenseman is at a great disadvantage not knowing what his attackman is about to do. My best advice for stopping a dodge is to know what your attackman's strong dodge moves are and then to prevent him from starting them. After a few minutes of play against a man, you can figure out what his strong dodges are and watch for them.

Feeders

I try to stop a feeder with constant poke checks to his bottom hand when it is on his stick. I use the time when he doesn't have his bottom hand on his stick to get in a good position for when he does. Remember that a feeder is not dangerous unless he has both hands on his stick.

Crease Defense

I front the creaseman strongside or ballside when the ball is out front. I play on the strongside or ballside of the man when the ball is behind. In both instances I favor the strongside which is the side of the field the ball is on, trying to keep my eyes on both my man and where the ball will be coming from. When two men are on the crease, I try to play one man with my body and the other with my stick. I prefer to play the strongside man with my body and the weakside man with my stick.

Defense

Team Defense

The important thing in team defense is TALK! TALK! TALK!!! There is nothing nicer for a defenseman to hear than, "Got your back right" or "Got your back left." It is also very discouraging for an attackman to know that if he beats his defenseman, he will be picked up immediately. Talk intimidates the offense! *[This is an excellent point Chris brings up. You will discourage many attackmen by talking. Keep in mind that even if you don't have your teammate backed, by calling out that you do you can make the attackman hesitate, break his concentration, and perhaps make him bungle the play.—G. F.]*

Head Checks

It doesn't matter how you go over a person's head as long as you keep your feet moving along with him. Then, even if you miss your check, you are up with your man and can recover. If you are not moving when you try an overhead check, it becomes a do or die check. Even though running astride your man means you must cross your legs and commit yourself, these are the chances you have got to take when trying an overhead check. I use this check a lot, but don't regard it as a safe check. It's very hard to master.

I go over the head when an attackman hangs his stick instead of keeping it close to his shoulders and head. An attackman hangs his stick most often when (1) I give him a forearm push, forcing him to push out his stick; (2) when he is changing direction behind the cage using a roll back move; and (3) right before he shoots—to get more power on the shot the attackman pulls his stick way back. If you watch for these opportunities, you'll have more success with your overhead checks.

Wrap Checks

I hardly ever use a wrap check because I feel you are totally committing yourself when you use this check. The only time I think it's feasible is when your attackman is backing into you and you are standing still. A wrap check should be followed by a forearm push and a hard poke check to the bottom hand. This way you don't stay in the wrap check and totally commit yourself.

Playing the Man Without the Ball

When the ball is behind, I make a triangle: ball-myself-man I am guarding. I stay ready for the back up if my other defenseman gets beat. When the ball is out front and my man is behind, I only go to the pipes. I do not guard my man behind when the ball is out front. (See Diagram 1 & 1a.) I usually fill in the weak side of the cage right before a

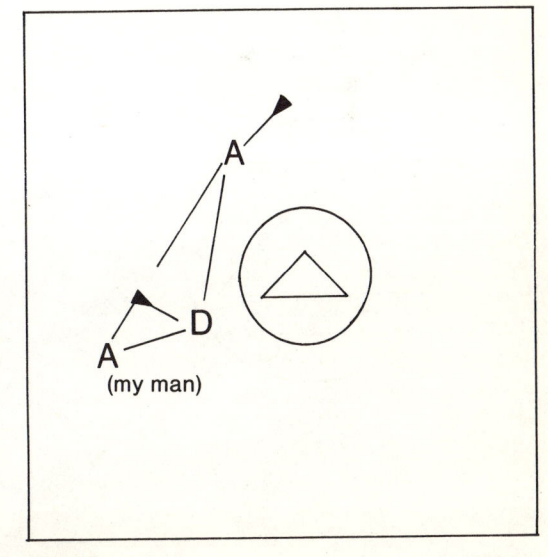

Diagram 1

middie is about to shoot, as shown in Diagram 2.

Future of Lacrosse

I think in the next five to ten years, we'll see increased playing of lacrosse in the southern and western United States. There the game can be played year round so I see the day coming when UCLA or Stanford can challenge Cornell, Hopkins or another big Eastern team for an NCAA championship.

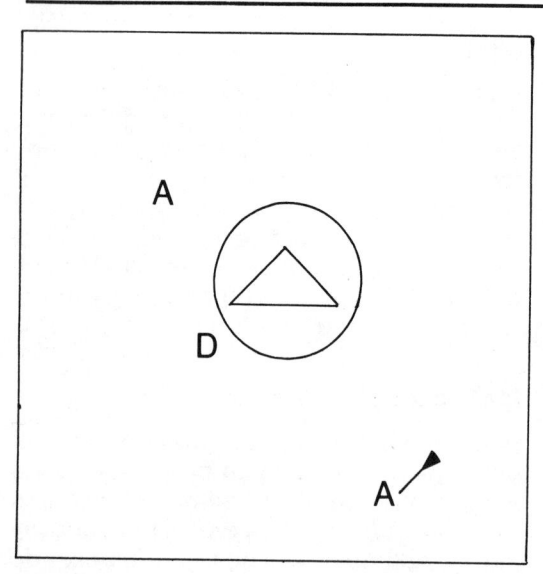

Diagram 1a

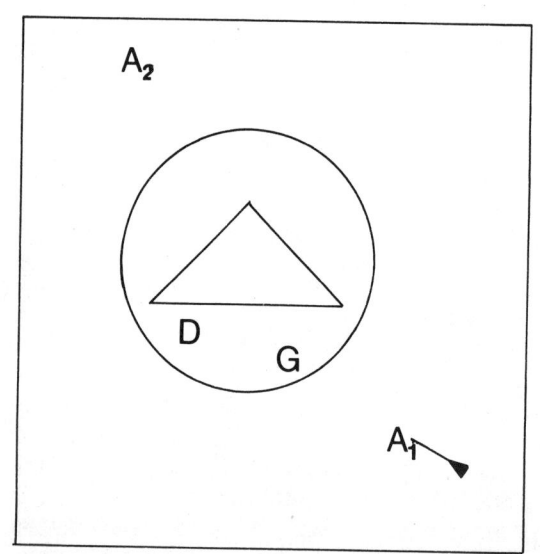

Diagram 2

Tom Keigler

EDITOR'S INTRODUCTION

Here's a really great defenseman who has been playing lacrosse since he was five years old. Keigs played for Towson High School and Washington & Lee University, where he was a two-time All-American and received the Hero's award as the outstanding defenseman in Division I. He also played on the 1978 USA National team. Since graduating from Washington & Lee, Keigs has been teaching at Maryland's Calvert Hall School where he also coaches lacrosse. He'll be following in his father's footsteps by joining the Mt. Washington Club.

Tom's concept of a good defense is that it's easier to win games with a good, consistent defense than to rely on the offense to score the additional goals needed to compensate for a weak defense. And good team defense, as he points out, starts with good individual defensive skills.

Philosophy of Defense

Defense is the most important component in any championship lacrosse team. For a team to be a consistent winner—whether it be on the club, college, high school, or little league level—it must have good, solid team defense. I believe this because there are many different variables which go into making a good offense, including timing, passwork, good shooting, ball movement, and a little bit of luck. But good, consistent defense entails only three important ingredients: fundamentals, talk and desire. It is much easier, therefore, to win with good consistent defense than it is to rely on the offensive squad to score fifteen or twenty goals a game.

Before we can talk about good team defense, we first must talk about good individual defense because *individual defense is the foundation upon which good team defense is built.* I will address three specific facets of individual defense—positioning, checking and fast break defense because they are the keys to good individual defense.

Position

Perhaps the most important component of individual defense is positioning. A defenseman who is a good position defenseman is much better off than the take-away defenseman or the defenseman who gambles all the time. Good positioning starts with the position of your body in relation to your attackman. First and foremost, you *always* should be between your attackman and the goal. Whether your man has the ball or not, it is your duty to take away the shortest distance to the goal. And, since the shortest distance to the goal is a straight line, you must make sure that you take away the straight line approach by being between your man and the goal.

In addition to always playing between your attackman and the goal, good positioning depends on how you break down when playing your attackman. Basic lacrosse positioning is no different than basic basketball or football positioning—feet approximately shoulder width apart, with your weight on the balls of your feet, knees and waist slightly bent. With this stance, you'll find you can smoothly and easily move forward, backward, or laterally to follow your attackman. It is essential that you always break down in good position whenever you address your attackman. If you rush him, if your feet are too close together, if your weight is too far forward, then the result will be that your attackman can easily dodge you.

Once you establish basic foot and body positioning, the next step is to add the stick. The stick is placed in poke check position. To establish proper poke check positioning, put your hands approximately twenty-four inches apart; your off hand (left hand if you're right handed) covers the butt end of the shaft, and your right hand is approximately twenty-four inches up the shaft from your left hand. Rest your right hand on your hip bone. The stick is turned over; the head of the stick faces down. Center the stick on the attackman's numbers. Thus, when you poke, your stick should hit your opponent's shaft right below the head of his stick. Poking is accomplished by sliding the left hand up to meet the top hand, using a quick, jabbing motion. When you poke, *do not lean forward!* Maintain proper position; all that is extended is your stick.

Obviously, this check will not work unless you are a stick's length away from your attackman. In other words, when you extend your stick, it will just touch the attackman's stick. If your stick will not reach the attackman's stick, you are too far away. Conversely, if your stick when extended in the poke check extends past your attackman's stick, you are too close to your attackman. Remember, you want to stay a stick's length away.

Once you've mastered poke check positioning, you need to know exactly where your body should be in relation to your attackman. Let's assume that your attackman is protecting his stick so that he is turned sideways behind the goal. He is right handed which means only one hand (his right hand) is on his stick. His left hand is out in a protecting fashion, and his stick is vertical.

Since his body is turned sideways, you must position yourself so that you take away the shortest route to the goal. To do so, first split the attackman's body with your own. (Remember, you have your feet shoulder width apart, weight on the balls of your feet, knees and waist slightly bent, and your stick in poke check position.) Now, make sure the attackman's body is exactly in the middle of your two feet. This way you'll be neither ahead of nor behind your attackman—you'll be right in the middle. By establishing this position, you make it hard for the attackman to get around you, because you have taken away the shortest and most direct route to the goal. In addition, you have positioned yourself in such a

Defense

Keigler

way that the attackman will have a difficult time dodging you. *[Remember the attackman is waiting for you to overcommit. Playing the way Keigs suggests certainly will go a long way in discouraging him from dodging.—G.F.]*

To summarize the first ingredient in individual defense, body positioning, let me emphasize a few major points. Your major duty as a defenseman is to make sure that you take away your attackman's shortest route to the goal. This means that you always play between your attackman and the goal. Next, your body and stick always should be in poke check position. Third, you always should split the attackman with your body so that it's more difficult for him to get by you.

Checking

The second important component of individual defense is checking. Many young lacrosse players are overly impressed with fancy checking; over the head checks, butt end checks, and wrap checks look fancy and are sometimes effective, but they should not be overemphasized. The most effective and most basic check which a defenseman can have in his arsenal is the *poke check*, because you do not have to sacrifice your positioning when using it. You are already in poke check position! Further, your stick is already aimed at your man's numbers so that all you need to do to make a poke check is to slide your hands together (the bottom hand sliding up to meet the top hand) which extends your stick and hopefully dislodges the ball. Implicit in the poke check is NOT stepping in when shooting the poke. Your weight remains on the balls of your feet and your feet remain spread shoulder width apart; all that moves toward the attackman is your stick. Consequently, if the check misses its target, you are still in good position and have not lost anything by implementing the poke check.

Some points to remember when utilizing the poke check. First, don't dangle your stick. The poke check should be a smooth, crisp check; and, after you have poked, you should immediately recoil your stick so that it is once again aimed at the attackman's numbers. This means that the entire time required to implement a poke check should be no more than one to two seconds. A second point to remember when using the poke check is not to be overly aggressive. What you are trying to do is to lull the attackman to sleep; hopefully, he will forget about *your* stick and expose *his* stick. That's when you strike. If you are constantly pecking away at the attackman's stick, he will be more conscious of your stick which decreases the chances of your being able to poke successfully. *[Most behind attackmen, seeing you play excellent position, will look to feed. Following Tom's rules will give you a better chance to poke the ball loose.—G.F.]*

The poke check is used most effectively when the attackman is jogging (not sprinting) behind the goal. As he jogs, shuffle your feet so that they do not cross one another. (Shuffle much the same way a boxer would shuffle his feet when boxing.) Whenever the attackman changes directions behind the goal, you need only push off on your outside foot to change direction.

An outgrowth of the poke check is the *slap check*. The slap check is used when the attackman is no longer jogging behind the goal but has started to sprint. This sprinting action makes it impossible for you to shuffle. Therefore, turn your hips and run hip to hip with your attackman. Although you're still only a stick's length away, the poke check is no longer a viable check because you are now running—hence, the slap check.

When you are running with a right handed attackman (assuming you are right handed also) maintain your stick in a poke check position (aimed at the attackman's numbers). Now, look for a rhythmic pattern set up by the pumping motion of the attackman's stick cradling. When you feel you have an accurate timing of this pattern and can predict where the stick will be, slap check. To slap check, extend your stick *through* the numbers by pushing out with your lower hand; at the same time, reach behind the attackman and try to dislodge the ball. The most frequent mistake when utilizing the slap check is stepping in when trying to slap check. *Never step in when checking!* If your stick cannot dislodge the ball, nothing is lost. You're still in good poke check position and haven't lost any positioning at all. Again, do not dangle your stick when slap checking; instead, slap quickly and return your stick to poke check position.

When running hip to hip with an attackman of opposite hand (for example, a left handed defenseman running with a right handed attackman), the slap check is a little more difficult to accomplish. Still push out with your bottom hand, but now reach in and slap a little bit with your top hand as well.

Tips for slap checking: Your hands when slap checking are closer together than when poke checking (six inches apart as opposed to twenty-four) to enable you to reach further with your stick. Another point to remember: The stick is still at the numbers. Do not aim higher or lower; the result will be either a penalty for slashing on the head or, if your stick is too low, not being able to defend yourself against a feed.

Another check which comes out of the poke check and the slap check is the *chop check*. The chop check is used primarily when an attackman who is either jogging or sprinting behind the goal steps back to feed. The most common reaction of the defenseman when the attackman steps back to feed is to step back with him. This is a dangerous move. If the attackman uses the step back and feed move properly, he can effectively set you up for a face or roll dodge if you step back with him. Be aware of this and, as the attackman steps back, step back cautiously with him. As the attackman puts his bottom hand on his stick to feed, bring down your stick with a chopping action on his lower glove. It is much easier and more effective to come down on the attackman's glove as he feeds than it is either to try to knock down the feed or to step in and try to poke his stick. It is extremely difficult for the attackman to feed if his bottom hand has been checked as he is initiating his feed.

Another check which is risky and should be used with discretion is the *over the head check*. Use it only when your attackman is in tight quarters around the goal. It should not be used in the open field because the attackman has too much time to react and too much field in which to run.

The most effective time to use the over the head check is right on the pipes, especially when a back-up is imminent from the midfield. In this situation, the attackman commonly has his stick back and not well protected and is being annoyed by the defenseman. (If he pulls back his stick properly, he will not have much time in which to shoot.)

When the proper situation arises for using the over the head check, use the following technique to implement the check. (First, though, remember that the poke check is easiest to use when guarding a man of the same hand.) In order to set up the attackman for the over the head check, first poke, forcing the attackman to draw back his stick. Then, quickly go over his head with the head of your stick. The danger of this check is that if you miss the attackman's stick, you have lost your body and stick position. This danger is minimized if you use the check sparingly and when the attackman is in tight and on the pipes.

As a defenseman, my favorite check is what I call the *ding dong check*. The ding dong check is nothing more than a fake poke, fake over the head, slap check. In other words, you half-heartedly poke, fake an over the head check (drawing the attackman's stick out in front of his body) and then quickly slap check. The beauty of this check is that you do not lose your positioning, and you can poke check instead of ding donging, or you can go over the head instead. Consequently, your attackman never knows what you are going to do. The check can be used when on the pipes, when jogging with the attackman behind the goal, or when running hip to hip with him behind the goal. It is a simple, yet effective, check.

Fast Break Defense

The next topic which I'll discuss is fast break defense. Fast break defense in this context consists of a four on three break. What is most important in fast break situations is the need for the defense to anticipate and to talk. These are the keys to successful fast break defense. The general principles which govern play during the fast break are as follows:

1. Maintain a tight triangle. The offense will try and spread the defense; don't let this happen.

2. Anticipate and talk. Fast break defense is predicated on anticipating your next slide and communicating it to the other players.

3. Never lose sight of the ball; this is the most important part of good fast break defense.

4. Never give up your body position unless you are 95% sure you can pick off a pass. Lead with a poke check but keep your feet.

5. Fast break defense is nothing more than a sliding zone defense. You no longer play a man but an area.

6. Always play the man in your zone from the inside out. This means keeping your body between the man and the goal.

7. Race to the backline on shots because the attackman is usually out in front of the goal, and you'll beat him if he misses the cage.

Once the goalie alerts the defense that a fast break is occurring, the defense turns and sprints into a tight triangle, never losing sight of the ball. The defense calls out their positions while dropping in using the following terminology, "I've got the left"; "I've got the right"; "I've got the point."

D3 and D2 are approximately three yards off the crease and three yards out. (See Diagram 1.) D1 is about eight yards from the crease favoring the side of the point attackman so that, if the point attackman receives the ball before D1 slides, he can still play that attackman.

When the midfielder with the ball (M1) hits the restraining line, the goalie yells "slide." D1 begins to slide on an angle so that he will meet the midfielder 10 to 12 yards from the goal. D1 is not directly in line with the midfielder; but, should the middie continue another two steps down the field with the ball, D1 will take two more steps

Diagram 1

Diagram 2

and poke check the middie. (See Diagram 2.) D1's stick is raised so that he will have a chance of knocking down the midfielder's pass. D2, who initially was three yards off and three yards out from the crease, now positions himself between the right attackman and the point attackman, but favoring the right attackman since he is closer to the goal. D2 has his stick to the inside ready and able to pick off a pass should the midfielder attempt a direct pass to the right attackman.

As the ball is passed to the point attackman, D2 slides to meet him. He slides to where the point attackman will be *after* he catches the ball, not to where he is initially. [When the point attackman receives the ball, his first move is toward the center of the field to try to create a 3 on 2. As Keigs says, by anticipating and going to where the point man will be after receiving the ball, you will put more pressure on him and make him force the

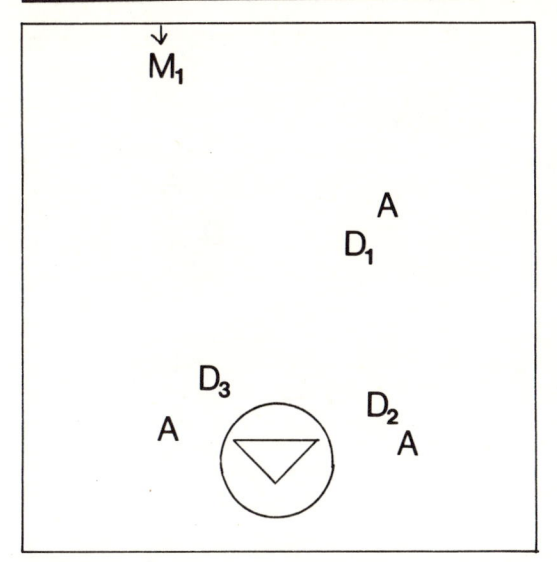

play. If you run straight out to him, he is likely to face dodge or sidestep you, making it easier for him to complete the play.—G.F.] (See Diagram 3.) D2 does not go any further than 12 yards out to play the point attackman. If the point attackman is 15 yards out, let him stay there. Don't let the offense spread you. D2's stick is up and ready to pick off any passes.

D3 is three yards out and three yards off the crease initially, but once he sees D2 positioning himself, then he, too, should reposition himself. D3 cheats as much as possible to the right crease while preserving his ability to cover the left attackman if the first pass is thrown to him. If the right attackman cuts directly to the ball while the middie has it, D3 also should be in position to play that attackman. (See Diagram 4.)

If the ball is passed to the right attackman from the point attackman, D3 should slide where the right attackman will be *after*

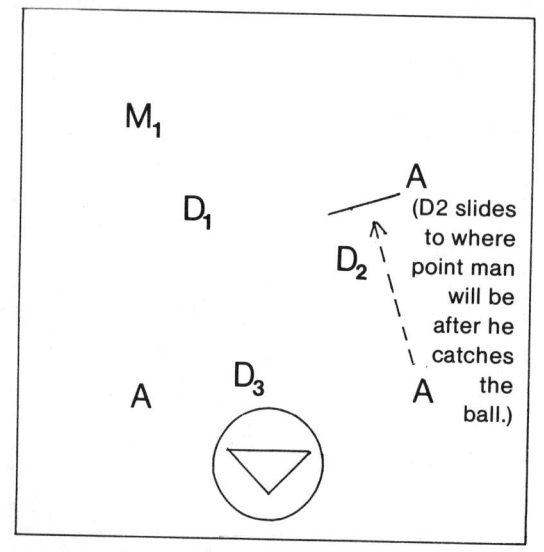

Diagram 3

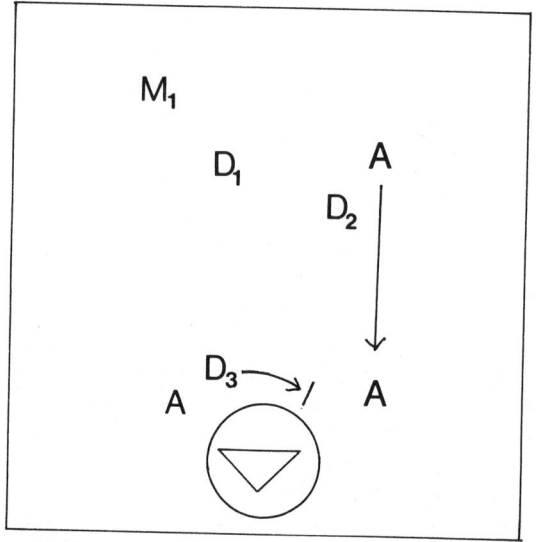

Diagram 5

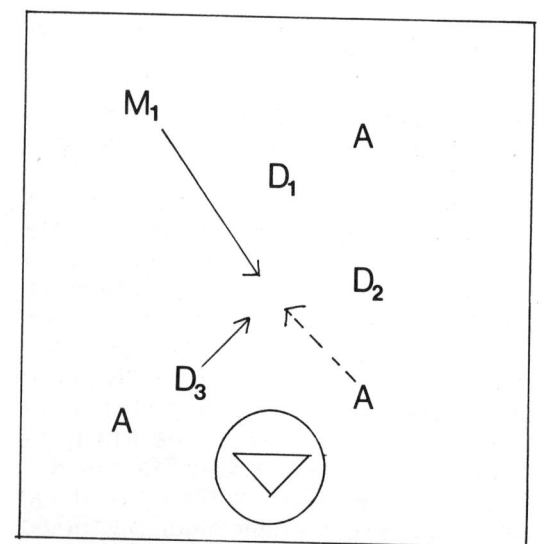

Diagram 4

he catches the ball, not where he is initially. (See Diagram 5.) Many attackmen attempt to set up the defense for a roll dodge in such situations because it is a common mistake for a defenseman to rush his attackman here. Don't let this happen. Lead with a poke but keep your feet.

Second slides: Once D2 has made his initial slide and the middie has passed the ball to the point attackman, D1 pivots on his foot and turns into the ball with his stick to the inside. D1 then aims for the opposite pipe in order to get in the passing lane between the point attackman and the left attackman as shown in Diagram 6. If the point attackman decides to throw the ball back to M1, then D1 again turns into the ball and plays M1. D2 begins to go back to the right attackman and D3 starts his slide to the left attackman.

The Reverse: If the middie throws the ball off before D1 begins his initial slide, D1 yells "Reverse" and stays on the point

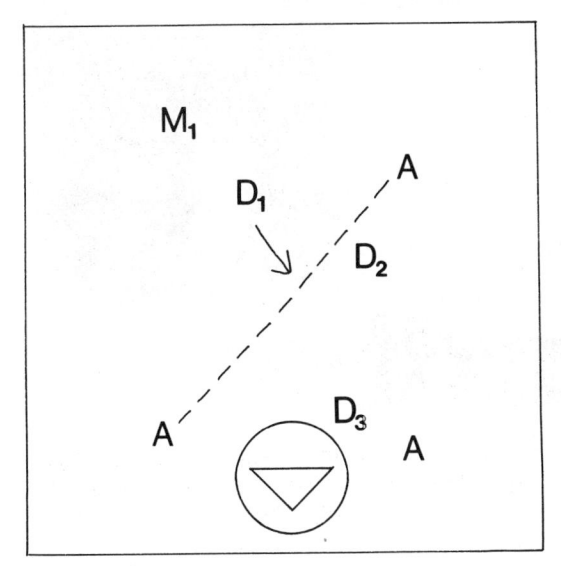

Defense

Diagram 6

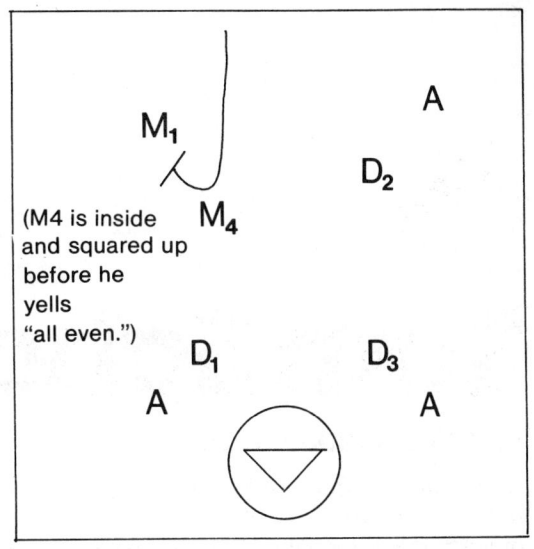

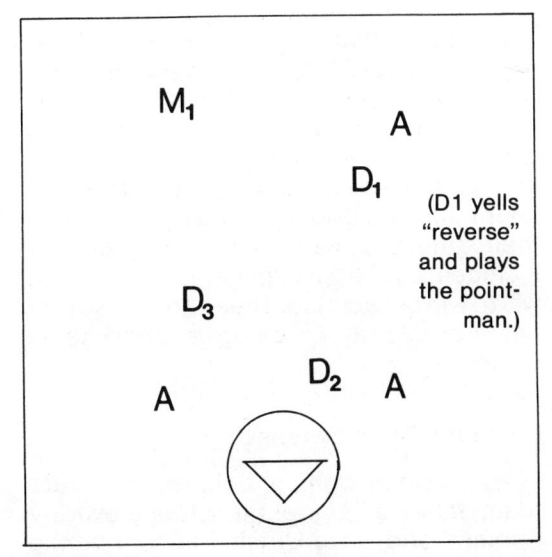

Diagram 8
(M4 is inside and squared up before he yells "all even.")

Diagram 7
(D1 yells "reverse" and plays the pointman.)

attackman. D1 is the ONLY player who can call reverse.

D2 and D3 anticipate their next slides. D3's slide will be to M1, so D3 will position himself between the left crease and the middie favoring the left crease. D2's slide will be to the left attackman; therefore, he should split the left and right attackmen still favoring the right attackman. (See Diagram 7.) The slides are all the same, simply reversed.

All Even: The defensive middie (M4) has as his job to get in the hole and play the offensive middie (M1). Once in the hole and squared up on the offensive side, the defensive middie yells "All even." This is very important because it is a signal to the defense that the defense no longer needs to slide; therefore, it is important that the middie does not yell "all even" until he is in the hole and has broken down in good defensive position as shown in Diagram 8.

Tom Schardt

EDITOR'S INTRODUCTION

Here's another real athlete who learned the game of lacrosse quickly. Tom had never played until he went out for lacrosse at Hobart. Under the guidance of coaches Jerry Schmidt and Dave Ulrich, he ended his four years at Hobart as one of the all-time great defensemen. He was second team All-American in 1976, after just two years of play, and made first team in '77 and '78. Hero's, Inc. named him college defenseman of the year for '77, and he was captain of Hobart's team during '78.

Tom is pursuing a career in lacrosse. He's currently in graduate school and will be an assistant coach in lacrosse at North Carolina State. He plans to end up coaching at the college level.

Tom's remembered by all lacrosse fans for his aggressive style of defensemanship, but let's hear it in his own words.

PLAYER'S INTRODUCTION

The game of lacrosse did not enter my life until I reached college. But it has been important in helping me learn to discipline myself and in meeting new people and making new friends. Lacrosse encourages a good type of competition where one is always learning and, most of all, trying to excel.

The game helps you endure the ups and downs of life, and I think it can really be beneficial to most people. It has taught me respect for individuals, discipline, how to deal with success and failure, and how to channel them properly.

I believe that attitude is 75% of the game. It is very important that a lacrosse player believe both in himself and in his team. If you "believe" in your mates, a good amount of success and reinforcement will follow. I have seen many teams with lots of talent perform poorly on the field because their attitudes were poor. Good attitude includes desire, discipline, pride and the will to win or sacrifice. These are the essential ingredients in being a good team player.

Pressure Team Defense

I call my philosophy of defense "pressure team defense." Under the tutoring of Jerry Schmidt and Dave Ulrich, I used it during my four years of play for Hobart. It's main

Defense

Bob Bradley

Schardt

features are:
  (1) Constant, total pressure on the man with the ball;
  (2) Total team defense consisting of slides, backing up, talk and double teaming; and,
  (3) Always looking to help your teammates.

There are a number of reasons for this philosophy of defense. First, when I played for Hobart, it was a fairly new concept so it gave us an advantage over teams that weren't used to seeing total pressure, double teaming, etc. Second, the constant pressure forces many teams to make mistakes that you can capitalize on. Third, it permits a total team effort and does not rely on just one or two individuals to carry the defense. Fourth, this type of defense creates its own offense by creating a lot of fast break situations. Finally, I feel that this defense allows the team using it to have a psychological edge because it forces the opposition to play your game. *[Every attackman ought to take notice!—G. F.]*

If I'm facing an offensive player who has the ball in our defensive half of the field, I try to play the ball very tightly (poke checking or slap checking at all times) from midline to endline and from sideline to sideline in all situations (out of bounds, all even defense, etc.). (The only exception is that I would not play pressure defense in a man down situation.) This constant pressure limits the offensive player in both his feeding and dodging.

Another key factor in playing successful pressure defense is backing up or sliding. With the defensive player playing the ball so heavily, there is a chance that he may get beat. Therefore, the other five defensive players become involved in sliding. It is essential that all five men be involved in the sliding process because if one defensive player faults, chances are a goal will be scored.

The five defensive players who are not pressuring the ball should stay in tight and not try to follow their men out too far. Always play position (between the man and the ball), but don't play your man behind the cage if he doesn't have the ball.

Note: When playing pressure team defense, play cross-handed defense both ways, not stick-on-stick. Two reasons for this are (1) if you're playing cross handed, it is more difficult for an offensive player to drive around you. The cross handed style gives more resistance. (2) When playing cross handed defense, you can turn a player back more easily into a double team situation.

Let's look at some pressure team defense setups. In our first setup (Diagram 1), here's what's going on:

D1: Is pressuring (poke checking) his attackman and forcing him to make a bad pass (and possibly taking the ball away).

D2: Is backing up D1 on his left. Notice that D2 is playing above the pipes (cage) and getting involved in team defense.

D3: Could be either a middie or defenseman, depending on the situation. D3 is sagging off his middie, keeping his eye on D1 because he is D1's back-up to his right. D3 is also watching his middie in case he cuts.

D4: Is sagging off his middie, staying in tight and watching both his man and the ball. He also is ready to slide.

D5: Is weak side middie and sags way inside, concentrating on both his man and the ball. It is important that he play his position with an open hip to both his man and

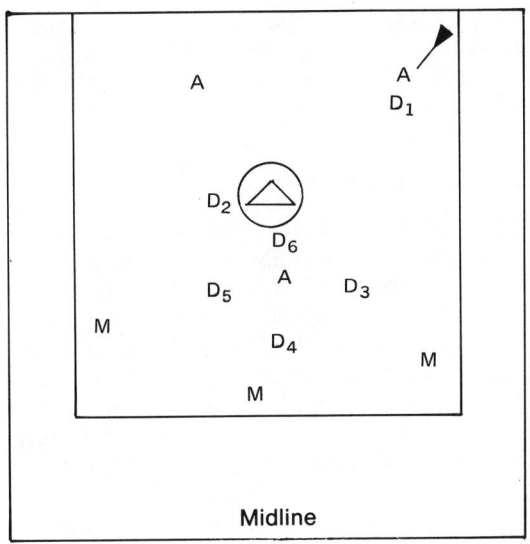

Diagram 1

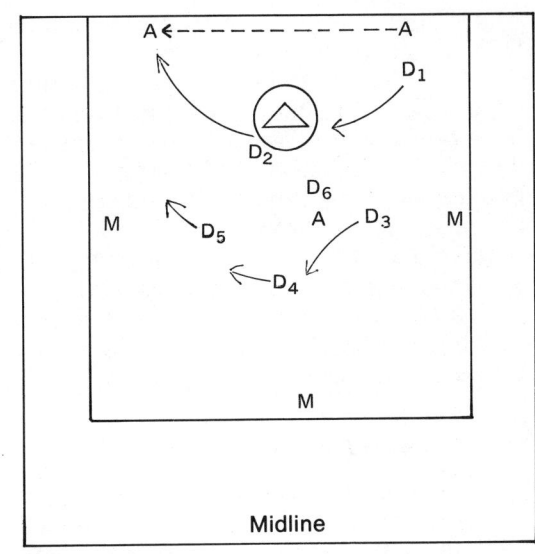

Diagram 2

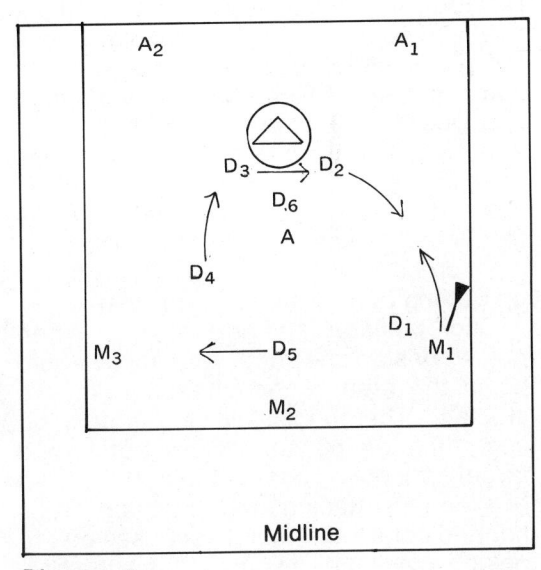

Diagram 3

the ball. He must also be sure to keep his stick up.

D6: Is the crease defenseman and is primarily concentrating on his man but also looking for the ball and calling out cutters.

Notice that the defense is tight, sagging off their men and in a position to move (slide) with an inside to outside line. Note, too, that all defenders are in a position to back up the ball in case D1's pressure forces the ball carrier to make a mistake.

Now if the ball should move, let's see what happens to the defense's positioning. Diagram 2 shows how the defensemen would slide to the ball as it moves across the field. Now let's assume that the ball moves again; this time out front as shown in Diagram 3. D1, in this case gets beat by his man. Here's what happens:

D2: Since D1 got beat by his middie, D2 backs him up and slides to stop the middie.

D3: Sees this happening and slides to D2's old position to cover A1.

D4: Slides from his old position and covers D3's old position. D4 must be cautious because he now has the responsibility to split both A2 and M3. D4 holds his position, splitting the two attackmen, until the next pass is thrown.

D5: Holds his position and tries to help D4 while also favoring his middie (M2).

The slides continue until the defense sets back up which may take three or four slides by everyone.

Playing Behind the Goal

In playing pressure defense, you are constantly poke checking your man (if he has the ball) so positioning is important. If you are playing a man behind who has the ball, you should be roughly four or five feet from him since your defensive stick is about six feet long. If your man is playing behind the goal and doesn't have the ball, play above the pipes while keeping an eye on both your man and the ball. Once your man receives the ball, go out to him, break down about six feet from him, and move with him, poke checking all the time from four or five feet away. Always keep a cushion of three to four feet. It is essential that you keep this cushion because if you don't you will end up getting beat or fouling your man.

Stick position is important also. When poking or slap checking, your stick should be in the area of the offensive player's stomach. The checks will vary in position according to a player's height, but a good target for a poke check is the bottom hand of a feeding attackman. Once again, cross handed defense is useful because you are poking at all times if your man has the ball; and, if the attackman gets too close, a forearm or butt end shove can aid you in keeping your cushion. Once your attackman starts moving, concentrate on him and set up your checks.

Playing the Dodger

The best way to stop any good dodger is with good body position and good footwork. If you can shuffle with an attackman and not open your hips, you will be in the proper position. Try to keep your body square with your attackman. If you have to open your hips and run with your attackman, make sure you are always anticipating what he will do—split dodge, roll back, drive, etc. Then act accordingly.

[I asked Tom how he would play the various types of dodges; here's his answer.—G. F.]

Split dodge: (change of direction) To stop a split dodge, your best move is a constant poke check. If you are anticipating well, you can see the split dodge coming and just poke the ball out. When poking, aim your poke stomach high.

Roll dodge: Good body position is important in trying to stop a roll or face dodge. Make sure you are giving the attackman his cushion because this cushion enables you to change direction and use a forearm or butt end shove to neutralize your opponent's momentum. The cushion also gives you your recovery time to hustle back and get in good position once again after checking.

Bull dodge: To stop this dodge use good body position and cross handed defense. What you are trying to do is neutralize your attackman's charge. You may have to give up your cushion in order to use your body (forearm, butt end, shoulder) to push against the attackman.

[Cross handed defense means changing

hands on your stick; there are advantages as Tom has pointed out.—G. F.]

Stopping the Feeder

The best way to stop a feeder is to use an extreme amount of pressure on him. If he is primarily a feeder, you might want to use more of your checks than usual because chances are he won't be going to the goal too much making the consequences of overcommitting yourself less critical. In stopping a feeder, poke checking his bottom hand is probably the best way. Do not give him a chance to look at his cutters; put so much pressure on him that all he thinks about is what you're doing.

Playing the Crease

In playing a crease attackman, you must be in good position at all times. This requires that you have constant contact with the crease attackman. Unlike the behind defenseman, the crease defenseman has very little cushion (about one foot).

To keep in constant contact with your attackman, put your butt hand on the attackman so you can feel his movements. Never play behind your man. Also, it is important for the crease defenseman to know where the ball is at all times. He must keep feeling his attackman, watching the ball, and be in a good enough position on his attackman to check his stick if he goes after a loose ball or gets a feed.

The crease defenseman is not totally involved in "team defense" because his main job is to watch the crease attackman. I feel slides should not come from the crease because the crease attackman is in the most dangerous position on the field and to leave him open even for a few seconds could be very costly.

The crease defenseman only slides or backs-up if it is the *only* thing left to do. Normally, he will just play his man. However, sometimes another player will be out of position and the crease defenseman *must* slide as a last resort against a sure goal.

Another job the crease defenseman has is to aid the goalie. First, if the goalie is being screened, the defenseman must use pressure on his attackman and move him to clear the goalie's view. This move requires a lot of finesse and savvy by a defenseman. He wants to get the job done without causing any fouls, and it's not easy. The crease defenseman also must clear the crease when there's a loose ball in front or around the crease. It is the goalie's job to get the ball; the defenseman's job is to move out any attackmen. The best way to do this is to lower your shoulder and drive out the attackman. A third job is to talk. Along with the goalie, the crease defenseman must call out all picks, cuts, and other plays.

Playing *two men on the crease* is difficult and requires lots of communication. If the ball is out front, I would play the men on the crease the same way I described in crease defense play. One thing you have to do is talk to the other defenseman (or middie) playing with you to let him know who is doing what. An alternative would be to zone. Have one defenseman cover one side, and the other defenseman cover the other side. The problem with this is that the crease defensemen have to "eye ball" their men, and this takes away from team play. Also, if the two offensive players come into only one zone, you have a *two on one* situation.

One thing that you should not do when playing two men on the crease is play them man to man and then switch all the time with the other defenseman who's playing the crease with you. It's an open invitation to open sticks or other problems.

Over the Head Checks

Going over the head is a difficult check, and I recommend to players who are just starting out that you wait until you mature before trying a check of this type. In using this kind of check, you must first set it up by poking and slap checking. You are trying to make your attackman hang his stick which means that the attackman is putting his stick too far above his head or away from his body, making it easy to get. There are two kinds of over the head checks:

Butt End Down: This check is done by first poking to set it up. When you feel your attackman is hanging his stick, slide your hand to the top (head) of your stick and swing it around your attackman. When doing this, it's important that you (1) clear your attackman's head on the sweep; (2) keep your stick perpendicular to the ground and parallel to the attackman to increase your chances of getting his stick and not fouling him; (3) pull hard on your stick once you feel the attackman's stick; and (4) keep a cushion so that if you miss the check, you'll have some room to recover.

Head Down: This check is also performed by first setting up your attackman with poke checks. (See photo, p. 171) Again, you're trying to get him to hang his stick. To complete the check (1) clear your attackman's head; (2) try to get your stick as parallel to your attackman as possible (and perpendicular to the ground); drop both hands to the butt end of your stick to decrease the likelihood of a hold; (3) once you are over your attackman's head, drop your stick down to jar out the ball; (4) once the ball is loose, scoop it up and (5) keep a cushion at all times. Note: I do not recommend that short defensemen try this check because of the likelihood of a hold resulting from the attempt. If at all possible do not leave your feet on this check.

The over the head check (head first) is my favorite defensive move. I'll set it up with a constant poke check and try to force my attackman into hanging his stick. I can't always do this because some attackmen don't hang their sticks, but if he does, I slide my hands down near the butt end of my stick, clear the attackman's head and try to jar loose the ball with my stick.

I prefer this check for a number of reasons. First, if used properly, it is not a home run, do or die check. It allows me to recover if my check is unsuccessful. Second, I can use it to fake an attackman. For instance, if I've used the check successfully on an opposing attackman, he'll be looking for it, perhaps even baiting me. So I fake an over the head (head down) and, when the baiting attackman pulls his stick in front of him to avoid the over the head check, I come down with my stick which is near the head area of the attackman. Usually, I can check his stick this way.

Over the head checks are especially good for tall and rangy defensemen. (I'm 6'3".) Height gives an excellent advantage. One further comment on technique: In going over the head, poke and then quickly drop your hands to the butt end, clear your attackman's head, *whip* your stick over the attackman's head, and look for his stick.

Wrap Check

A defenseman can use this check effectively and not alter his position too much. The two kinds of wrap checks that can be

Defense

used most effectively are the stick on stick and the cross handed wraps. Both are done pretty much the same way. The wrap check is used when an attackman is holding his stick too tight to his body, or if his stick is too far out in front of him. The steps are as follows: (1) Shuffle with your attackman; (2) drop both hands to the butt end of your stick; (3) wrap your stick around the attackman, trying to hit his stick; (4) keep your cushion and, if possible, stay square on your man; (5) when wrapping, try to snap your wrists; don't try to overpower your attackman with cocked up slashes with your arms; and (6) once you have wrapped your attackman, snap your wrists a few more times to get in a few more wraps.

Note: Once your attackman rolls back, pull back your stick and play position. The wrap check should be executed in the stomach or lower chest area, not near the hand.

Future of Lacrosse

I feel that with the no faceoff after goals, the game will be higher scoring and the defensive phase of the game will be stressed more and more. The game of lacrosse is developing fast and I'm sure we'll see new sticks, faster players, and quicker phases of the game. Defense will become more and more sophisticated.

In my four years of playing lacrosse, I've seen it grow by leaps and bounds, especially in central and upstate New York. I truly hope that many more states will adopt this super game so, hopefully, some day we will have something known as the Lacrosse World Series.

In closing, I would like to give a very special thanks to Mr. Dave Ulrich of Hobart College. Without his help, guidance, and superior knowledge of the defensive phase of lacrosse, I would never have been as successful as I was in my four years of playing for Hobart.

TOM SCHARDT'S 7 KEYS TO PLAYING AN ATTACKMAN

1. See if he favors a particular hand. If he does, force him to go to his weaker hand.

2. I find that the size of an attackman tells you things he will do. Smaller ones are quick and will split, face, and change directions better. A big attackman usually is a bull dodger or will roll dodge well.

3. If an attackman comes running straight at you, you can bet he will face or split dodge. A poke check is an effective countermove. Try to hold your ground.

4. If an attackman is really forcing his way to the cage (bull dodge), use your body to try to keep him away.

5. If an attackman holds his stick high and comes at you, he most probably will face dodge. A poke check works well here.

6. If an attackman is studder stepping at you, you can bet a split dodge is coming.

7. Watch your opponent's stomach when playing him. This way, your chances of being faked are less. Also, if possible, check your attackman's stick position. If he has two hands on his stick, he's about to either feed or shoot. This is when you should try to be all over his bottom hand and stick. It's amazing what a poke check will do to an attackman—and for you!

Dom Starsia

EDITOR'S INTRODUCTION

Dom Starsia entered Brown University in the fall of 1970 as an excellent football prospect. His leadership and athletic abilities led to his captaining his freshman team. One of his teammates who was also a lacrosse player convinced Dom to try out for the sport. Dom had never even seen a lacrosse game, but he decided it would be a good way to keep in shape during the spring and tried out for the team.

From the start, Dom and lacrosse proved a perfect match. He gave up football and devoted his full time efforts to lacrosse. The result was that (after only two years of play) he was named to both the All Ivy and All New England teams and by the time he graduated he had been named All-American twice. In 1974, he was captain of the Brown team, captain of the North for the North-South game, and captain of the New England All Star Team.

Since graduating from Brown, Dom has played club lacrosse. He was named to the All Club team in 1976, '77 and '78 and was on the U.S. National team in 1978.

Dom carries on his enthusiasm for lacrosse to the next generation of stars by serving as assistant lacrosse and soccer coach at Brown while working on a Master's degree in sport studies at the University of Connecticut.

Here's Dom's description of how a winning lacrosse defense is organized and played.

PLAYER'S INTRODUCTION

There are some very specific areas in which lacrosse has affected my life. It has helped me decide on career goals and introduced me to a great number of fascinating people. It has taken me to the St. Regis Indian Reservation in New York for some box lacrosse games, to Atlanta for the North-South game, to Montreal with the N.L.L. and to Europe with the U.S.A. team.

As a student at Brown, I was always able to detach lacrosse practice and games from the regular pressures of everyday life. It was not very often that I carried a personal problem onto the field. Lacrosse was always a great outlet for me, and I would often escape to the field to be alone. Somehow, nothing seemed quite as serious after a brisk workout.

Club ball serves the same purpose for my professional career. If it has been a

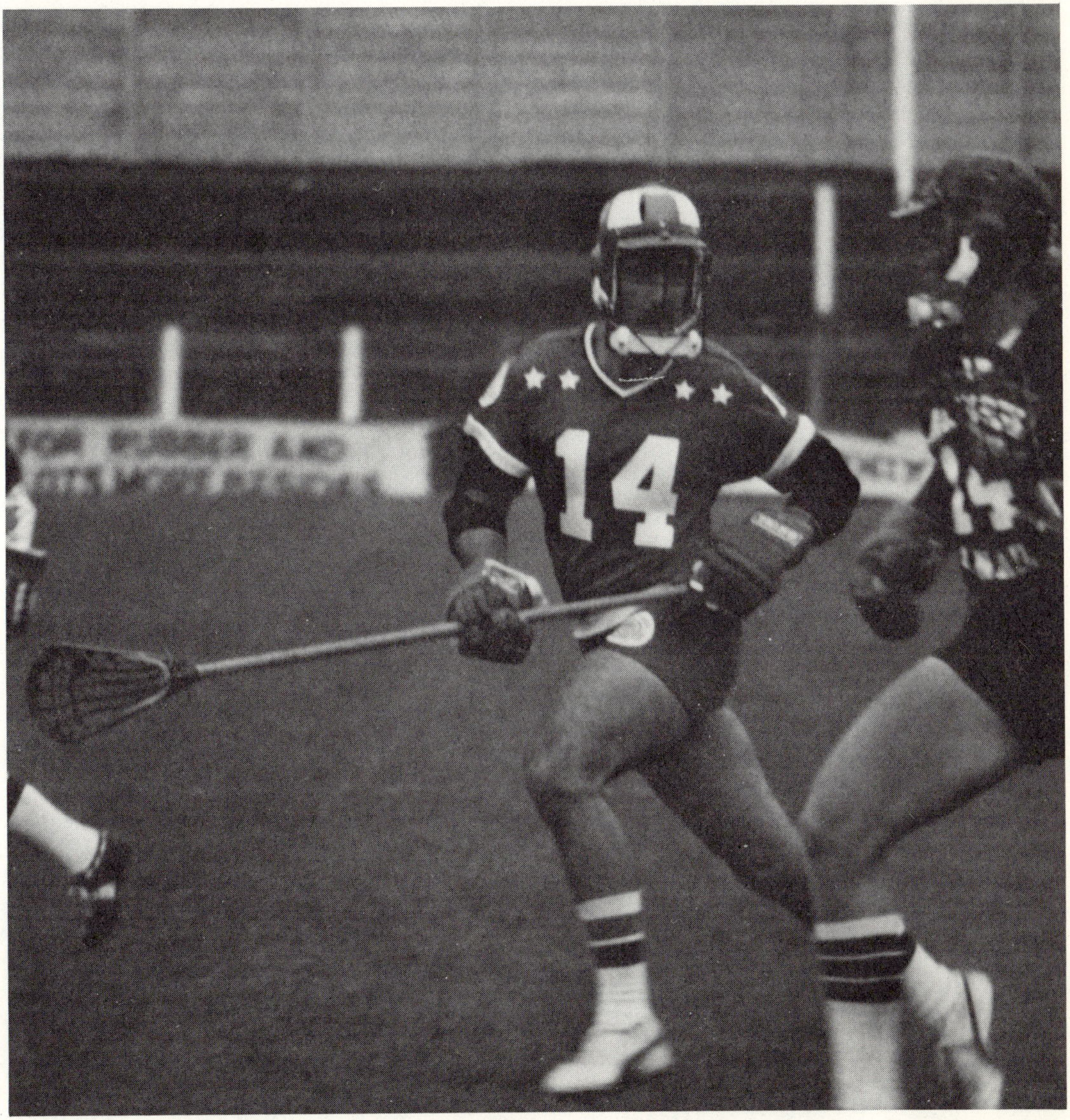
14

tough week at work, I really look forward to those Sunday games. Lacrosse has also forced me to maintain good physical condition because I want to extend my playing career as long as possible. Finally, lacrosse has added to my family life; they enjoy seeing me play and all turn out whenever they can.

Starsia on Defense

My philosophy of defense is that it is a very active position whose trademarks are speed and finesse. It requires top flight athletes who understand the fundamentals but who are aggressive and like to initiate plays on the field.

A top defenseman appreciates one-on-one play and wants his man to have the ball. He wants to handle the ball so he can move it upfield. He takes calculated risks to intercept a pass or break up a play. When he crosses that midfield line, he makes the smart play, the easy pass, but he also tries to capitalize on constructive offensive opportunities. He is involved in the complete flow of action on the field.

While it may sometimes seem to defensemen that lacrosse favors the attackman, there are certain keys a defenseman can use to help him to gain an edge.

Some attackmen have an obvious style or series of moves that can be discovered if you're attentive. For example, big, strong attackmen tend to have fewer tricks and are more liable to challenge you outright. Others may be quicker and shiftier, with less obvious patterns to their play. A smart defenseman will use the early part of a game to study his attackman, feel out his strengths and weaknesses, and look for any clues that will tip off an upcoming move.

The defenseman must look at all facets of an attackman's repertoire. The answers to the riddle of how to play your man will come from his stick, hands, feet, trunk, eyes and head. Ask yourself these questions: Which is his strong hand? Nine times out of ten an attackman will go this way in an important play. Does he carry his stick differently depending on which hand it's in? Is he more susceptible to a back check when he goes one way or the other? Does he stutter step before a face dodge? Does he naturally swing or rock his stick? Does he expose the butt end? Does he respond to your checks and fakes? Does he drop his head when he is *really* going to the goal? Ninety nine percent of all attackmen must look at their target while shooting or feeding. Learn to follow your attackman's eyes. They are often the key to his intentions.

At Brown, I construct our team defense on the premise that the man playing the ball will be beaten. Of course, we don't want that man to get beat, but we build our defense around the fact that the offensive player has a distinct advantage and will try to exploit this whenever possible.

With this in mind, we stress a team play concept of support and back-up on defense. This concept combines the principles of man-to-man and zone defense. Each defensive player is responsible for his man, but there is also right and left support for the man playing the ball.

In a typical setup, shown in Diagram 1, we bring our behind defensemen to the pipes. They are the first slide if the wing middies get beat to the outside. These defensemen try to maintain their position on the pipes and do not chase their men behind. If, when D1 slides, the ball is dumped off to his attackman, (A1) the next slide would come from D2. If the ball went to

Defense

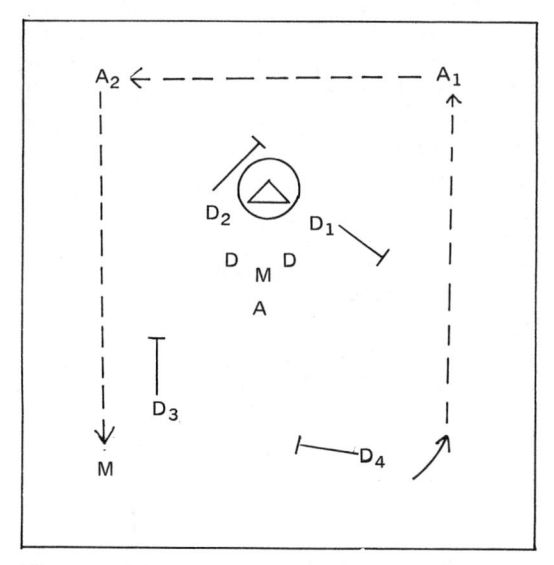

Diagram 1

D2's man, D3 would slide down and pick up A2. If the ball went to D3's man, D4 would pick up there, and the rotation would start again.

It is important for the defensemen and middies off the ball to be sloughing into the middle to make their slide easier. This also will put them in position to cut off the more dangerous passing lanes. Good team defense requires that each player always knows the location of the ball and his man. And, finally, the most important item is communication between the players on defense. It is essential that defensive players tell each other who has the ball, where the support is, when they are in trouble, etc.

This is a very basic look at our team defense, but it does illustrate our most fundamental tenets—back-up and support. Actually, what we are trying to do on defense is protect a 10 square yard area in front of the goal. If the defense can keep the offensive players with the ball outside that area, they should accomplish their job—preventing a score. Our goalie will make the save on shots from outside that 10 square yard box.

[But Dom isn't only a great student and teacher of how lacrosse should be played. His theories derive from his own style of play. To show how one great defenseman handles himself on the field, I asked Dom to describe how he plays under a variety of field situations.—G. F.]

General Style of Play

My style of 1-on-1 play is a bit unorthodox. Most defensemen use a stick that is between 5' and 6' long. This permits them to maintain a sufficient space between themselves and their attackmen. This cushion (the distance determined by the length of a defenseman's stick and arms) provides him with a margin for error; and, if he can keep the attackman outside this area, he should have enough time to react to any move.

My stick is 55 inches long. Although it is the shortest defense stick I have seen in major college lacrosse, I do not feel it hampers my play. In fact, it enhances my style which I characterize as the "position" game. I am confident enough in my own athletic ability to believe that I cannot be beaten unless I overextend myself. (This is not always true, but I do approach each game and each play in that frame of mind.)

I play lacrosse defense a lot like a basketball player plays defense. I like to get up close to my man (a lot closer than most lacrosse defensemen) and use my hands and forearms to maintain position. If I lose a step, I use my stick to make my recovery and a check. *[The closer you can stay to your attackman when he has the ball, the more you'll succeed in worrying him. He then has to think about what you're going to do instead of what he's going to do. This really puts an extra burden on your man.—G. F.]*

Contrary to the belief that the stick should be kept in an attackman's face to hinder his vision or block passes, I feel it can be wielded much more effectively if the attackman does not know where it is. The defenseman should always keep his stick moving. Most attackmen can see around and through a defenseman's stick and can easily drop step and pass (to avoid contact) if they know what is coming. A good defenseman wants to create a situation where the attackman constantly must concern himself with the location of the stick and the next check.

The defenseman should think of his stick as a foil and should use a lot a quick, strong checks—quick check behind and a slap in front; poke in front and a slap behind, etc. Wielding the stick in and out and front to back allows you to have your stick in position to check your attackman's hands when he attempts to pass or shoot.

The defenseman's main responsibility is to prevent the man he is covering from scoring a goal. This continual one-on-one struggle with the attackman is the essence of defense play. Although the attackman has the formidable advantages of facing the goal and planning his approach, a defenseman with sound fundamentals can control an attackman's dodge. Here's how I do it.

Controlling a Dodge

Approach: When my attackman starts a dodge, I move out onto my man quickly but under control. I "balance up" by assuming a stance with my feet about shoulder width apart, knees bent, weight slightly forward on the balls of my feet and one foot back half a step. My hands are comfortably in front, away from my body, and the head of my stick is as high as my attackman's chest.

Poke Check: If the attackman is coming straight on, the first task is to slow him down. As he gets closer, I try to induce him to move to the right or left before he gets right on top of me. A good, hard poke check at his hands will coerce the attackman into his move and often dislodges the ball.

Forearm and Butt Hand Push: If the attackman does break down the cushion and goes to his right, I use a right forearm check such that my right forearm and stick are perpendicular in order to push the attackman back out. If the attackman goes to his left, I use a butt end push (left hand on the butt of my stick) and slap to move him out. In both cases, it is imperative to maintain footwork control. Do not step in when performing these checks. Use your arms and upper body to do the work.

[This is an extremely important point. The smart attackman when making his move will wait until you have committed yourself before he chooses which way he'll go. Following Dom's advice here certainly will help you turn back your attackman.—G. F.]

Drop Step: The reason for saying earlier that the proper approach stance is to have one foot back half a step is that it facilitates the drop step and recover technique. A good defenseman must be prepared to give ground and re-establish his position. If he loses a step to the attackman with his original move, he drops back a step and takes a direction that will cut off an attackman's approach to the goal. He then picks up his attackman once again. (See Dia-

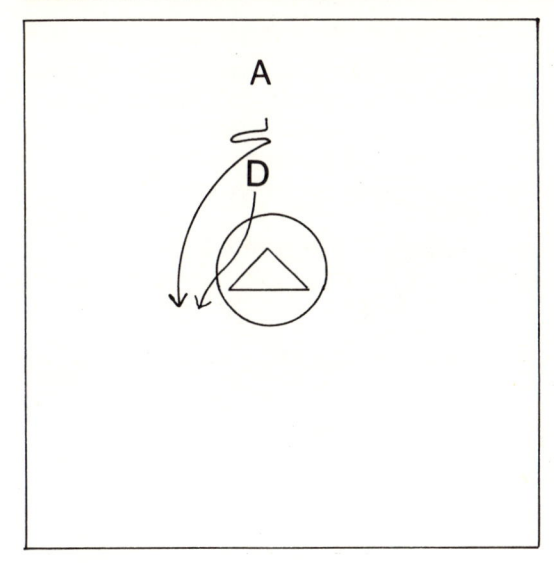

Diagram 2

gram 2.) *Never chase an attackman from behind.*

Playing a Feeder

Obviously, the best attackman is the one who can dodge, score and feed when men are open. However, many attackmen are either good feeders or good scorers. I make certain defensive adjustments in each case. When playing a feeder, I slightly decrease the distance between us. In this way, I can become even more physical, using forearms and stick to disrupt his patterns. Any defenseman must be careful not to be foolish, however, because even a mediocre attackman will exploit glaring defensive lapses.

I also increase the number of checks, especially those of the poke, slap and backslap type when playing a feeder. These checks are particularly bothersome to a feeder and do not carry the risk of poor positioning. They also allow me to keep my stick in a good area to make a check on the attackman's hands when he does try to pass the ball.

Crease Defense

Playing crease defense is one of the toughest jobs in lacrosse. I dread playing a crease attackman or being switched onto the crease; intense, single-minded concentration is required. When playing the crease, there are some basic rules that you should follow. When the ball is straight behind, play your man face to face, stick to stick. Listen to the goalie; he should let you know when a feed is coming or when to slide. You cannot afford to let up for a moment because you're often covering the quickest and best shooter on the opposing team. A short concentration lapse can cost a goal. When the ball is in the midfield, maintain a position between the attackman and the ball. Be in position to cut off any attemped passes.

Another situation that creates problems for the creaseman is the question of when to slide. Should he be the first back-up for the wing defenseman and middies? Because he is covering the best shooter on the attacking team, the crease defenseman should only slide in a real emergency situation. A good idea here is for the goalie to let the creaseman know when to release his man since the goalie has a better eye on the play.

The crease defenseman also has the prime responsibility for clearing the crease on loose ball and screening situations. When the ball is rolling around in front of the goal or the offensive players are screening the goalie, the crease defenseman has to move their bodies out of there. He has to be very physical; upper body strength is a real asset when playing crease defense.

Perhaps the only thing tougher than playing an attackman on the crease is *playing two attackmen on the crease.* Having two offensive players in front of the goal is the most difficult situation for the defensive team to control. The play is tight and very physical; the slightest defensive hesitation will result in an open man and, perhaps, a goal.

Neither a straight man to man or zone defense is entirely effective here; what's needed is a combination of the two. Even for this combination to work, there must be communication between the two defensive players. This is the most important aspect of double crease play. The two players must be talking all the time in order to alert each other to position and responsibility.

If the offensive pattern is a *double high post,* the defensemen must position themselves on either side of the low post. (See Diagram 3.) The onside defenseman is responsible for the first cutter to his side, and the backside defenseman picks up the second. In this type of coverage, the defensemen must not let the top post man get too high because he is in position for a good shot if he can receive a pass.

A *double low post* pattern presents another set of problems. (See Diagram 4.) The offensive players will continually be setting picks, and the defensemen must either switch or fight through. There will be an immediate foul up unless the defensive players are talking. The defenseman whose attackman sets the pick calls for the switch. If the defenseman being picked does not hear a switch call, he must fight through the pick to cover his man. A continual switch-

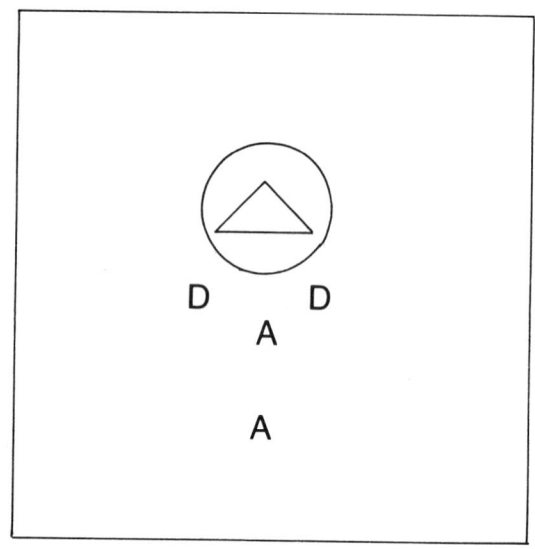

Diagram 3

ing situation can be confusing, however, and it is advisable to remain man to man as much as possible.

The two defensemen on the crease are ultimately responsible for the two men they are covering and should listen to the goalie to follow the position of the ball. They have enough problems of their own without having to worry about sliding unless there is an emergency situation.

[Checking is the single most important weapon available to a defenseman. Here is Dom's advice on when to use and how to execute each type of check.—G. F.]

Over the Head Checks

There are about five variations of over the head checks. The one I use most often is a straight, two handed check. (My hands in a normal position on the stick.) A right handed defenseman uses this check on an

Defense

The Wrap Check

Many coaches teach the wrap check as a front side move using the head of the defenseman's stick. It is used, most often, on the corners of the goal to prevent an attackman from shooting or feeding. This is a sound maneuver, but I do not feel comfortable reaching in when my attackman is in such a dangerous position. Here is my variation of this check:

As my attackman winds down a left handed run with the ball behind the goal, I begin to close down the distance between us. In a balanced up position, my right hand slides midway up the shaft, and I remove the left hand. At the instant when the attackman changes from left hand to right, I step in with the right leg and quickly wrap my butt end around the attackman on the backside. The stick is moved like a baton and is quickly removed so that there is no chance of a hold being called. I throw the wrap check on the backside to limit the possibility of impeding the attackman's progress. Often, a front side wrap will entangle your arm and stick with the attackman's and a holding foul results. It is also important to keep the stick low. Referees will surely call a penalty if you so much as even brush the attackman's head.

Both the over the head and wrap check are very exciting and can be very effective if done correctly. However, I have found that only the most experienced defenseman has a high enough degree of timing and efficiency to make these two checks an integral part of team play. Too often, an inexperienced defenseman will throw one of these checks regardless of his position on the field or the game situation. In my playing experience, these checks are not a fundamental part of the game. I will use

Diagram 4

attackman going to his right. The essence of this move is to reach over the attackman's head and make a stab for his stick.

However, it is a difficult maneuver, and there are three important techniques I have worked on. The first is to lift the hands high enough to get completely over the attackman's head. This enables me to avoid a penalty and get as much of my stick as possible into the area of the attackman's stick. The second is not to stab directly for the stick but to start the check in the area through which the attackman's stick must pass. Most attackmen will tuck their stick when someone comes over their head. By anticipating this movement, you can turn it to your advantage. The final technique is to throw the check quickly and, if missed, return quickly. This check can be made without putting yourself completely out of position and should not be thrown in a do or die frame of mind.

Starsia

them regularly on an attackman who hangs his stick behind his head or carries it away from his body. I also use them to take advantage of the element of surprise or in a situation where my team needs the ball (especially, late in the game). But these checks should not be used late in a game when your team has a one or two goal lead.

Playing a Man Without the Ball

[One of the most difficult skills for a defenseman to master is playing an attackman without the ball. No matter how well the principles are taught, it takes a lot of experience to do correctly. Any defenseman can be taught to cling to his man, with or without the ball, all over the field. But a defenseman who can help out in the overall team pattern when his man does not have the ball is a real asset. A team that has seven (including the goalie) players thinking this way, probably plays excellent team defense. I asked Dom to comment on this.—G. F.]

How I play a man when he doesn't have the ball depends on the location of the man *with* the ball. If both attackmen are behind the cage and close together, both defensemen must be tight enough on their men to perform any switching, double teaming or checking required.

If the ball is behind and the attackmen are in the opposite corners, the defenseman away from the ball should lay off his man and position himself on the corner of the goal. In this way, he can help out in front, cut off a pass, pick up a cutter, etc.

If the ball stays behind and the attackman without goes to the crease or cuts out front, he must be played like you would play a crease cutter. (See Diagram 5.)

If the man without the ball stays behind and the ball goes up the side, the defense-

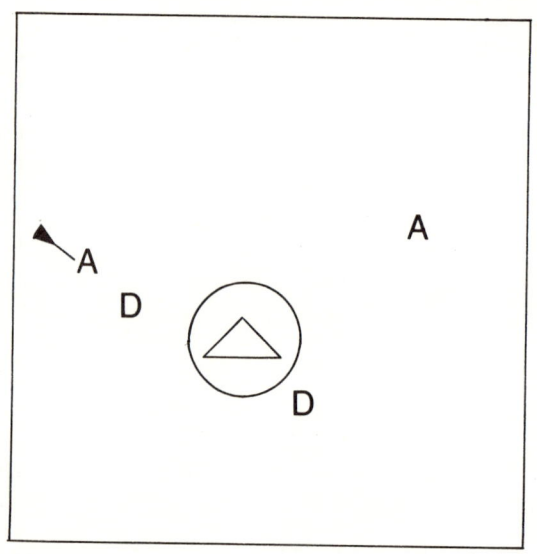

Diagram 5

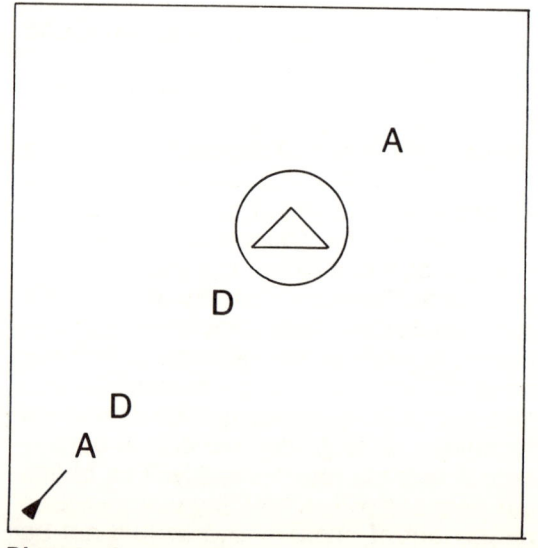

Diagram 5a

Defense

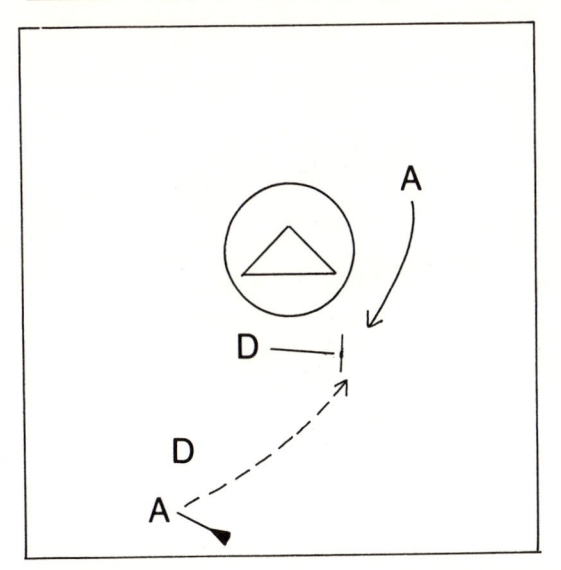

Diagram 5b

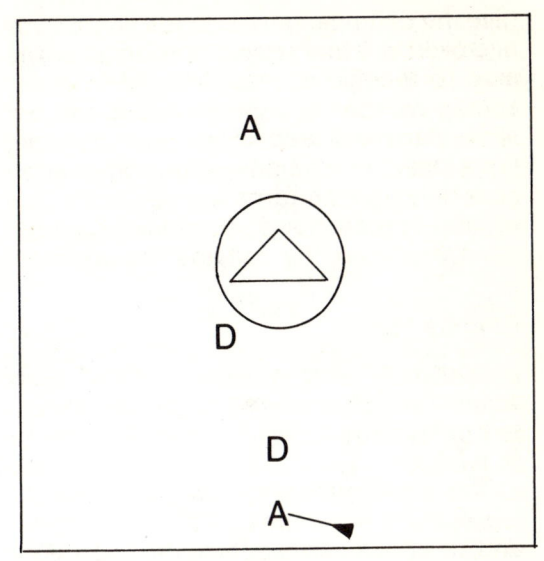

Diagram 5c

man covering the attackman without the ball comes to the corner of the goal on the same side as the ball. (See Diagram 5a.) Now, the defenseman will be in position to back up on a dodge out front and still be able to pick up his man as he comes around for a feed as shown in Diagram 5b. It is important for the defenseman to position himself so that he can see both the ball and his man with his peripheral vision. His stance should be open, and he should be facing the action.

If the ball is directly out front, the defenseman covering the man without the ball plays up on the corner of the goal on the same side as his man. (See Diagram 5c.)

If his man is directly behind, the defenseman should play on that side of the field where his team is defensively weakest. In this position, he can back up on the dodge out front. (See Diagram 5d.) A high, looping pass to the open man behind should

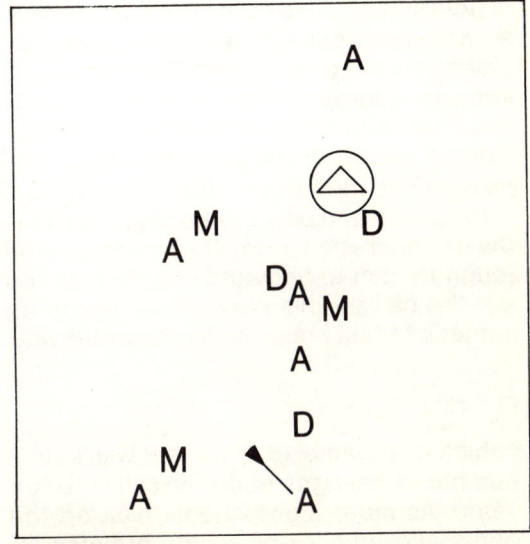

Diagram 5d

give the defenseman a chance to get back and pick up. If that attackman comes up the side to receive a pass, the defenseman should be able to pick up. Again, the defenseman must keep an eye on everything, but a smart attackman will take off as soon as a defenseman turns his head. For this reason, I recommend short, darting glances at your man, the ball and the action.

Favorite Plays

[I thought all lacrosse players could learn something if Dom shared his favorite defensive game moves with us. Here is his reply.— G. F.]

The situation for my favorite defensive move arises when the ball is in the midfield and my attackman is behind the cage. If he is the only attackman behind the cage, he probably feels compelled to stay there and back up. Meanwhile, I move out to the corner of the goal. I keep my eye on my man and the midfielder with the ball. As that middie moves to his right, he can spot me in a non-threatening, stationary position alongside the goalie. (See Diagram 6.) As soon as he turns back to his left, I am on him in a flash with a double-team on his backside as shown in Diagram 6a. My attackman behind the cage is often the only man who can see the play developing, and he is the farthest man from that middie. It is tough for him to get word out. Also, if I do get the ball on this play, it can create an immediate fast break going the other way.

Future of Lacrosse

I think our game of lacrosse will see a number of changes in the next five to ten years. As more high schools pick up the game, the number of quality athletes in-

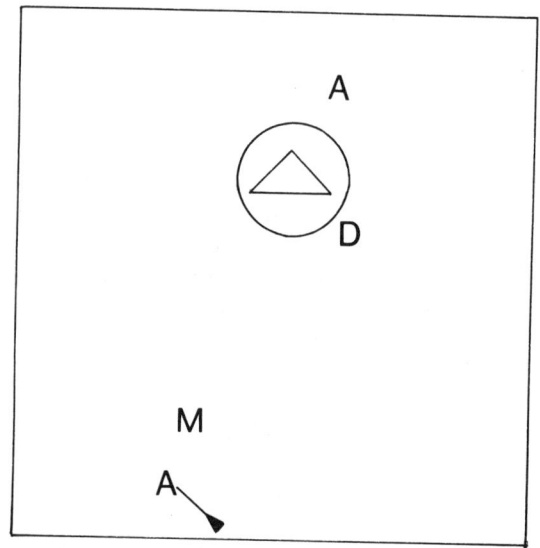

Diagram 6

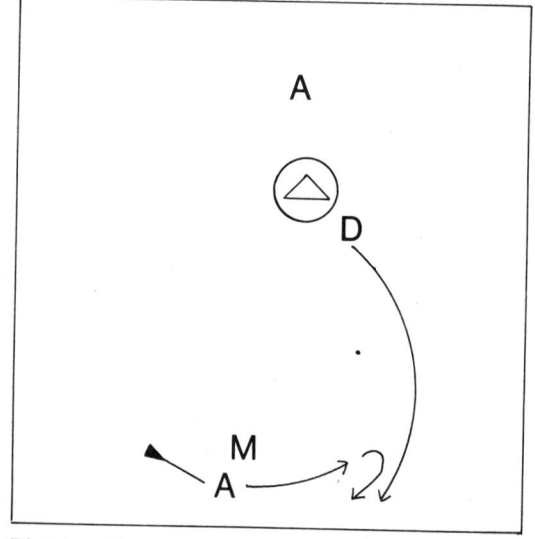

Diagram 6a

volved will increase. As this happens, play will get faster and the game will improve.

However, as the play gets faster, injuries will become more numerous and severe. It is imperative that the equipment industry keep pace with the quality of the game. In ten years, the lacrosse player may look completely different, with a solid helmet, mandatory shoulder and arm pads, and some thigh protection.

Removing the faceoff will also have a profound effect on the game. Play will become more concentrated in a six-a-side action, and coaches will spend more practice time teaching the half-field game. I feel that the additional half-field work will make the positions less specialized. Coaches will have to take advantage of midfielders behind on offense and attackmen out front. This implies that attackmen may have to get back on defense and spend time on these skills. I envision the evolution of a free flowing offensive pattern with all six players cutting, weaving, and moving in all directions.

At the other end of the field, in settled situations, we will have six defensive players who work well together. They all must be able to work behind, on the crease, or in front of the cage. When they gain possession of the ball, they will have to go on the fast break and initiate some offense.

Bones Waldvogel

Editor's Introduction

Bones Waldvogel began his lacrosse career as a freshman in high school. He played for four years for Cortland State (SUNY) and was named First Team All-American in 1968 and 1969 as well as the Outstanding Lacrosse Player in Upstate New York for both those years. After graduating, he played club lacrosse first for the Long Island Athletic Club and currently for the Central New York Lacrosse Club. During his club years, he has been the only defensive player to serve on two USA National Teams—first in 1974 and then again in 1978.

He presently coaches the defensive team at Cornell and is one of the reasons why Cornell won 42 straight games, including three straight trips to the NCAA Finals—winning two straight.

Bones shares with us some of the defensive strategies use by his Cornell teams. His 18 Keys to Better Defense should be memorized by every lacrosse player.

Player's Introduction

I believe that the most important part of good defense is mental preparation. I mean "mental" in the sense that you're physically ready to play, as an individual and as a team. I like to play defense by attacking my opponent, make him go where I want him to go, and then take away the ball. In today's game, if you let an attackman stand back and feed, he'll pick you apart. A good defenseman must study his man's moves. Notice what things he likes or doesn't like. Does he only shoot one way? Does he only force the cage one way? Does he hang his stick or only use one type of dodge? You must capitalize on these weaknesses.

The second major point to good defensive play is how you use your stick. *Use your stick like a foil, not like an axe.* On defense, the stick is used primarily to keep your man off balance by constant poking, slapping, etc. Movements must be quick and graceful; stab, don't bludgeon, your opponent.

Slough and Press

At Cornell, we use two systems of man to man defense: the loose man to man slough and the tight man to man press. We employ some variations of these in order to cope with the different offensive strengths and patterns we have to face.

The *slough* or loose man to man is our primary defense and is played as follows:

1. The man playing on the ball picks up his man and plays him in the normal defensive fashion.
2. The men playing off the ball sag off toward the goal while maintaining good man/goal position. The closer their man is to the ball, the tighter they must play him. They must be able to get their man and offer a balanced check just as he receives a pass. It is essential that each player watch his man *and* the ball. If a dodge should occur, the closest defensive player *between* the ball and the goal should slide and assist with a solid back-up check. On the dodge, the rest of the defensive unit should anticipate a coordinated slide into the ball if the dodger should attempt to dump the ball off to an open man.

The *press* or tight man to man defense has as its purpose reducing the freedom of the offense to move the ball and/or to gain possession. The theory behind this defense is that the offense will have to put its full attention on trying to hold onto the ball rather than scoring goals. Here's how it's done:

1. The man playing the ball presses and tries to take the ball away from his opponent or to force him to throw a poor pass which might be intercepted. He does not overextend himself and must learn how hard he can press his man before turning him into a dodger. *[This will take a lot of practice, but it's a must. As Bones infers, a smart attackman waits for his defenseman to overcommit before making his final move. So, when playing defense, you must learn how much pressure you can exert.—G. F.]*
2. The men playing off the ball tighten up on their opponents to such a distance that if the ball is thrown to one of them, the respective defender will reach his man *before* the ball does. The two defenders on either side of the ball must play the tightest in order to make the short pass very difficult to complete.

There are several offensive weapons that can be effective against the press offense. If you are fully alerted to these, your defense is much more likely to succeed.

1. The *give and go* play. You must be ready to play the quick break for the goal; control your man by delaying his cuts.
2. The *good dodger.* Be sure you know exactly how much you can press your man and how effective he is at dodging.
3. Close *picks* and *screens.* Playing a man tight makes you vulnerable to the pick and/or screen. Be ready for the switch call and know how to execute it. Talk!!!

There are times when press defense is absolutely necessary. For example, if, late in a period or game, your team is behind by a goal or two, it is imperative that you gain possession of the ball in order to score. Press defense is your only hope.

Defensive Areas

I use the various defensive areas (See Diagram 1) to key certain defensive maneuvers.

"D"—Outer Perimeter. In this area men are played very easy unless (1) the defense has an extra man; (2) the defensive plan calls for pressing tactics, or (3) the team is behind.

"C"—Perimeter Area. In this area, the ball is picked up on the outer edge. Defensive play is deliberate, steady, but no leisurely feeds, good shots, or screen shots should be permitted. Use this area as a cushion against a hard-driving attackman

Waldvogel

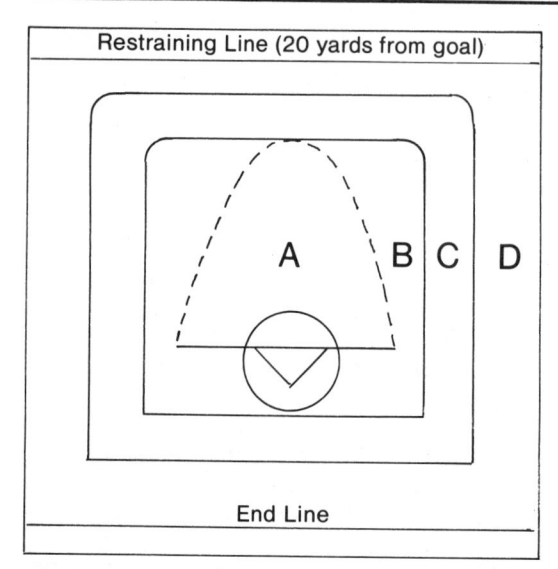

Diagram 1

or middie or to regain lost position. Give ground rather than commit yourself at the outer edge.

"B"—Pressure Area. No attacking player can be allowed to control the ball unmolested. An open stick here is a potential goal. The defense must regard this area as the *last* line of defense, forbidden territory to loose attackmen. Hard checking, tight playing, and rugged body contact are called for.

Rules that apply in this area are (1) play cutters through tight favoring stick side; (2) feeds into this area should always be followed by checking; and (3) penetration into this area by the ball carrier calls for close playing to prevent a shot, forcing the attackman out of the area, and preparation by men nearby to slide and back-up.

"A"—The Hole. No one in this area should be left standing if the ball is within five yards.

Good team defense depends on every member of the team knowing the fundamentals. Talk, look and think. Here's how I tell men to handle the basic defensive situations.

Picking Up

Approaching the attacker as he receives a pass is a very important part of defensive play. A poorly timed or careless approach to the attacker immediately makes the defender vulnerable to certain offensive maneuvers.

As a pass to your man becomes more imminent, you must close the distance to your man in such a way as to force him out of the perimeter area. *Cover the last two steps to the attacker as the ball is in flight, not before, not after.* This is very important. Arrive in position, a stick's length from your man, under control, squared up and balanced. Your stick should be no higher than the numbers on the attackman's jersey. Annouce your move loud and clear, "Got the ball."

A premature approach to the ball removes you from your off ball position and leaves your territory open to a dodge. It also opens you to a break by your man.

A late approach, arriving after the attacker has control of the ball, opens you to several types of dodges. It is better to give a few yards and pick up on the inner edge of the perimeter than to try to rush out and redeem your mistake when you find yourself late picking up.

Playing the Cutter

With or without the help of a pick, your man will occasionally cut for the hole area in an attempt to elude you and take a pass for a shot. As he moves from the perimeter into the hole area you must gradually tighten up so you are on him tightly when he penetrates the hole. Play strong to ball side and keep your stick up and in checking position. If your man goes by you, trail from directly behind him so that when he raises his stick, you will be in position to check. As your man goes through the hole, yell "Man cutting."

Fast Break Defensive Maneuvers

A well controlled defensive team is the best way to minimize fast break situations. Always keep one or two middies in a back-up position by the offensive restraining line. When a fast break does occur, the key to good defense is a tight triangle. The goalie should direct the defense, and each man should sound off his position. Be alert for the interception and the hard stick check.

Do not overcommit on your attackman. If you do, you may allow him to face or roll dodge for a point blank shot. Be prepared to race to the backline on a missed shot since attackmen are not often in a good position to back up a shot on a fast break.

Once the break is stopped, each defensive man must be alert to check up and call out the number of the man he is guarding.

Responsibilities: On a fast break, each position has certain responsibilities as follows: The *midfielder* must hustle full speed to catch the breaking middie. Try to check his stick as he passes off or go to the crease to jam crossfeeds. At times the middie can pick up the point attackman or intercept the pass off to him.

The *goalie* calls out "Fast break!" and the name of the defenseman who will take the point position. Make sure the point man drops in far enough before picking up the

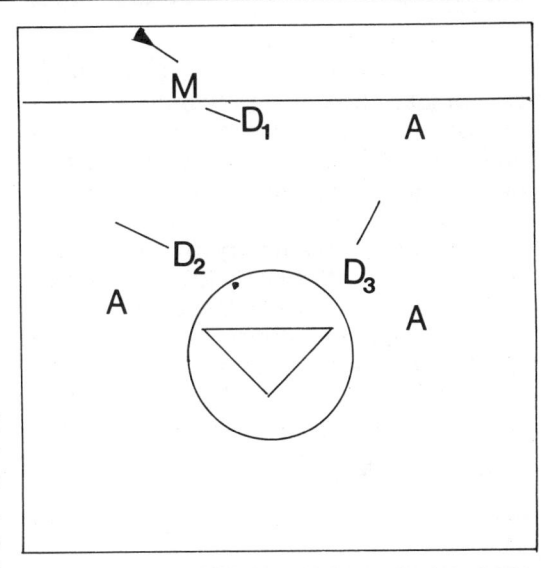

Diagram 2: D1: POINT MAN should pick up no further than 15 yards out, stick up. Force middie to outside. If he goes let him, as long as he is going away from the cage. D2: LEFT WING stick to outside prevent pass; body position should be 5 or 6 yards in front of the cage and as close to the pipes as possible, ready to rotate over. D3: RIGHT WING in this situation must 'cheat' up and toward the ball to prevent pass to back attackmen.

ball; also tell him when to pick it up.

The *point defenseman* (D1) is the defenseman nearest the ball as it is advanced. He must call out, "I've got the point." He will look over his shoulder at the ball as he drops into a position 12 yards from the goal. (See Diagram 2.) He will square up on the ball carrier from a position close to the center of the field and meet him no deeper than 15 yards from the goal. Try to block the pass off or stick check the ball carrier if he cranks up to shoot. With the pass off, turn toward the ball and sprint to the goal, keeping a high stick and looking for the interception. (See Diagram 2a.) *Never* turn your back to the ball.

The *wing defensemen* (D2 and D3) who do not take the point will hustle to a position on the left and right crease—about two yards in front and two yards outside the pipes. (See Diagram 2) Each is alert to passing off in his area. If the ball is thrown to an inside attackman, try to block the shot and then follow through with a hard check. Don't overcommit and allow a dodge. Each winger's position will be adjusted to the position of the ball carrier and where the first pass can be anticipated. Once the first pass is made, the two wingers rotate toward the ball with *sticks up*.

[The following diagrams show the proper positions for various types of defense strategies. Try to follow not only the defensive moves but how you might react if you were an attackman.—G. F.]

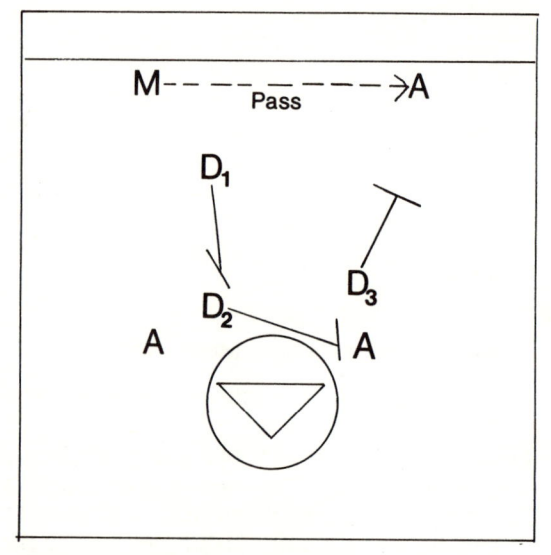

Diagram 2a: Rotating to the ball.

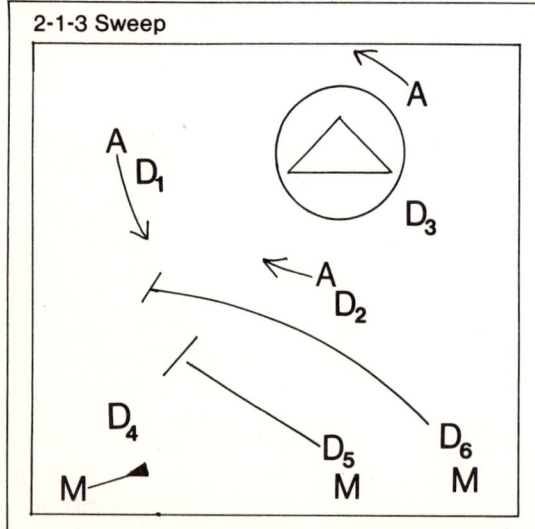

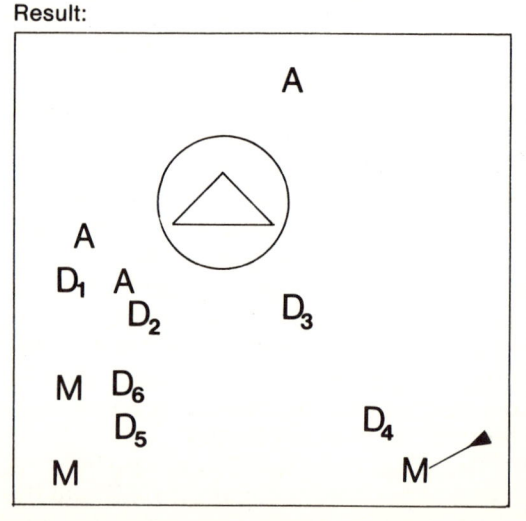

Diagram 3

Defense

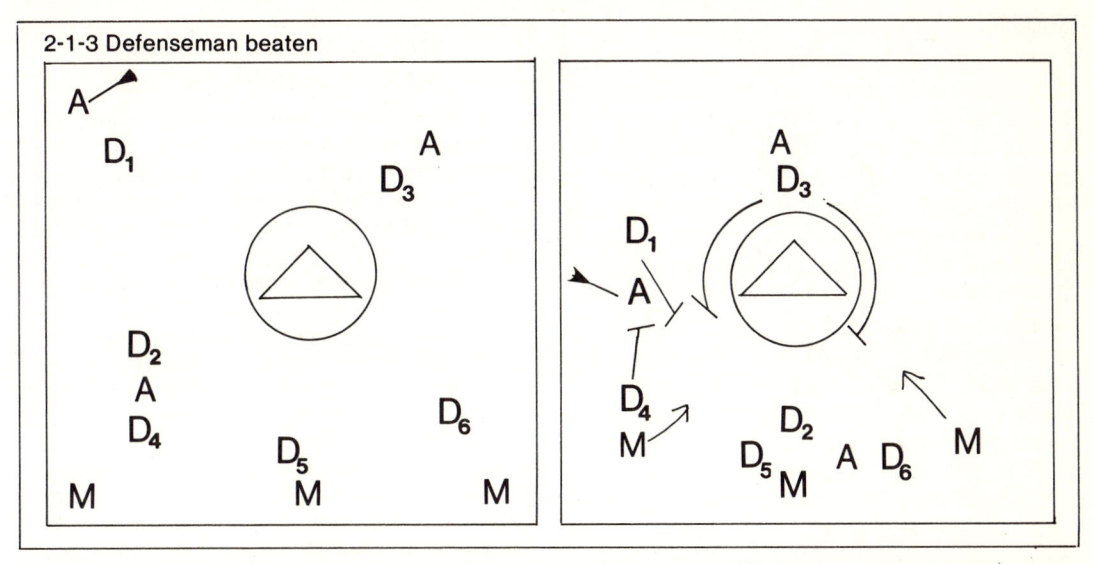

2-1-3 Defenseman beaten

Diagram 4: D4 must slide, maybe D2 also if middies are taken out of play with D3 and D6 backing up the crease. D5 must play zone for cutters or a pass to M1. If D3 cannot get back, he should cover the far corners of the cage.

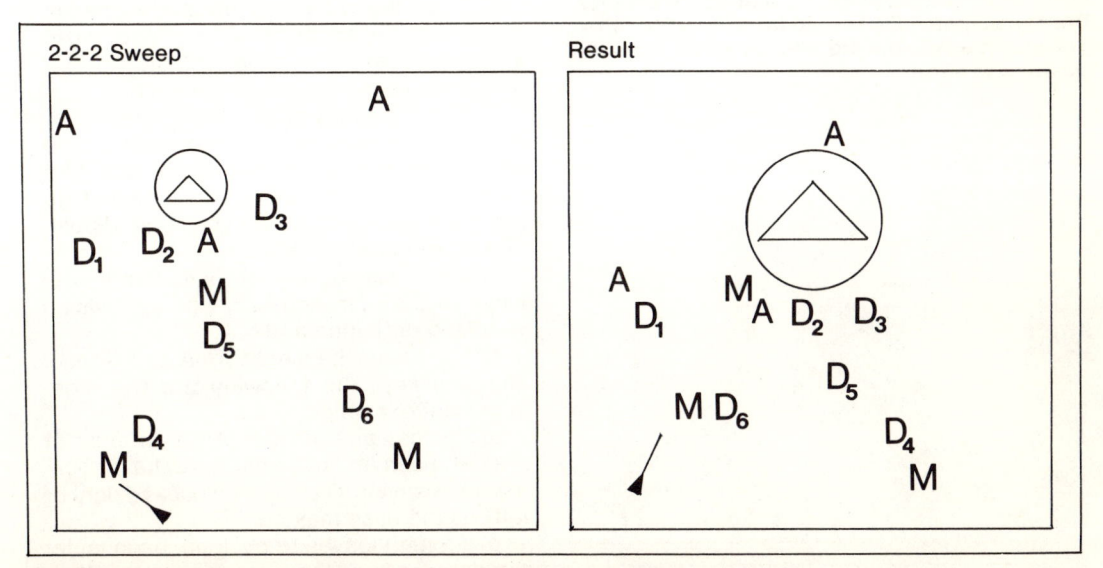

2-2-2 Sweep

Result

Diagram 5: If D4 is beaten, slide comes from CREASE D5, with D1 and D3 backing up on crease, watching for sneak.

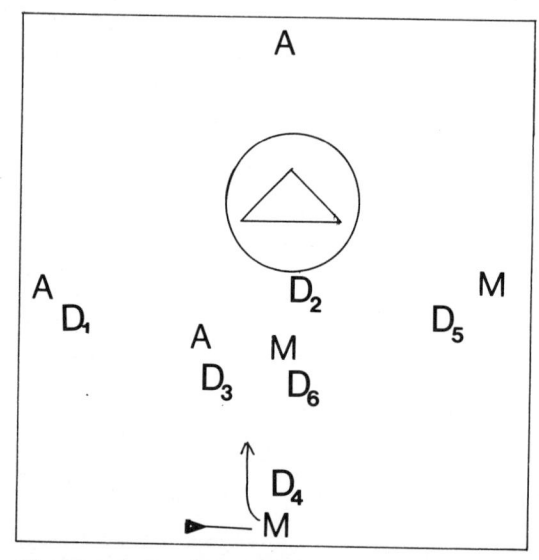

Diagram 6: Backup in a 1-4-1 must come from the CREASE with the man furthest away from the ball telling the men in front to go. In this example, D4 is beaten. D2 tells D6 "I got your back—GO!!" D2 also tells D1 and D5 "Watch for the sneak man." D6 should be telling D4, "I've got your back" And he should be in a ready position to slide.

THE DEFENSEMAN'S BIBLE
18 Keys to Better Defense

1. As a pass is made to the man you are playing, move out to cover him as the *ball is moving to him,* so that you are in position as he catches it. Do not wait until he has caught the ball, and then move out on him. It's too late, then.

2. Once the attackman has the ball, worry him plenty by flicking, etc. Don't give him much chance to look over his field; make him worry about you and plenty. *Do not force or rush him.* There is a big difference between worrying a man and forcing or rushing him. *Make the attackman make the first move.*

3. NEVER take a step into a man while playing defense; this forces the man to dodge you. Set the man up so that he moves in the direction *you* desire him to.

4. When not playing the man with the ball, *keep your stick a little above the height of your attackman's shoulder.* Don't ever carry it at your side; keep it up.

5. Be willing to give ground, until warned of danger by your goalie rather than stepping in and giving the man an opening. Listen to your goalie. He is the key to the defense.

6. When playing off the ball, *always play slightly to the ball side* of your man so that you gain a step as he cuts towards the ball. If he cuts away from the ball, the pass must go over your head which puts you in good position to intercept or check.

7. When playing off the ball, stand sideways to the man and ball. Use split vision watching both man and ball.

8. There must be plenty of *talk* on defense. *The real key.* The following are the most important examples:

   a) The man on each side of the ball must let the defenseman on the ball know he is backing up by saying, "I've got you backed right or left" as the case may be.

   b) If a man leaves to back up, he must let the defense know he is leaving, so that they may shift to leave the man farthest distant semi-open.

c) The man playing the ball must holler "I've got the ball, who has me backed up?" If no one answers, then he calls again and continues to call until he gets an answer.

d) If a man cuts, the man playing him should holler, "man cutting" so he can alert the rest of the defense for a possible shift and/or pick. The entire defense must *watch for the cutter*.

e) If a switch is necessary, the *back man* calls "switch", although both men should call it whenever possible.

f) The goalie must talk constantly; he is the key to the defense. Listen to him and react as he directs regardless of your own ideas.

9. Always *use your shoulder* when backing up, forcing the man away from the cage. Never cross your feet when playing a man, unless you are forced to run to keep up with him.

10. When you check, make your *check short and hard* across the man's stick and gloves and follow through with your shoulder. *Never raise your stick high to check* as this is a giveaway as to where the check is coming; plus it is a waste of time and energy.

11. When a man dodges you, keep after him. You should catch him as your backer comes in from the front. Trail him from the rear.

12. After your man passes the ball, step back two steps quickly and be ready for a cut. Also always look in the direction of the pass as you drop off. Do not turn your back on the ball or your MAN. Make use of your split vision.

13. If the ball is out front and your man is behind the goal, play on the front edge of the crease on the side of the goal your man is on. (Play the pipes—between the ball and your man.)

14. If the ball is behind the goal and your man is behind also, although without the ball, go behind with him; this is only as a general rule and will change depending on the game situation. Use your extended stick to force the man out of feeding range.

15. If you do switch, stay with that man until your team gets the ball or you have a very good chance to switch back. Always be in a position to back-up. *Do not allow your man to pull you out of the play.*

16. Always clear the crease whenever the ball is within five yards. Never let an attackman clamp your stick. If you are on the crease on a screen shot, check sticks down and listen to your goalie. Be alert not to screen your goalie.

17. Once the other team has cleared the ball, all defensemen must run to the hole fast. Run hard; this is the time you cannot loaf. Be alert and ready!

18. On clears, make all passes sharp, away from the rider and, as a general rule, to the nearest open man. When making a pass to a man coming at you, throw the ball at his face, so that he catches the ball in front of him, making it hard for a rider to check him.

Jeff Wagner

4 Goalie

The goalie is the pivot on which a lacrosse team turns. It's up to him to lead and inspire his team by both word and deed. Like a grandmaster in chess, he must position his defense to counter the opposition's moves and to try to seize the initiative by taking advantage of any offensive weakness.

As you'll see by reading the individual articles, a star goalie can't afford to ignore the psychological aspects of the game. Lacrosse is a thinking man's game, and the goalie is the brain of the team. He must analyze the opposition; he must never blame his teammates for a mistake; he must foster a spirit of teamwork and team play. He must involve himself in clears and rides. And he must be absolutely and without question fearless. If he wavers or lets down, the entire team will sag.

As with defense, there are two basic philosophies of goaltending represented in this book. One is the reaction goalie, who waits for the offensive player to shoot and then relies on his reflexes to save the shot. The second type is the more popular position goalie who takes away as much of the goal as possible. Even though both styles are fairly similar, you have to decide which best fits your own abilities and overall team philosophy. If you are an offensive player, reading this section will help you develop strategies for dealing with each type of goalie.

Goalie

Jeff Wagner

Bill Beroza

EDITOR'S INTRODUCTION

B.B. tells a good anecdote about how he began a really brilliant career as a goalie. His first day of practice the coach gave him an attack stick. A ninth grade defenseman checked his stick and it cracked. The next day the same defenseman checked him again and the repaired stick broke in two. The next stick he was handed was a goalie's stick.

So began a career that so far has seen B.B. named All-American, receive the Hero's Award for Outstanding Goalie two years in a row, set NCAA play-off records for saves and be named 1978 Outstanding Club Lacrosse Player.

After a great record at Roanoke College, B.B. is now playing for the Long Island Lacrosse Club.

One additional note of interest about B.B. A goalie is not usually the biggest man on the team, but B.B. is 6'1½", with a speed and quickness that lets him throw his frame behind almost every ball. He's a real thrill to watch or play against.

PLAYER'S INTRODUCTION

Because there's no pay involved in playing lacrosse, the effort and hard work I have put forth for so many years can only be attributed to my love for the game. And I do love it, although I've had my share of ups and downs.

As a freshman at Roanoke College (1978 NCAA College Division Champions), I became the starting goalie towards the end of the season. But, during my sophomore year, I found myself playing third string and warming the bench. The let down had me thinking to myself, "Is all this hard work worth the insult to my pride?" Fortunately, my parents had taught me to keep fighting, to never give up if you believe in yourself, and to do your best. I stuck with it and my junior year I was the starting goalie, tri-captain of the team, and made Honorable Mention All-American.

The rewards, honors and accolades I have received can be attributed to a certain amount of natural athletic ability, a great deal of practice, and a strong desire to excel in lacrosse.

Now, as a businessman, I am aware of the need to work hard to be successful. My lacrosse experience has reinforced my feeling of competition and my desire to achieve off the field as well as on the field.

The game has given me so much that when the day comes to hang up my cleats and give way to the younger players I'll be sad, but I will not have any regrets. I'll always have a deep love for the game of lacrosse.

Playing Goal

Playing goal for a lacrosse team is similar to being a quarterback in football. The goalie has to be thinking continuously. He must direct the defense; and, when he's not directing the other players, he is doing the most important part of his job—stopping the ball.

It doesn't matter if you have to use your arms, legs or any other part of your body—you're supposed to stop the ball. If you are not into getting hit with the ball, you don't want to play goalie.

Position

When the ball is *out front* I stay on my toes, always keeping my stick high. I am constantly feeling the goal pipes with my stick in order to make sure I'm in position. I try to stay close to the crease to help cut down the angles of the shooters. *[Playing in the position that B.B. uses when the ball is out front often causes a shooter not to shoot or to hesitate and throw his shot off.—G. F.]*

When a feeder is *behind my goal,* I stand high near the front of the crease, keeping my stick head high so that the top of my stick is touching the cross bar. I sometimes wave my stick to distract the feeder, holding the face of my stick parallel to the goal line in order to knock down any feed within my range.

It is better not to try to knock down a feed if it means getting out of position for the oncoming shot. If you concede the feed and prepare yourself for the shot, your position probably will be better, increasing your chance of making the save.

As the feeder gets closer to the goal line, I start to tuck my body against the pipe to try to eliminate the chance of his scoring an easy goal.

A feeder looks to shoot when you least expect it. A good goalie anticipates this. Since an expected feed can easily turn into an unexpected shot, I look for the person out front with the ball to shoot, then I worry about him feeding.

I always keep my stick high, because this is my ready position before I make a save.

Clues

I never watch the shooter's eyes; I watch the head of his stick and the ball. If you know the opposition's shooting preferences, it's a real help. But nothing can substitute for being 100% alert 100% of the time.

Coming Out

A goalie is not supposed to come out of the goal except to chase a ball to the endline or sideline after a shot. However, in riding and clearing, I do the unexpected. The goalie who is going to come up with the big play or turn a game around, is the one who takes a calculated risk. I try to anticipate and use speed when I believe I can steal or intercept the ball on a long pass. After a save or interception occurs, I frequently take off up the field with the ball when there's an opening. Other goalies prefer to look for an outlet pass.

When a goalie has confidence in his stick, he can do whatever he wants to or feels comfortable doing. The unexpected is what I enjoy. But I don't want you to get the idea that I'm in the game only for

Goalie

myself. The team effort is what's important, not individual superstars. So the ability to communicate is a real necessity. In order for a goalie to succeed, he must talk to his players, not only when the ball is within shooting range but also when the ball is being cleared by the opposing team.

And remember that not everybody is standing right next to you. Give your directions loud and clear, using short statements. Don't confuse your team by giving long and confusing directions.

Screening

I'm often asked, "How do you avoid screening?" You don't! There always seems to be somebody in my way. Being screened is part of the game and the best way of dealing with it is to get practice in stopping screened shots. Your middies and defensemen can be effective in minimizing the chances of being screened, but *you* have to give them their directions. They can't tell you're being screened and, as a matter of fact, it is not always the other team that screens the goalie!

Traits of a Good Goalie

There are two factors that go into the making of a good goalie: psychologically you must be relaxed and at the same time aggressive. You should be able to psych yourself for the tough games so that you don't lose your confidence even when your team isn't performing up to expectation. Also, you must not be afraid of body or ball contact.

Physically, a good goalie needs agility, keen eyesight, exceptional reflexes and the ability to concentrate.

One further thing that's needed is attitude. Attitude is everything. With a good attitude, a poor player can be good and a good player can be great, but a great player with a bad attitude plays very poorly.

Drills

I prefer drills that get me moving. For example, three or four players standing five yards off the crease passing the ball and shooting or one-on-one drill. My own favorite drill consisted of spending hour upon hour throwing a ball against a wall.

Future of Lacrosse

Lacrosse certainly will grow in popularity within the next five to ten years. I foresee the Midwest teams becoming perennial powers and an accelerated growth of lacrosse in the West.

This growth is inevitable as long as the rules committee doesn't take away from the excitement of the game. I believe eliminating the after goal faceoff will make the game less exciting.

The faceoff in lacrosse can't be compared to a faceoff in hockey, a jump ball in basketball, or a drop ball in soccer. A faceoff in lacrosse is different from any other type of fight for possession of the ball. In hockey, basketball, and soccer, it is relatively easier to take the ball or puck away from an opposing player. In lacrosse, once you have control of the ball, it is easier to retain possession. The elimination of the faceoff will put a damper on the come-from-behind wins, something that makes lacrosse particularly exciting.

Tips on Becoming a Good Goalie:
1. Have confidence in yourself.
2. Be a leader.
3. Be smart on the field and off.
4. Always know that you are going to be the best at what you do.

Rick Blick

EDITOR'S INTRODUCTION

USILA Goalie of the Year for three consecutive years, Rick Blick is one of the best around. He played four years on Hobart's two-time championship team. Rick was First Team All-American in 1976, '77 and '78 and a member of the '78 USA National team. He's now playing club ball for the Central New York powerhouse.

Rick has the quickness and mental agility it takes to be a superior goalie and lead a successful defense. His advice to new goalies comprises a point by point narrative of how to be a topnotch player.

For the player just starting to play goalie, Rick feels that you should master two very important elements before you ever step into the goal—foot stepping and hand movement (stick control). And, because of the fast pace of the game and the tremendous shooters, quickness is an essential ingredient. Rick feels that there are a few things to help you develop this quickness—squash, racketball, jumping rope, and playing with a weighted stick.

In addition to lots of practice, Rick says it's important to be able to visualize in your mind the total game situation and learn to react to it with your stick. Here's how he puts it all together.

PLAYER'S INTRODUCTION

Lacrosse has meant a great deal to me. It has opened doors for me that I never would have had opened. It helped me get into college, helped with the financial aspects of college, and gave me the opportunity to play with a winning team. Unlike basketball or football, the game is suited to those who aren't big in size. It also is fairly easy to master—with practice. It's a great all-around sport.

Philosophy

My philosophy of goaltending is really very simple. STOP EVERY SHOT. Do it any way you can. Always feel that each shot is a potential goal no matter how wide it may look to you. And always feel that you CAN stop a shot no matter how certain it looks. If you start thinking that there is no way you can stop it, you will start believing it and find that more and more goals are being scored on you because you didn't try.

Always praise your defense when they make a good play. When they make a mistake, don't overreact and start yelling at them. Good defense requires good teamwork; you have to work at it together. If you

Scott White

antagonize the defense, they won't work with you in preventing goals.

Positioning

I keep my hands about 7 or 8 inches apart (measuring from the bottom of the top hand to the top of the bottom hand). I keep my elbows out and arms loose. My knees are slightly bent and my back is almost straight. I stay on my toes with my back heels about an inch and a half off the ground and turned in slightly (pigeon toed). This can save a second of reaction time when I start to step because instead of going from toes to plant to step, I can just plant and step. Remember that when stepping, never bring your feet together because it will throw you off balance.

I hold my stick about shoulder high, even if the shooter is in close. If the shooter is at the restraining line, I drop it to waist high.

When I first get into the goal, I make an arc from pipe to pipe. Next I mark the center of the crease line to help me remember where the center of the goal is. During warm-ups, I practice moving along the arc while never letting my feet cross. (See Diagram 1.) The most important thing to practice is stepping across; learn that you must always step across and not just out. (This is shown in Diagram 2.) I make this mistake frequently, and it can be very costly. If you step out too far and not across, the shot will be by you before you can even finish stepping. If you don't go across when you come out you also limit the chances of the ball hitting your body because your body won't be in the direct path of the shot.

When the *ball* is *out front,* stay on your arc and follow the ball, not the shooter's body. As the shooter goes to his right or left, take a half step for every two steps the shooter takes. Look down and follow him to the

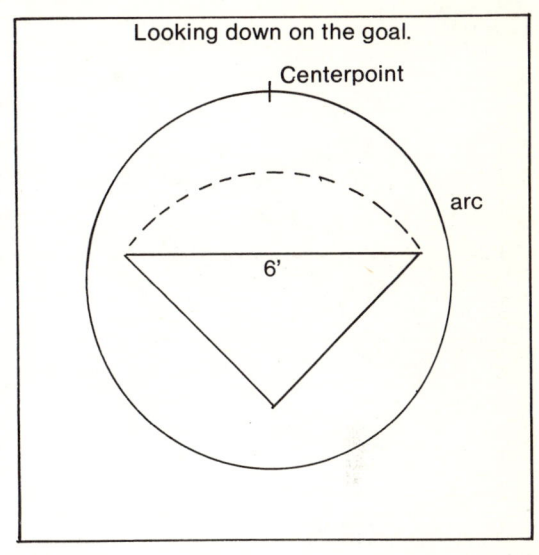

Diagram 1

center point of your arc. You want to cross the center line as the ball in the shooter's stick does. Then position yourself using the goal pipes as your reference point. (See Diagram 3.)

When the *ball* is *behind,* keep your stick up. Don't rest it on the top of the goal. Stay on the arc, *opposite the feeder.* Diagram 3a shows how I play a feeder coming from behind.

[The way Rick plays the feeder behind is really unique. Notice that he is on the opposite side from the feeder. This cuts down on backside feeds. Even if the feed is thrown on the same side as the feeder, you won't have any problem trying to meet the shooter. I definitely think you should learn this technique. It will improve your game.—G. F.]

If the feeder begins to come around and is becoming dangerous as a shooter, follow him with your eyes until he is almost parallel with the pipes. Then step to the pipes. Put the heel of your forward foot tan-

Blick

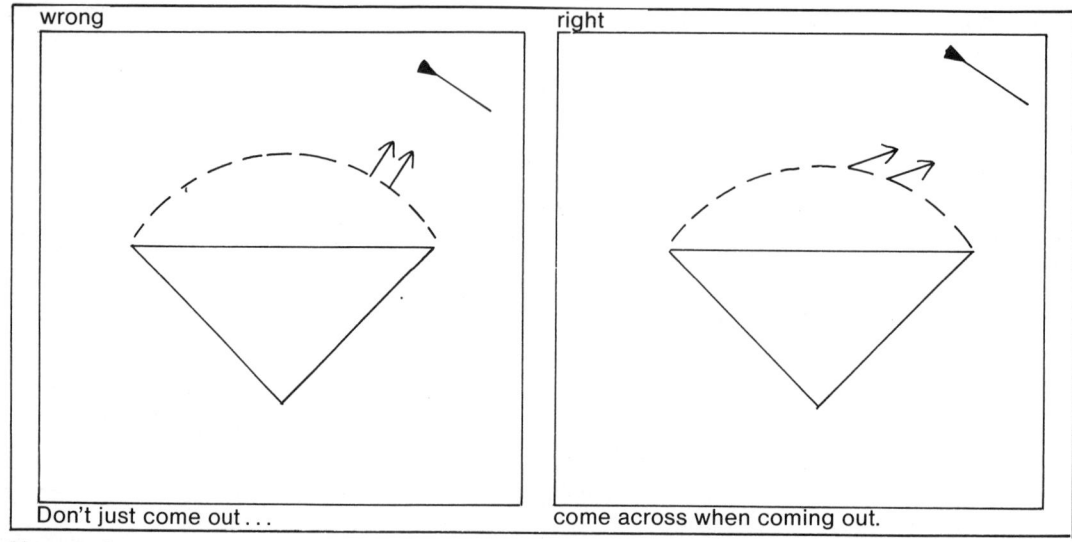

wrong

Don't just come out...

right

come across when coming out.

Diagram 2

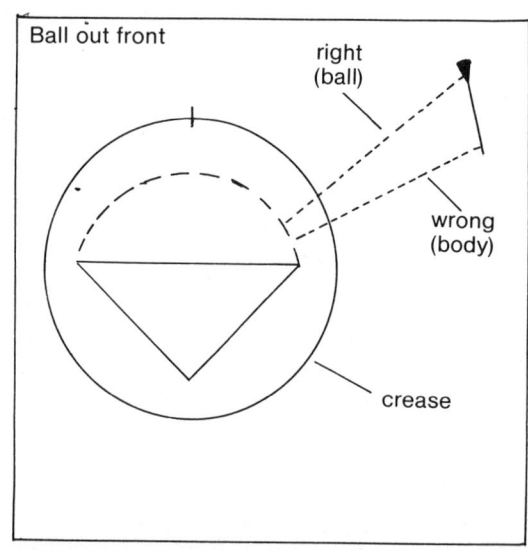

Diagram 3: Ball out front.

gent to the pipes. Now, raise your stick shoulder high, elbows outside, and be prepared for the shot. If he keeps going, take half steps, trying to play your stick on his. (See Diagram 4.)

When faced with this situation, I bend my shoulders to leave a spot in the goal very open that I am strong at stopping. My hope is that the shooter will see this opening and aim his shot there. As the shooter releases the ball, I step to the spot and meet the ball. This is very discouraging to a shooter but is a great move for a goalie. Instead of the shooter faking the goalie, the goalie has faked the shooter. But it requires a lot of practice before you can do this successfully in a game.

Screening

When you are screened, tell your defensemen to move the attackman opposite the shooter, as shown in Diagram 5. If the screen can't be moved, look around him

209 Goalie

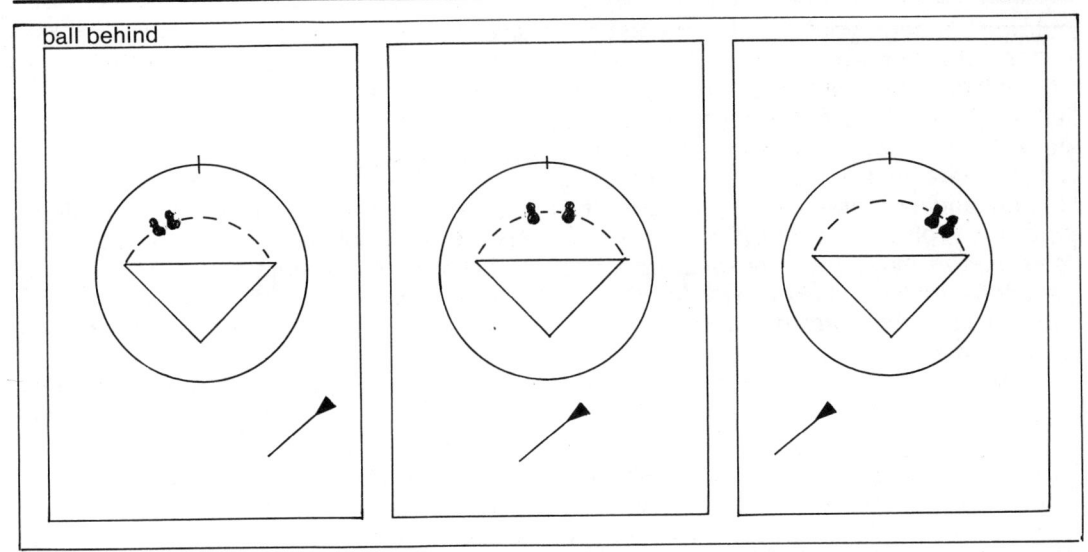

Diagram 3a: Ball behind. Stay on your arc, opposite side from the man with ball behind.

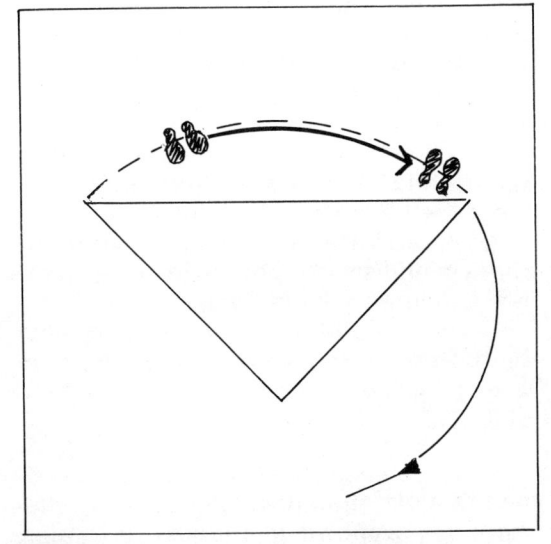

Diagram 4

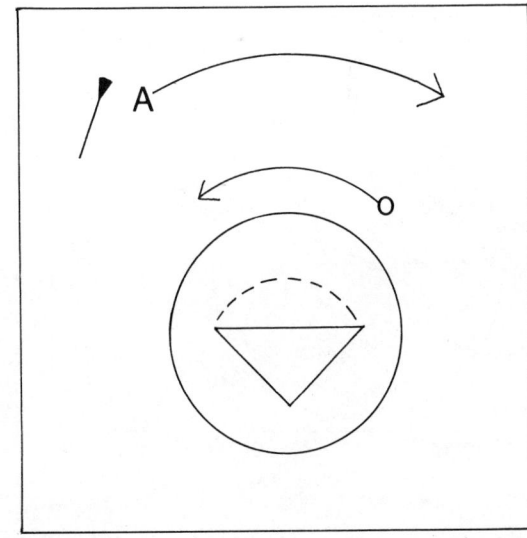

Diagram 5

but don't change your positioning just because of the screen or you may be way out of position when the shot comes. Keep telling your defensemen that you're screened. Work on screening during practice. Put a teammate in front of you to act as a screen and practice looking around the screen and blocking shots. *[Getting your defensemen to move the attackman opposite not only takes him out of the way, but also removes your defenseman who can be a potential screen.—G. F.]*

Drill

I think the best drill for a goalie is to have a shooter shoot over you against a wall. As the ball rebounds, your job is to catch it. (See Diagram 6 for a sketch of this drill.) In the beginning of the drill, you should be pretty far away from the wall; but, as you progress in catching the rebounds in your stick, move closer and closer. At times, try it without your stick using body blocks to stop the ball.

Team Defense

One of my main jobs as goalie is to direct the defense. My philosophy on this is:

(1) Talk all the time and very loud to let your defense know where everybody is.

(2) Praise your defense as much as possible.

(3) Come together before each game and each quarter to stress teamwork. Tell your defense anything you notice about offensive players.

(4) When someone scores, let your defense know he scored on *all* the defense and not just on one man. If you start blaming one, then you won't be effective as a team.

Clearing

Clearing is a very important aspect of being a goalie. The key here is to get the ball out after you save it as quick as you can with the idea of starting a fast break. If the fast break isn't there, set up your defense. When clearing:

(1) I first look at my middies; if the riding team is middie on middie (three-on-three), I clear the ball using my defensemen.

(2) If two of their middies are splitting my three middies and my defensemen are covered, I clear to the middies.

Remember, when you clear, take your time. Don't rush. Use short passes whenever possible. Keep moving. Don't stand still.

Special Tricks

[Here are some of Rick's own techniques which you might want to try to improve your

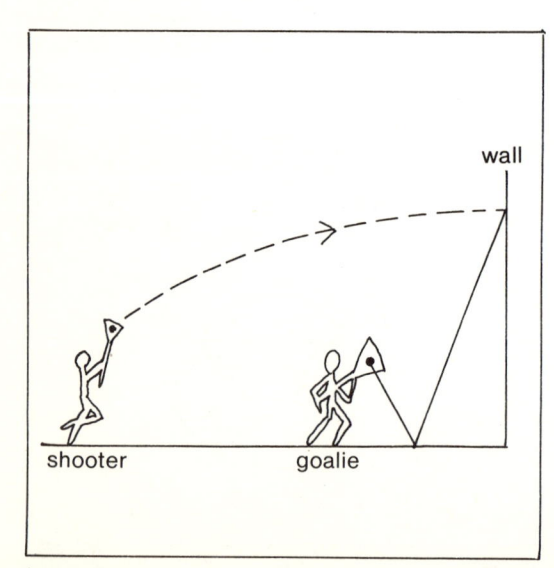

Diagram 6

own goaltending.—G. F.]

I put grooves in the wooden handle of my stick to make it easier for me to handle. (See Figure 1.)

I put a deep pocket in my stick. This keeps the ball in better. If the pocket is too tight, there's a chance the ball may pop out. I want as few rebound shots as possible coming back to me.

I always warm up *without* my stick to help me practice stepping in the arc I've drawn in front of the cage.

When I'm warming up before a game, I like to take shots right in the face mask to practice not blinking. *[Rick calls these headers.—G. F.]*

The day of a game I take it fairly easy. I do nothing that might tire out my eyes.

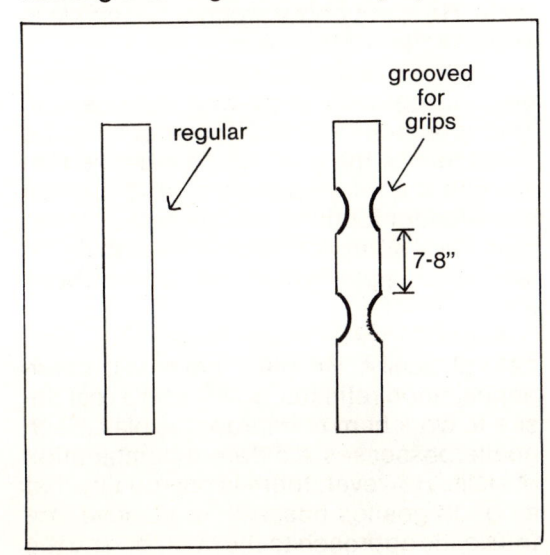

Figure 1

Skeet Chadwick

EDITOR'S INTRODUCTION

Confidence and poise mark this all-star goalie. Skeet began his playing career at Towson High School and went on to Washington & Lee where he was largely responsible for Washington & Lee's '73 upset victory over Navy (13–12 in sudden death overtime) by piling up 28 saves during the game. He was named to the All-American team twice while at college. In 1974, he received the C. Markland Kelly Jr. Award, as the outstanding goalie in the country, was named his team's Most Valuable Player and played in the North-South game.

He now plays for the Chesapeake Lacrosse Club and was named the club's Most Valuable Player in 1976 and '77, as well as All-Club for those same years. Skeet works for Peterson, Howell & Heather in suburban Baltimore.

PLAYER'S INTRODUCTION

Lacrosse has done a great deal for me. It trained me to make quick decisions, gave me the self-confidence that comes from hard work and mastering your subject, helped me learn the meaning and value of teamwork, and perhaps most of all, has given me many life-long friendships.

Philosophy of Goaltending

The goalie is the team's quarterback. He should be the leader of the defense and the team. He is not only a stopper but active in and a leader of the clear.

To be a good goalie requires a certain mental approach to playing the position. This approach includes: (1) overcoming the initial fear of the goal; (2) confidence that you can and will stop every shot; (3) being a cheerleader for the team by always having a positive approach; and (4) the ability to lead by example—your hustle and enthusiasm.

A good goalie must have more than natural ability. He must have self confidence, good reflexes, agility and a real desire to work hard to improve his play. Each goalie possesses a different combination of skills. However, there is one quality that all good goalies possess—a positive, enthusiastic approach to the position and the game. Few goalies became good on their ability alone.

The first step in developing this positive, confident attitude is overcoming the natural fear of the ball. The best approach to use is to realize that this is indeed a natural

Goalie

Chadwick

fear and overcoming this fear is a great accomplishment in itself. A goalie should take pride in having disciplined his reflexes to the point of overcoming what most others cannot.

The second step is to train yourself to be confident at all times. Every shot taken at you is a challenge and an opportunity. First of all, if the challenge is met and the save made, you get a great deal of personal satisfaction. This rubs off on the entire team. Second, each shot is an opportunity to show everyone else (as well as yourself) that you have worked hard and have the character to overcome the natural fear of the ball. You must be certain in your own mind that you can and will stop every shot.

As the team leader, it is very important that you be positive about your performance. Guard against showing negative responses when scored on. Forget the last play and begin to concentrate on what must be done next. If you dwell on the last goal, you will not be ready for the next shot. If a goal is scored easily, the entire team has a tendency to let down, and one letdown can lose a game. But, if the team sees that you did your best to stop the shot, you can prevent the normal sense of let-down by exhibiting a positive attitude, by showing your team that you're ready to try again. *[At times, your defense will seem to break down. It is your job to bring them together. As Skeet says, showing negative feelings or yelling at them is to no one's advantage and can certainly hinder future defensive play.—G. F.]*

Enthusiasm and a positive approach can more than make up for some physical weaknesses. But a negative attitude will make even a good goalie mediocre at best.

Positioning

My basic movement pattern is along the arc, depending on where the shooter or ball is. Diagrams 1, 1a, and 1b show how I position myself when the ball is out front. If the ball is behind I play the same positions except that I play a little closer to the goal. My stick position is waist high when the ball is out front. I hold my stick higher the closer the shooter gets to the goal until, when the shooter is within 5 yards, I hold it up head-high.

A goalie must position himself in relation to the shooter's stick, not the shooter's body. Watch the head of the stick; wherever it goes dictates the path of the ball.

I find that a feeder can be bothered by your presence on the arc. You must make the feeder aware that you can intercept his feed. If you are successful, the feeder's effectiveness will be diminished. However, you must be sure that you don't decrease your overall effectiveness by trying to do too much in this area. Don't get so caught up in trying to block feeds that you come out too far and leave yourself open for an easy shot.

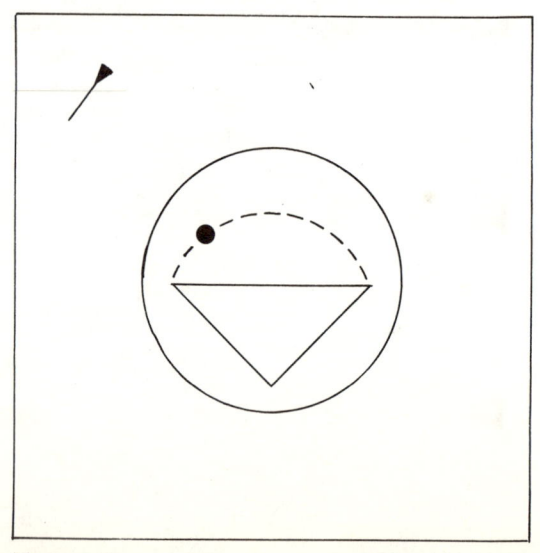

Diagram 1

Goalie

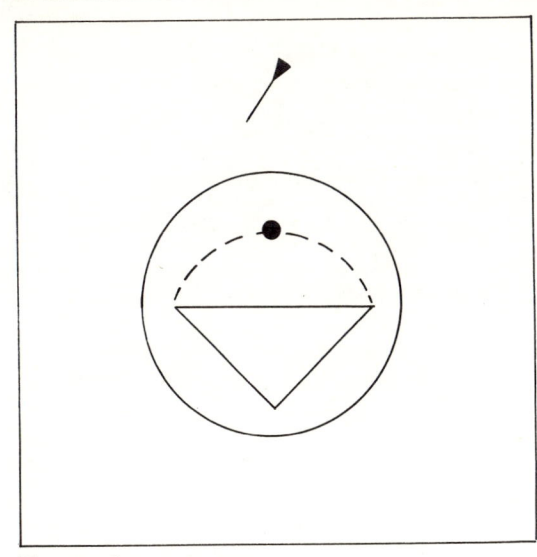

Diagram 1a

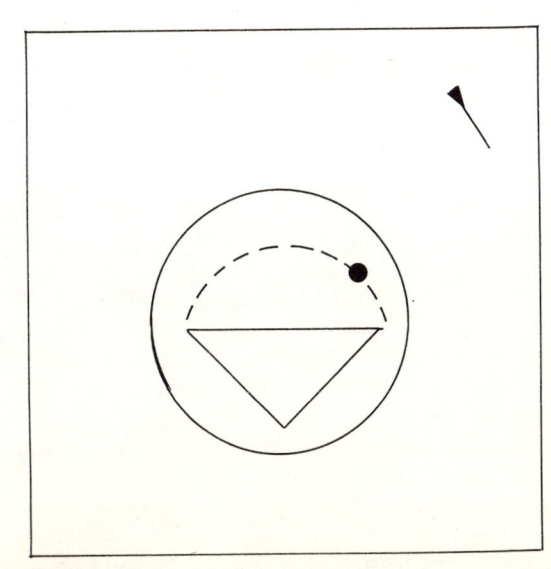

Diagram 1b

[Making the feeder think of you certainly will take part of his game away from him. Anything that can deter your opponent is smart lacrosse.—G. F.]

In fact, I only leave the goal when I'm positive I can reach the offensive player before the offensive player catches the ball. In a one-on-one situation, I don't leave the goal. Instead, I try to bait the shooter into shooting where I can anticipate the shot and make the save.

Leading the Defense

In order to effectively direct the defense, the goalie must earn the respect of his defensemen and middies. (If he doesn't have this respect, the defenseman who does have the respect of the other players should direct the defense on clears, while the crease defenseman should assist the goalie in directing the defense when the opposing team has possession of the ball.)

Calling out ball position is the most important responsibility of the goalie. Beyond that he should constantly try to think and anticipate for the defense. He does this by watching the play away from the ball and communicating to the defense what is happening and what the defense should be doing to react.

On a clear, when the goalie doesn't have possession of the ball, he should act as the eyes of the player who does have the ball, telling him where to make his next pass. He must also direct the other players on the team to position themselves properly on the field.

Screening

Avoiding the screen is difficult and requires extreme concentration and a great deal of unpleasant but necessary practice. The best way to avoid a screen is to lean slightly to one side or the other of the screen, while always staying aware of how far out of position you are. Practicing this requires taking a great number of shots off of the body. However, there is no easy way to learn this important skill.

Another drill that is useful is the turning drill. Have a teammate stand behind the goal and feed a shooter in front of the goal. Both the feeder and shooter should vary their positions constantly. Try blocking the feed and then stopping the shot. Complicate the drill once in a while by using a third teammate as a screen in front of the shooter.

Future of Lacrosse

Over the next five to ten years, I think lacrosse will become a more specialized and professional sport. The sport's growth will be slow because of the high start up costs involved—especially burdensome at the high school level.

Dave Creighton

EDITOR'S INTRODUCTION

This truly great player started his lacrosse career under Jerry Schmidt, who was then lacrosse coach at Calvert Hall school. Dave went on to play under Jerry at Hobart where he was a three-time All-American. Dave is now teaching at Calvert Hall where he's also lacrosse coach.

In addition, Dave is one of the mainstays of the Mt. Washington Club, having served as co-captain for the '74 through '78 seasons. The Cricket's overall playing skills, especially his ability to motivate his teammates by making truly remarkable saves, was instrumental in helping the Mt. Washington Wolfpack to three straight club championships.

Concentration

My experience in both playing and coaching the goalie position has taught me that there are four basic areas which must be mastered by anyone who wants to be a successful goalie. These areas are concentration, positioning, technique, and leadership. The most important of these is concentration because a breakdown in concentration usually leads to major breakdowns in other areas. Concentration is essential to maintaining position because your position must be adjusted according to field conditions, ball position and the habits of particular shooters and feeders. Game concentration begins in the warm-up period when you must make sure that you are absorbing the proper steps and reactions until they become instinctive. It is better not to warm up at all than to do it in such a way that bad habits and attitudes are reinforced. During the game, work on concentrating on the present situation, not on past mistakes or missed saves. Lingering on past mistakes only causes future ones.

Positioning

After concentration comes positioning. Each goalie's position is somewhat different, depending on his size or quickness, but there are some basics which apply to all goalies. Position yourself so that you are in the middle of the goal with respect to where the ball is. This is usually accomplished by following a small arc inside the arc of the crease. (The arc should be altered

Creighton

slightly according to the surface of play. A harder surface usually dictates a slightly higher arc.) Your stance should be comfortable, with feet shoulder-width apart and body weight off your heels. *[Dave suggests a higher arc (one closer to the crease line) because he knows shots off a hard surface will bounce higher. The closer you are to the crease line, the better chance you have of saving the ball. If you stay too close to the pipes, you'll watch the ball bounce over your shoulder and into the net.—G. F.]*

Stopping the Ball

Stopping the ball is, of course, the most important aspect of goalie technique. To be a good shot stopper, I feel you must work at mastering the proper techniques until you can repeat them instinctively on every shot. After correctly positioning yourself on the arc, you must be able to move to either side with equal skill. You must be able to stop any shot taken to your left with your left foot and vice versa. Step forward at approximately a 45° angle to a position where, if you miss the ball, it will hit you. Then, bring your back foot up to a position approximately shoulder-width from your front foot (as in the goalie starting position described earlier). I don't advocate closing your legs for several reasons. First, with the feet again in a starting position, it is easier to play rebounds and other shots. Second, with the stick between the legs, more area is covered for bounce shots. Third, you are in a better position for chasing shots or loose balls than if you were standing with your feet together. Use the step to take care of the direction of the shot, and the stick to cover the height of the shot.

To stop low or bounce shots, bring the stick perpendicular to the ground; then, by extending your arms, push the stick *toward* the ball. Your body should be slightly hunched over the ball so that rebounds fall in front of you. After the ball has made contact, a slight twist of the stick will help retain the ball in the pocket. Always concentrate on locking the ball into the pocket. Avoid sweeping the stick across your body because even the slightest mistake in timing will result in a goal. Also remember to keep the largest stick area presented to the ball. Don't twist the stick; it decreases that area.

Low shots to the right or left should be stopped using this same technique.

Shots up the middle can be stopped by stepping with either foot, although I prefer the offside foot because it prevents overstepping.

High shots to the off side should be stopped by bringing the stick under and out toward the ball.

The hardest shot to stop is one to the off stick side between the thighs and ribs because the stick must travel the furthest distance from its natural slanting position. On these shots, you must decide whether to bring the stick across, over or below. As a general rule, I try to bring the stick across high whenever possible.

In playing close shots, it is important to try to limit the shooter's selection by concentrating on stopping high shots. To do this, don't commit yourself too early. Have the stick in position by your ear and in close to your body. As the shot is made, step with the proper foot toward the shot and push the stick out to cover the shooter's stick. If, when released, the shot turns out to be low, you must rely on your step (at a 45° angle) and stick quickness to recover and make the save.

Try to make the shooter shoot a difficult shot or one that you expect and hence

Goalie

Russell Sport Photos

have a good chance of stopping. For example, as a right handed shooter comes around the goal, a right handed goalie should hang on the pipe as long as possible with his stick in a position to stop any type of high shot. This tends to force the shooter to shoot to the lower left side of the goal. Although this is a tough save, by anticipating and stepping correctly, you should have an advantage.

Whenever a shot misses the goal, you should automatically turn with your stick up, anticipating a feed or looking for an opening to run out the shot. *[Running to the back line and beating an attackman will really demoralize your opponent. Look for this opportunity in fast break situations because all the attackmen are out front which gives you the advantage.—G. F.]*

Playing a Feeder

Position is very important in playing a feeder. With the feeder behind the goal, try to recover in the middle of the goal with your stick up to discourage all difficult feeds. If your position is too far to one side, you never will be able to react properly to a shot coming off a feed from the backside. Do not attempt to pick off feeds which pass outside the pipes unless you are positive you can catch them. On the other hand, you *must* stop all feeds which pass between the pipes. Failure to stop this type of feed will result in a shot by a shooter who is directly in front of the goal with most of the goal as an open target. In reaching for feeds above the goal, use a poke check technique. *[Dave plays the feeder behind the goal just as he plays the shooter in front of the goal, that is, he doesn't let the ball go between the pipes. This certainly helps your defense and will prevent an easy goal.—G. F.]*

If a feed gets past you, shout "check" and quickly turn, never losing sight of the ball. As you turn, you should establish your position with respect to the shooter using the same basic stance as you use for close shots. (Remember to keep your stick up.) The key to stopping this type of shot lies in the quickness of your turn. You must learn not to lunge at the shooter but to set yourself after the turn, be patient and follow your usual shot-blocking techniques—stop all high shots and force the shooter to try to shoot low because this is the most difficult shot from in close. *[As Dave says, patience is critical. Don't give the opposition an easy shot. Play your position; make him think about you and where he's going to shoot.—G. F.]*

Clearing

In clearing the ball, you must remember two things. First, don't rush the clear unless the game situation dictates. Unless you are down a man, the clearing team always has a man advantage. Second, as long as your team controls the ball, the other team cannot score.

After a save, look to get the ball out quickly. Know how and where each of your teammates likes to break. If no one is open, don't force it. Try to pass the ball out yourself. If forced to slow down the clear, set up your regular clearing patterns. Off a shot, most rides are man to man, so force the quickest 2 on 1 you can.

In clearing the ball from out of bounds, determine whether the ride is man to man or a zone. (To do this, check to see whether the middies are covered man to man.) Try to keep all your clearing men on your side of the midfield line to keep your man advantage. Remember that when you clear you must use all your men, especially yourself.

[This is important. Stay in the clear. In most cases, you're starting with the ball, so you're in an excellent position to see the entire field. Create the situation and direct your team. Do as Dave does—talk and communicate with your players. Let them know what's going on and where the openings are.—G. F.]

Leadership

The last major aspects of goalie play I'll discuss are leadership and direction. Of the two, leadership is more important because without it you cannot direct your team. To be a leader, you need not be the team captain, but you must be respected. Most goalies earn this respect by the hard work and courage it takes to play the goal. The goalie should be the ultimate team player, for without the proper team support you are helpless.

Direction of the defense is especially important during unsettled situations. Here, you must follow general precepts. Get all the defense inside the ball. The key to stopping breaks is telling the point man when to pick up the ball. Picking up too soon can make the defensive slides too long. Try to make the offensive team pass as much as possible so your team has a chance to recover.

On all even situations, keep communicating with the man playing the ball. You have to tell him ball position, where to pick up the ball, and when to force the ball out. It also is important to keep the defense in good sliding positions. Encourage your teammates to call out back-ups and slides. The more people communicating, the better. Also be firm in your commands to back up.

During man down situations, you must keep the defense in tight. Do not try to call individual slides, instead concentrate on the ball and calling its position.

In closing, remember always concentrate on the *next* shot—which could win or lose the game.

Cookie Krongard

EDITOR'S INTRODUCTION

Cookie Krongard will long be remembered as one of the best goalies who ever played the game. He began playing in 1955 while at Baltimore City College, played four years at Princeton and has played club ball ever since for Boston, Mt. Washington, New York and Long Island.

During his long lacrosse career he's received many honors and awards in recognition of his outstanding abilities in the cage. Here are a few of them: All-Ivy '59, '60, '61; First Team All-American 1961; USILA's Sydney M. Cone Trophy to Outstanding Goalie in U.S., 1961; USCLA Outstanding Player Award, 1968 and again in 1974. A real international player, Cookie played for Cambridge University while studying in England in 1965. He was named to the All South of England Team and the All English Universities Team that year.

Cookie's talent and long experience puts him in a good position to explain how a real "pro" handles the goalie position. Unlike many of today's new players, he is a "reaction" goalie—but I'll let him tell you what that means in his own words.

PLAYER'S INTRODUCTION

Lacrosse has been a source of tremendous pleasure and satisfaction and of lasting friendships. The ability to continue to play a team sport in post-college years on a non-professional basis but yet at the highest level of play probably does not exist in any other sport. Both physically and mentally it has kept me fit. I derived a substantial "psychic income" from lacrosse. The accomplishments and sense of self-satisfaction and gratification I received from playing helped reduce the need to "prove" myself in other areas of life thereby allowing me to pursue these other areas in a more balanced and relaxed manner.

Lacrosse excels at creating friendships and fostering a spirit of cooperation, because everyone is participating because he loves the game and enjoys playing. Few, if any, are playing because it provides a livelihood or as a full time job. This common bond of doing something you all enjoy doing is a unique feature of club lacrosse. The spirit of teamwork, of respecting the abilities of others, of trying jointly to accom-

223　　　　　　　　　　　　　　　　　　　　　　　　　　　　　　　　**Goalie**

Jeff Wagner

plish a common objective, and of relating one's own need for pleasure and gratification to the needs of others is something I have found invaluable in other areas of my life.

Playing "Reaction Goalie"

My philosophy is that the opposing team must put the ball by me in order to score. I will challenge them on each shot, and they must beat me. I will not beat myself—or let them score on a mistake. Once they beat me, that play is over and we start even again. I cannot worry about a goal that is already scored. I want the opposition to know that they will have to work for every goal and that I intend to stop every shot they take. For the most part, I am a "reaction" goalie—you shoot, then I will try to stop it.

My "normal" playing position is feet comfortably spread, toes pointing slightly out, knees bent enough so I can jump to cover upper corners without first bending more, hands spread on stick about shoulder width, stick about waist high (higher as ball comes closer to the goal or against high shooters), face of stick wholly open and parallel to goal mouth, elbows and arms as loose as possible and elbows bent. When moving to a shot, I believe it most important to get the body behind the ball and, therefore, frequently move sideways rather than forward. Many coaches *always* want the goalie coming forward diagonally but I disagree. Moving sideways gives an extra split second to get behind the ball, and sometimes this is more important than coming forward. As I move, I always keep my stick face completely open so it covers the widest possible area. My movement is limited to *one* step with the lead foot and the sweeping or dragging of the back foot —never two steps. Eyes should stay on the ball as long as possible, hopefully seeing it hit in the stick. (Even if it is not physically possible to "see" the ball, this will have the effect—on low shots, for example—of keeping your head down and preventing premature lifting and jumping.)

Although I want to be ready to throw the quick clear as soon as I get the ball, I look at the crease attackman's stick as I am starting to throw to avoid a blocked or intercepted clear.

Playing the Ball

When the ball is out front, I play the same semi-circle as most goalies but an extra half step further out between points A and B. At the posts (C and D) I am always *next* to the pipe, never in front of it. My left heel will be against post C and my right heel against post D (See Diagram 1).

When the ball is behind (see Diagram 2), I am out almost to the crease, facing the ball, with one foot in front of the other so I can pivot on that foot and be in "shot-stopping" position without taking any steps. I will normally move to the same side of the goal as the feeder (X1) so as to cut him off at point Z before he can get to the plane of goal (dotted line) and also to cut down feeds to the open side of the field. (For example, I would move toward point R as right-handed feeder X1 moves toward Z.) However, in certain situations, against certain teams or feeders, the feed behind the goal is more dangerous, and I may play at point L against X1.

In both cases—ball out front or behind— I may overplay one side so as to induce the feeder or shooter to go where *I* want *him* to go. [Cookie has been very effective in making

Goalie

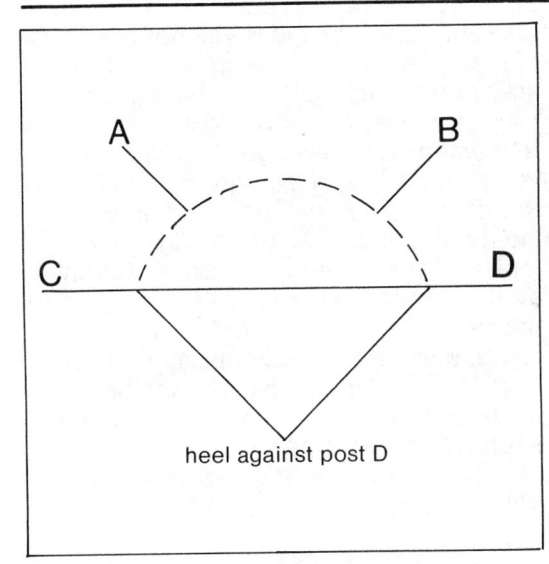

Diagram 1

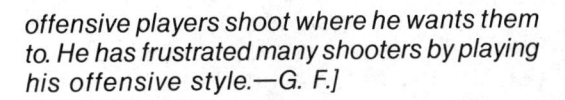

heel against post D

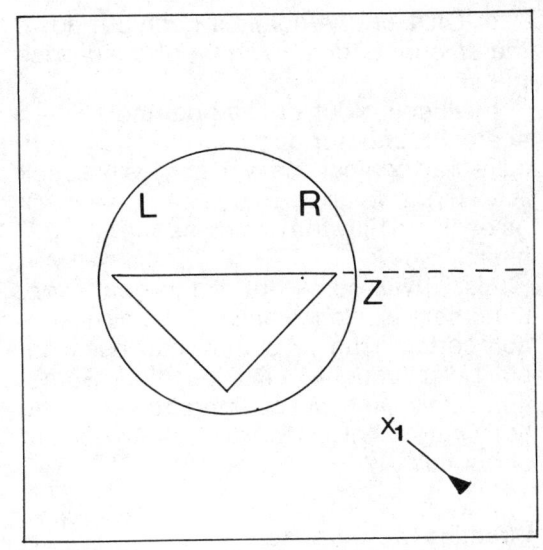

Diagram 2

offensive players shoot where he wants them to. He has frustrated many shooters by playing his offensive style.—G. F.]

Anticipating the Shooter

The plane and position of the head of the stick are the best indicators of where the ball is going. Also important is the vertical height of the shooter's hands, particularly in relation to each other. For example, a "lazy" right arm (one that hangs straight down) on a right-handed side arm shooter means a high shot.

Playing a Feeder

I don't really "play" a good feeder. Instead, I try to take away what is most dangerous considering the feeder, the situation, and his offensive team. I play back at the crease (inside so as not to get knocked down), stick not fully extended (I do not want him to know my full reach), and knees slightly bent so I can spring up if the opportunity arises. If the feed comes where I am looking for it and where I can get it, I spring at it. If not, I get into shot-stopping position. I never gamble on going for a feed; it's too easy to wind up out of position. *[Playing this deep can add an extra defensive player to your team. Many times, the goalie can help cut off a good crease attackman—G. F.]*

Coming Out of the Goal

I come out of the goal:
    a. On a dodge from behind if I can get to the plane of the goal at the same time or before the dodger.
    b. On a 2-on-1 where I can arrive at the same time the ball does, or if I can cut off the pass, or if I think the shooter will not be expecting me.

c. On 1-on-the-goalie if I can cut down the amount of goal to shoot at or surprise the shooter.

I will come out of the goal more often against a shooter carrying his stick vertically than against one who carries his stick in a more side arm position because it will be easier to play the end of his stick ("stuff" him).

Also, I will come out of the goal every time there is a loose ball that I am reasonably certain I can get or that I can lose without being caught out of position. Sometimes this means scooping towards the baseline so that if I lose the ball, it goes out of bounds.

Directing the Defense

I direct a defense by words and by example. A goalie cannot be yelling too many things at once. The important things to communicate are: (1) Where is the ball? (2) What is the position of the man playing the ball? (About to be picked off? Too loose? Too tight? Not squared up?) (3) Who is the back-up man and when is he needed? Feeds and loose balls must be yelled by the goalie. I think most good defensemen know far more about defensive play than the goalie and, in any event, cannot digest too many instructions "in-play." Therefore, the best direction I can give is by example. I want to be aggressive going after loose balls; I want to emphasize team defense; and I don't want to get down on myself or my defense when a goal is scored.

Screening

The best way to avoid screening is not to let anyone know when you are screened. *Very few* offensive players really know how to screen or when the goalie really *is* screened—unless the goalie is yelling to his own players that he is screened. Therefore, I stay quiet. I also let my defensemen play *their* game without worrying about me. Defensemen don't like goalies who are always yelling they're screened. To cut down the effects of screening, I might back up closer to the goal to get a slightly longer look at shots, I remind my crease defenseman to always be moving his men around, I may play more body and less stick on shots, and I may anticipate more bounce shots when I am being screened because most shooters use screens for bounce shots. *[This is an excellent point; most offensive players are taught to use bounce shots when they have a screen.—G. F.]*

Reflex vs. Position

I have two unorthodox traits: I was almost entirely a reflex goalie and I used a sweep for all off-side shots, even opposite shoulder. I tried to follow every shot and react to it, pitting my reflexes against a shooter's accuracy. Perhaps the offensive players are getting too good because there are very few reflex goalies around. (Creighton is probably as close as any.) However, being a reflex goalie meant I generally did not make the first move and put myself out of position. I forced the shooter to beat me. From what I see today, there seems to be too much anticipation on the part of some goalies and too much reliance on position by some others and not nearly enough reaction to individual shots.

As for the sweep, perhaps shooters are too quick today to permit a complete sweep. Most goalies use a "windshield washer" for high shots. By becoming a left-handed goalie while being a natural right-hander, I was able to have my "off" side arm be my stronger arm, thus I am able to sweep very quickly, even one-handed. I also had an unorthodox sweep with the butt of the stick winding up behind my head, my elbow extended to give added blocking space, and my body and head facing directly forward to maximize the area covered.

The best drill for me was playing bounce shots without a stick to improve my body positioning. I also worked on using the butt end of the stick and my right fist to make saves.

One minor unorthodox thing I did on saves was to point my toes slightly out and bring my heels together but not my toes. By keeping my feet in a "V," I stopped a few shots every year with my toes.

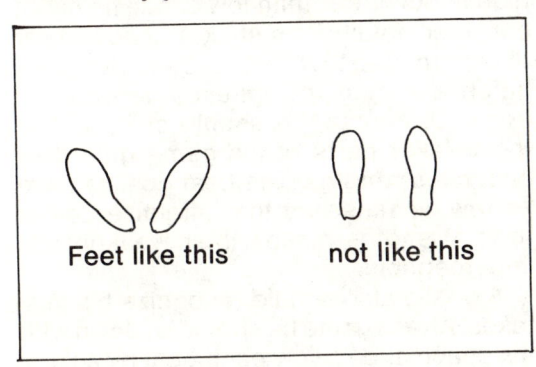

Feet like this   not like this

Traits of a Good Goalie

A good goalie must have loose arms, particularly the elbows. The elbows are the key to arm movement, and I believe I can pick out a good or potentially good goalie by watching his elbows. Obviously, sharp eyes, good reflexes, and quickness are indispensable. Mentally, it is important to *really* understand lacrosse and, basically, to be smart. When a shot is taken, a goalie (particularly a reflex goalie) is like a computer—his mind should instinctively evaluate what he knows about the shooter, the weather, ground conditions, the position of the shooter and his stick, how fast he was moving, etc. The better equipped the goalie is to do all of this while maintaining his poise, confidence and body relaxation, the better equipped he will be to make the save.

Attitude

Mental attitude is more important in the goal than at any other position. The goalie must believe he can stop every shot and yet be prepared to be scored on without losing that confidence. Everyone has heard of the "hot" goalie. This is often just a reflection of a "confident" goalie. That confidence can intimidate shooters. Confidence also lets the goalie stand in just a little longer as the shot is taken. The quick move by the goalie is often the result of anxiety and allows the shooter to beat the goalie.

Future of Lacrosse

I cannot foresee substantial growth in the acceptance of lacrosse as a "big time" sport in the next five to ten years. The start-up costs, the sophisticated nature of the game, and the difficulty in projecting well on television are the biggest drawbacks. As far as the game itself goes, the equipment will improve, and the rules will more or less stay the same. I do foresee a drop to eight men on a side (by eliminating crease attack and crease defense) and a possible decrease in the size of the field.

Dan Mackesey

EDITOR'S INTRODUCTION

Dan Mackesey currently is coaching lacrosse at the University of Virginia while he attends UVA's law school. (His former teammate from Cornell, Bruce Arena is assistant lacrosse coach at Virginia.) While at Cornell, Dan was First Team All-American in 1976 and '77; received the Hero's award those same two years and played on the '78 USA National team. In addition to these honors, he received the coveted Ensign C. Markland Kelly Jr. Memorial Award as the Outstanding Goaltender his Junior and Senior years.

His goaltending style depends on his mental attitude and, as he says in his article, the positioning he learned from Cornell's coach, Mike Waldvogel.

PLAYER'S INTRODUCTION

I believe that while each person who plays goalie will have his own style, there are some things which all goalies should think about. They must analyze their strengths and weaknesses and force the opponent to play to their strengths. If a goalie saves high shots better than low shots, he might consider holding his stick a shade lower than normal so that when the shooter looks before shooting, the upper corners appear open. Of course, he should still practice the weaker parts of his game until they become strengths. The best goalies have so few weaknesses that effective use of their strengths makes their weaknesses imperceptible.

A goalie also should recognize his mistakes. After a game he should sit down with his coach and review each goal by asking himself four questions: Was I caught out of position? Did I fail to anticipate a shot which I should have seen coming? Was my execution or technique poor? Would the shot itself have been prevented if I had directed the defense more effectively?

This last question is one which most goalies fail to ask. The best goalies, though they may not have the highest save percentages, ultimately allow fewer goals because they have fewer shots taken on them. Their verbal direction and their leadership results in better defensive play by midfielders and defensemen.

Philosophy of Goaltending

A sound mental approach is necessary for top notch goaltending. Because so many goals are scored in lacrosse, many goalies become defeatists and concede to themselves that certain types of shots will score. Anyone who approaches the goalie position in this frame of mind has admitted that he cannot control the outcome of the game and that he does not have the potential to be a great goalie.

I believe that I am able to save every shot taken at me. Like "position goalies," I think of the goalie's job as one of reducing the probability that a goal will be scored. But unlike some position goalies, I believe that I can reduce the probability of a goal being scored to zero. If I establish perfect position, anticipate well, and execute properly, I will save the ball.

This approach serves me well in two respects. First, it creates a positive attitude toward saving the ball every time I step on the field. Secondly, it encourages resiliency after a goal has been scored against me. I can remain confident by analyzing my error, realizing that the save was within my capabilities, and telling myself that I *will* save the next shot.

Of course I do not save every shot; if I save three-fourths of the shots taken on me, I feel that I have played relatively well. But on certain types of shots and in situations where goals would be especially demoralizing to my team, I am satisfied only if I do not allow *any* goals. I set the following aims for myself:

Never allow a goal to the nearside. It is much easier for attackmen to shoot accurately at the nearside than the farside. If they are going to score on me, they will at least have to take a difficult shot.

Never allow a goal on a feed over the goal. Most defenses rely on the goalie to protect against feeds over the goal. It is discouraging for the defense to see goals scored which they could do little to prevent.

Never allow a long shot to score. Most defenses are designed to prevent close in shots; the goalie is supposed to save long shots. When long shots score, the defense is disrupted because the defensemen have to prevent long shots as well as close in shots.

Never give up a goal with less than a minute left in a quarter. It is demoralizing for a team to end a quarter shortly after having a goal scored against them. In a sense, the team has no chance to retaliate. For this reason I try to concentrate especially well at the end of a quarter.

Never allow a goal on a rebound. A goalie should control every shot. If I let my teammates down once by giving the ball back to the opponent on a rebound, I had better be sure that I do not let them down again by giving up a goal on the subsequent possession.

Never allow a goal while or immediately after my team has been a man up. A goal in this situation is a great boost to my opponent and utterly demoralizing to my teammates.

Leadership

A goalie may develop his leadership ability in several ways. He should be knowledgeable about lacrosse generally so that he can recognize situations and basic offensive patterns early in a game. This lets him anticipate offensive plays in time to direct his defense to use the appropriate cover-

Mackesey

Jeff Wagner

age. (It also will allow him to anticipate shots for which the plays are designed.)

[I suggest you re-read the previous paragraph. The only way you CAN lead a defense is by having totally undisturbed field vision, that is, an awareness of the entire action. You're the leader. You're the one who can see everything. You must direct your team.—G. F.]

A goalie should also be familiar with his opponent's strengths and weaknesses. If he observes his opponents closely during the first quarter, he can communicate their individual characteristics to his teammates. If number 33 has had the ball three times and used his right hand for shooting each time, the goalie should alert the defensive midfielder playing him: "You've got 33. He's a shooter. He want's his right."

A goalie also should know his teammates' strengths and weaknesses. For instance, he might direct his best defensive player to pick up his man farther from the goal than his worst defensive player.

A good leader is both encouraging and demanding. He should never blame anyone for a goal; after all, *he's* the one who should tell his teammates to buckle down and inspire them with his example. But, after a goal is scored, the goalie should leave the criticism to his coach and help his defense regroup for the next play.

His voice should be calm, loud, and varied in pitch. He should call out ball position in a calm, rhythmic monotone which is punctuated by calls at a higher pitch alerting his defense to the developing play: "Right behind; left behind; left side; *cutter!* Left front; *watch the sneak!* Right front." When he is giving his defense a command such as "check" or "slide", his voice should remain calm but rise an octave so that the defense will key into him instantly.

General Technique

My technique is a reflection of the excellent coaching of Cornell's Mike Waldvogel. It is a bit unorthodox, and I'll take credit only for those aspects of it which he disowns.

The fundamental rule of technique taught at Cornell is that the goalie should always try to save the ball with his stick. A stick save is preferable to a body save in two ways. First, it prevents rebounds. Secondly, a goalie who catches the ball can give his team an offensive advantage by starting a fast break.

I try to follow the same pattern in nearly all my movements in the goal: *I lead with my stick and follow through with my body.* This is not a new concept, but some may disagree with the particular way I follow this pattern. First, I simultaneously thrust my stick into the path of the ball and step laterally (at about a 15° angle) with my near foot. Ideally, my foot will intersect the line of the shot, and my stick will be about 12 inches in front of my foot. Then, as the ball hits my stick, I follow through by bringing my far leg or trail leg forward until I have resumed my natural stance. Thus, when a shot hits my stick, my arms are outstretched, my near leg is extended with my foot pointing at about a 15° angle, and my trail leg is just starting to close the rather large gap between my legs.

Leading with the stick improves my speed and range. Obviously, it's quicker to move just the stick and one leg than the entire body. It improves my range because I can cover a greater area with my stick than with my body. Following through with my trail leg helps me to catch the ball because, as my trail leg comes forward, it releases the muscle tension caused by my outstretched position so that not only my arms but my entire body relaxes or gives when the ball hits my stick.

Catching the ball is the result of a smooth follow-through, not a quick cradling motion. As my trail leg follows through, it allows the momentum of my initial stick thrust to carry my stick and arms beyond the point where I caught the ball. On saves low to the offside, I continue my sweep all the way up to chest level. On high shots (regardless of the side) my follow-through carries my stick at about a 45° angle backward and to the side.

Positioning

Most coaches and goalies have the mistaken idea that the goalie's body should always be directly behind the ball when a save is made. But in many instances this makes catching the ball more difficult (as any lacrosse player knows, the easiest way to catch a ball coming at his head is to step to the side) and reduces the chance of making a body save. Let me illustrate what I mean using the example of a shot to the goalie's offside, a type of shot which most goalies find very hard to stop.

On offside shots most goalies step forward with both feet almost simultaneously. Because the goalie has stepped forward, his feet are pointing upfield. The stick is thrust forward so that when the ball hits the stick the goalie's arms are fully extended. With this technique the goalie's range has been reduced from its maximum. Because his feet are pointing forward and his body probably still is moving forward, anything outside his shoulder is extremely difficult to save. If he stepped laterally instead, his range would be increased because he would be able to extend his arms and stick to either side of his body.

Stepping forward with your body behind the ball is not conducive to catching shots. As the goalie explodes forward his arms must counteract the forward motion of his body by giving backward as the ball hits his stick. But even the best goalies rarely master this technique. Usually, the goalie attempts a choppy cradle and the ball pops out of his stick.

The chance of making a secondary save with the body is actually reduced when the goalie has his body directly behind the ball. A good goalie rarely misses a shot to which he has time to react and which never hits the ground. But, if the ball is not saved cleanly, it usually deflects off the goalie's stick. By standing directly behind the point of deflection, he has placed most of his body where a deflected shot will never travel. Because the goalie's upper arms are outstretched, his shoulders cover less area than they ordinarily would; therefore, when his body is behind his stick, a deflected shot will almost always deflect *around* him unless he has an unusually broad build.

By stepping laterally and only slightly forward, I have a better chance of saving with my body a shot which deflects off my stick. Because my sweep always carries beyond the shooter's angle and because my stick naturally slants slightly in toward my body as I sweep through, most deflections are to the center of the goal. (Deflections off the outside of my stick almost always go wide.) As I follow through with my trail leg, I bring my body directly into the path of deflected shots that are potential goals.

As I move farther out, I reduce the shooter's angle and also the angle at which a deflection will score. Once I know a player is going to shoot, I like to assume a high position—sometimes as far out as the crease line. On wide or fast shots, I often find myself reaching slightly backward for the save. This is actually the best position for catching the ball because the momentum of my stick and body is fighting the ball even less than if I were stepping laterally. But there is a trade off here. By stepping backward, I have taken my body out of position for deflections. I have upon occasion watched shots headed well off cage deflect off my stick and into the goal.

I also have found stepping sideways an effective way of saving troublesome bounce shots. On skim shots which go underneath my stick, I use my foot to make the secondary save. Because my foot is almost perpendicular to the path of the ball (and because I have unusually large feet), this method has been effective for me. Of course some shots are so wide that I cannot get my foot behind them; but neither could I get my body behind them by stepping forward.

Shots which kick up over the stick also are hard to save. I find that my best chance for stopping this kind of shot is to step laterally. Because a high bounce slows the ball, I have time to cover up by accelerating my follow-through. The key is to bring the open hip (open because the foot is pointing to the side) over the lead foot very quickly. If a goalie has trouble reaching these shots with his hip, it is probably either because his foot is pointing forward instead of to the side, or because he is not concentrating on following through quickly with his hip.

This style of goaltending is not for everyone. But this style of lateral movement is less limiting than any other style I have seen. Not only does it enable the quick goalie to catch every conceivable shot, but it also extends his range to shots well off goal.

Drills

In practicing this technique of lateral movement I have found two drills extremely helpful. The first is a quick stick drill. My coach (or another player) and I stand about five yards apart and gently quick stick the ball to each other. If I am not following through well, I find that working my way down field instead of resuming my original position after every save forces me to bring my trail leg forward. The coach should throw the ball to the same spot until the goalie is correctly and comfortably moving to the spot. I like to take about five shots to my stickside high, then five to my offside high, and continue until I have had shots to my stickside hip, offside hip, stickside low and offside low. This drill is excellent for teaching a goalie to lead with his stick and near foot and to follow through with his trail leg. I do the drill every time I practice because it forces me to catch the ball. I try never to cradle but to hold on to the ball by following through with my stick and body.

The second drill is a wall drill. Here the goalie stands about five yards from a wall and works on his technique by shooting the ball off the wall and saving it. This is a good drill for developing a quick follow through and is particularly good for learning to bring the near hip quickly over the near foot.

Feeds From Behind the Goal

I was taught at Cornell to stand in the middle of the goal whenever the ball was behind the goal. I feel that this technique is superior to that of moving around the crease as the ball position changes. It is easier to consistently turn around in good position if you are always standing in the same position. Also, from the center of the goal, the goalie has a chance to intercept any feed over the goal which is not too high. From the middle, the goalie always can be in position to save a shot off of a feed with just one step. The only advantage a goalie gains by shading toward the ballside is that he makes it more difficult for an attackman to pass over the nearside of the goal. But in so doing, he has conceded a pass over the goal to the weakside (and a goal should the play be completed). It is not appreciably more difficult to step to the near goalpost from a position in the center of the goal than from a position closer to the goalpost; it is only a one-step move from either position. *But,* it is very difficult to get back to the far goalpost with just one step if you have shaded to the ballside.

Turning: The mechanics of the turn involved in following the ball behind are simple but difficult to master. I pivot on the foot which is closest to the ball when it passes me. (I prefer to take long steps and therefore my pivot foot is stationary.) On passes moving across the face of the cage, a shorter goalie may want to take a slight drop step with his pivot foot. *[This style is becoming more popular with goalies. With more and more teams using back side cutters, goalies are having to adjust their stances to meet this challenge.—G. F.]*

A simple rule helps me check whether I have turned to the correct side—I follow the ball with my eyes. If I have been able to follow the flight of the ball from stick to stick, I have turned to the correct side.

As the ball passes me, my shoulders are parallel to the path of the ball, and my stick is reaching for an interception.

As I continue my turn, I am able to see the attackman for whom the pass is intended and plant my lead foot in proper position. At this point, I am ready to make a stick save. Then, I resume my normal stance by following through with my pivot foot so that I am standing with my shoulders perpendicular to the shooter's angle.

Unlike most goalies, I try to reduce the shooter's angle by turning to a position about a foot inside the crease on passes to the front of the goal. I do this by standing about three feet off the goal line when the ball is behind the goal and by taking unusually long steps forward on my turns. This style requires an awareness of the play going on behind my back. If the pass is to a moving cutter, I am better off in a shallower position where I can adjust to the cutter's changing angle once he has the ball. When I am caught out of position, I hold my bad position anticipating that the shooter will probably shoot to the resulting opening. Then, as the shooter shoots, I move to cover that opening. I do not move into proper position because I am most effective when I am absolutely still right before a shot. I also believe that I will always save a shot if I know where it is going.

Common Errors

Goalies commonly make several errors. Many goalies forget to lead with their stick. The stick should be well out in front of the body so that even if the goalie has not turned fully into position, he can still make a stick save.

Most goalies have a tendency to dip their stick below shoulder level as they turn. A goalie should hold his stick so that the top is slightly above the crossbar throughout the turn (whether or not he chooses to rest his stick against the crossbar). By holding his stick high and thrusting it forward, the goalie can take away the attackman's best shot even before he has completed his turn. Of course, if the feed is a low one around the side of the cage, the goalie may want to drop his stick to cover the shooter's stick. This should be done only when the shooter is already committed to shooting low. Remember that it is always easier to drop the stick on a shot than to fight gravity and raise the stick.

Many goalies give away their range of interception by holding their stick high above the goalpost. If the goalie holds his stick only slightly above, the feeder is less likely to be wary of the goalie's range and may throw a pass which is easy to intercept.

A goalie should not lunge for an interception unless he is sure he can reach the ball. Otherwise, he should concede the pass and turn quickly. A shooter standing on the crease has very little goal to shoot at if the goalie is in good position.

Finally, many goalies do not turn around quickly enough. Once the mechanics of turning are mastered, the quickness of a goalie's turn depends largely on anticipation and concentration. The goalie is not reacting to the flight of the ball but to the feeder's stick position and eyes. Thus, as with saves, the goalie should be starting his turn before the ball leaves the feeder's stick. A reasonably quick goalie can establish good position on every feed. A coach should insist that his goalie concentrate on anticipating feeds if the goalie's turns are too slow.

Close In Shots

On close in shots I can only cover the entire goal by positioning myself aggressively. This can be done in one of three ways: (1) by reducing the shooter's angle by standing farther out from the goal line, (2) by baiting the shooter to shoot to a particular spot, or (3) by knowing enough about the shooter to anticipate his shot.

A goalie must carefully choose the situations in which he plays high angles because a good attackman usually will beat him by passing or shooting around him.

There are two situations in which the shooter does not have time to do either. First, when a player driving to the goal is so pressured by defensive players that he cannot change his shooting angle by moving his stick. In this case I step forward just as he is about to shoot and make myself as broad as possible. In this way, I cover virtually the entire goal. (Here I am committing the woeful sin of sacrificing the stick save for the body save, but I rely greatly on anticipation by "reading" the shooter's stick. Moreover, when the shooter is being harrassed and is in an awkward position, it is often impossible to read his stick. A quicker goalie than I am should rely more on the stick save in these situations.)

The second situation in which I play an extremely high position because the shooter may not take sufficient time is when there is a feed from the wing or from in front of the goal to a creaseman who is standing still. As long as I can see the attackman and he is not moving, I can anticipate the pass so that I smother him as he quick sticks the shot. However, playing high in this situation can be very dangerous. If I misjudge the pass, the attackman easily can take a step backward or to the side and shoot into the open goal. Again my reliance on this technique is a weakness; I would rather catch these shots.

Baiting the Shooter

There are two situations in which I try to improve my anticipation by baiting shooters

Mackesey

to shoot to particular areas. As I mentioned earlier, I try never to give up a goal to the nearside. Whenever the shooter is on the wing, I try to force him to shoot to the farside. I do this by holding the near post longer than most goalies and, as the shooter moves out front to a better shooting angle, giving him very little to shoot at on my nearside. This technique forces the shooter to take a farside shot that is very likely to miss the goal and enables me to anticipate where the shot is going. Timing is essential here, and perfection of the technique takes hours of practice. But it demoralizes a shooter to see half of the goal wide open only to have his shot saved.

When a shooter comes straight in on the goal, I prefer that he shoot high. To bait the shooter, I exaggerate my crouch, drop my stick to make the lower corners appear open, and then explode upward as the shooter releases the ball. I try to remain ready to make the low save. If the shooter drops his stick early, I drop my stick to make the stick save. But on an overhand low shot, I usually have to rely on my feet to make the save, although I would prefer to make a stick save.

I also occasionally bait a player to take his favorite shot. Often the hardest shooters shoot to the same spot repeatedly. By making that shot appear open and moving early to stop it, I block many apparent sure goals. This is a cocky technique, but occasionally it give me a psychological edge over shooters as they see that I am stopping their best shot.

if he does not allow any more goals, he goes home a winner. In order to accept this challenge of shutting out his opponent, a goalie must use a technique with which he feels he can save every shot.

My technique is not for everyone. But two points hold true for all goalies. First, a stick save is better than a body save, and a body save is better than no save. A talented goalie should strive to make every save with his stick. Undoubtedly, some goalies are not as adept at making stick saves and should develop their own techniques which rely more on body saves. Secondly, a thinking goalie who analyzes his play carefully can make himself a better goalie. If he learns to position himself according to his strengths and weaknesses, and if he becomes a good leader of the defense, a goalie can drastically improve his effectiveness.

Conclusion

A goalie must accept the challenge of his position, if he saves every shot his team will win. The game rests in the goalie's hands when the score is tied in the fourth quarter;

Kevin Mahon

EDITOR'S INTRODUCTION

Kevin Mahon is 5'11", weighs 160 lbs., and was called "Elf" by his teammates at Hopkins. He is also one of the best goalies to ever play for Hopkins. He began playing lacrosse his first year in high school and now helps coach varsity lacrosse at Baltimore's Loyola High School, where he first learned to play. Elf also plays for the Maryland Lacrosse Club and is still one of the top net tenders of the game.

While at Hopkins, he was a three-time All-American and helped the Hopkins team to one of he most hard-fought and exciting NCAA Championships ever.

Anyone who has seen Elf play knows that both his body and his mind work like lightning. Not only is his playing exciting to watch, but he's thought a lot about what it takes to play goalie without loosing your mental poise.

PLAYER'S INTRODUCTION

I believe that to be a successful goalie, you need—more than any other attribute—the ability to keep a clear and level head, even when you're being scored on. This philosophy of keeping a level head definitely carries over into everyday life. If you can keep a level head, it can give you a definite advantage and help you make it through difficult situations.

My Philosophy of the Good Goalie

It is tough to describe a good goalie because each goalie has a different style. But, as a rule, the most important prerequisite for being a good goalie is the ability to efficiently execute all of the fundamentals, in and out of the goal.

Equally important is the ability to keep a level head throughout the game. If a goal is scored, you should not become overly upset. If you do, your anger will affect the rest of your game. Instead, you must be able to forget about that goal.

The defense counts on its goalie, and he cannot get upset; he must at all times stay calm. It is a level head that separates the great from the good goalie. In my opinion, 90% of goalkeeping is levelheadedness.

A level head helps a goalie perform consistently, and it is the consistent, not the spectacular, that wins championships.

I should point out that my own experience as a player helped me form my philosophy. Each player who plays the position develops his own style and philosophy to help him cope with the goalie position and,

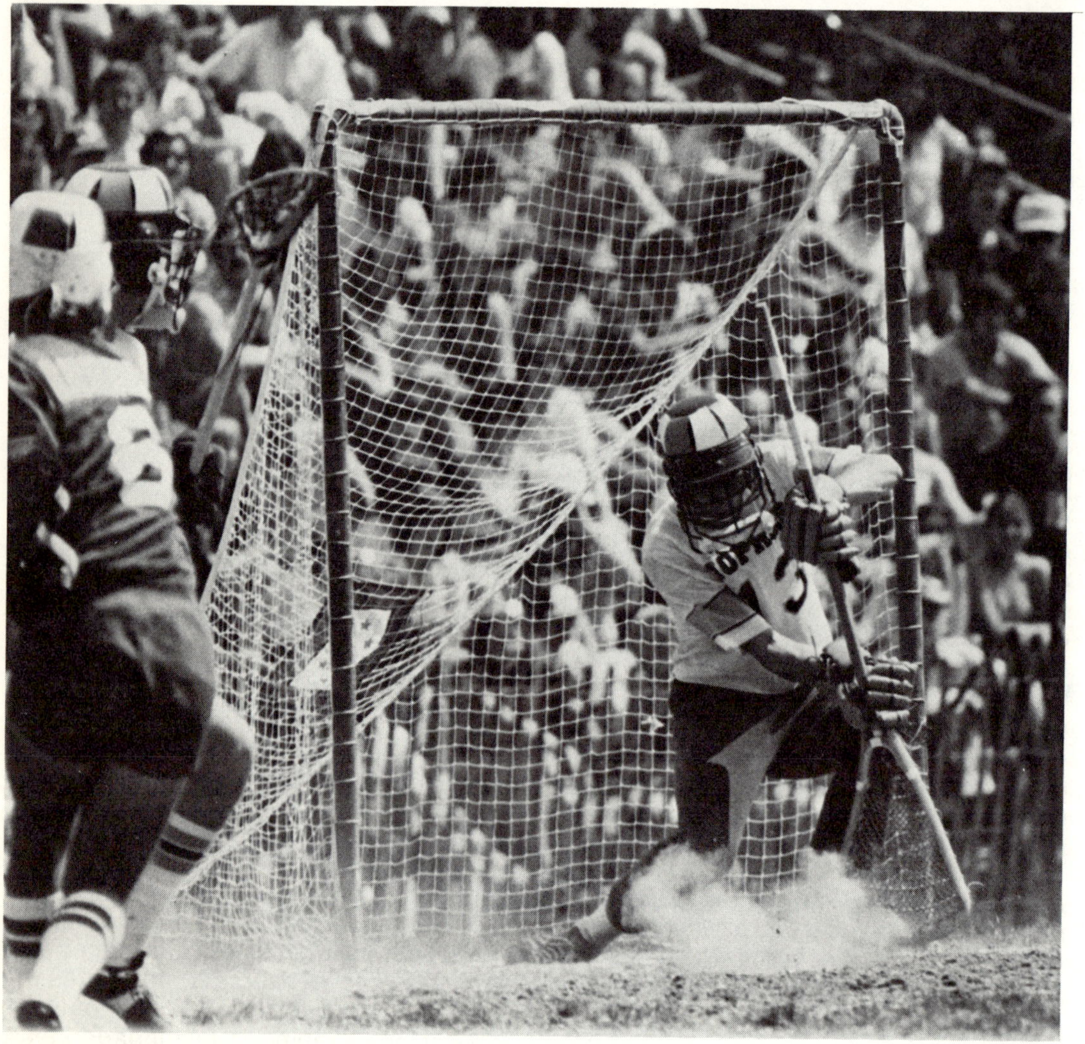

hopefully, make him a better goalie. Since everybody is different and one person's style and experiences will not be valid for everyone, I'll be talking about how *I* play lacrosse not about how *you should* play. If what I have to say helps you be a better player, then use it. If it doesn't help—well, just remember that everyone has his own style. Use what works best for you.

Positioning

When the *ball* is *out front* (15 to 20 yards), I keep my feet about as far apart as my shoulders with my legs slightly bent at the knee. I hold my stick away from my body, hands apart to allow free movement of the stick; the head of the stick is in a high position (just about even with my shoulders). The head of the stick is *flat* towards the shooter in case of a quick shot. (Never turn the face of the stick; always have the webbing pointed at the shooter.) *[A small point but an important one. It may make the shooter hesitate since he sees more of the goal area covered.—G. F.]*

As a potential shooter moves, I match my position on the semicircle with the head of his stick, not his body.

The closer the shooter comes toward the goal, the more erect my body and the higher my stick. This is very important—always straighten up in close with both body and stick.

When the *ball* is *behind* the goal, my body and stick position are basically the same as when the ball is out front, but I stand taller with my stick held slightly higher in order to give myself a better chance at snagging feeds.

I *never* lunge or abandon my position on the semicircle to knock down or catch a feed. If I miss, I'm out of position, and the shooter has an even greater advantage.

An important fact to remember when playing the goalie position is that *your feet should never cross*. When moving on the arch, move your feet as if you were playing defense in basketball. Never stand with your feet right next to each other. This is an off-balance position and limits your ability to move toward the ball.

When playing a shot to the off-side, don't cross your feet. Make the first step toward the ball with the foot that's closest to the side to which the ball is shot. (If the shot is to your left, take the first step toward the ball with your left foot, followed by your right.)

To a great extent, position is determined by what the opposition is doing. I'll try to give some general insights by talking about how I play different situations.

When a shot is taken, attack the ball, that is, step to the ball in order to get your body in front of it. Your body and stick should move together, but getting your body behind the ball is more important.

Many times, especially in close, the shot comes so fast that attacking the ball is impossible. This is when your body position on the arc and high stick position can really help you.

On feeds from behind the goal, turn with the feed, keeping a high body and stick position. (A basic fault of young goalies is that they drop their sticks when they turn with a feed.) Most shots off of a feed are high and will be thrown right into your stick providing you have maintained your high stick position when you turned with the feed.

Shooting Tendencies

Some players execute a specific shot at different points on the field and other players shoot just one type of shot (for example, the worm burner or the high hard one). But the basic rule is that *a goalie should react to the shot itself.* Anticipating a specific shot can, at times, hurt you. But you can (and must) learn to anticipate *when* a shot will be taken and *where* the ball will go.

The position of a shooter's stick can help you. If a shooter drops his stick below his waist, then the shot usually will be low. If the shooter keeps his stick in a high position, the shot will be either a high bouncer or a high hard one.

But, there are no absolutes concerning shooting tendencies. Good shooters will shoot to open areas. Thus, you must concentrate only on reacting to the ball when it is shot.

The exception to not relying on anticipation comes when you're one on one. In my opinion, there are two ways to play the one on one situation. The first and most effective way is to hold your position and make the shooter execute a good shot to score, then try to block it. The second way is to dictate, as far as you can, the direction of the shooter's shot. To do this, set yourself up favoring one side of the goal, leaving the other side open. Most good shooters seeing the open area will shoot at that area. The goalie, knowing he has baited the shooter, can reduce his reaction time because he can anticipate that the shot will come to a particular side. Remember, in the baiting method you must set up before the shooter is in a position to shoot. Thus the use of the baiting method is dictated by the playing situations. Usually, in a one on one situation, you must wait to see where the ball is going.

Running the Defense

An important aspect of a goalie's play is his ability to direct the defense around him. Communication between the defense and the goalie is imperative. The goalie must constantly call out the position of the ball as it moves around the perimeter. Once an offensive player moves toward the goal, the goalie's talk is directed specifically at the defensive player who is covering the threatening offensive player. The goalie must tell the defensive player how close his man is to the goal and must make sure the defensive player remains in a good defensive position at all times. When the goalie believes the shooter is in shooting position, he must tell the defenseman to "hold" his man and direct the rest of the defense into a back-up situation if applicable. Thus, in a settled situation, the goalie's talk is concerned mainly with the position of the ball and with talking a specific defensive player through an offensive threat.

The Spontaneous Clear

Once a shot is taken and the goalie makes his save, his concern is with clearing the ball. First, he must gain possession of the ball, if the save wasn't a clean one. (When the ball is loose around the crease, the goalie should always play the ball while the defensemen play their men, *never* the ball.)

Once you have possession, your problem is to get the ball upfield. I always look first at the area from which the shot came. Many times the shooter's momentum leaves him off balance and his defensive counterpart is already streaking up the field. If this man isn't open, my next look is to my wing middies who are breaking up and out to the sidelines. If the wing middies are not open, I look to my wing defensemen who are breaking perpendicular to the face of the goal. Always take your time when clearing: a bad pass can be disastrous this close to home.

One final note: There is another version of the spontaneous clear. Many times a goalie makes a save and the offense automatically begins to drop back. In this case, he may be able to sprint out of the crease and up the field, thus initiating a fast break and clearing the ball at the same time.

Unsettled Situations and Fast Breaks

A majority of goals are scored during fast breaks and unsettled situations. Thus the goalie must learn to direct his defense through these situations. Here's how. After alerting his defense to the fast break, the goalie must try to stop the ball by telling the defenseman closest to the ball to take the point of the defensive triangle.

Once the ball is stopped, it is important that the other two defensive players fill out the rest of the triangle. Their positions should be to the right and left of the goalie. The triangle should be tight with the point about 10 or 12 yards from the crease area.

After the triangle has been set up, the defense usually makes the required slides on its own while the goalie concentrates on saving the ball. If the defensive slide is slow, he might help out on the side by playing an offensive man.

In the unsettled situation, many times there is no one around to stop the ball. Thus, to limit unsettled goals, I always keep at least one and preferably two defensemen in the hole area when the ball is loose.

SPECIAL NOTE: In all phases of the game there is one call that is my best weapon. That call is "CHECK." When I call it, I make it the loudest of calls. Throughout the game and especially in unsettled situations, there are defensemen who are sliding and playing their men without any idea of the position of the ball. They rely exclusively on my "check" call. Outside my own ability to save the ball, the check call is my most useful tool in preventing a goal.

Screening

To avoid being screened simply look around the screen, leaning your upper body and head around the offensive player. When I lean, I don't like to move my feet from their position on the semicircle. But many times I have to sacrifice position in order to see the ball. In my opinion, this is permissible if it is the only way I can get to see where the ball is.

Coming Out

As a rule, I always strive to maintain my position on the semicircle, so I hardly ever leave the crease area while an offensive thrust is in motion. But there are times when it's to my advantage to leave the crease area. Here are some examples:

In the *fast break* and *unsettled situation,* offensive players will sometimes go unnoticed by the defense and consequently be in a good position to convert a feed into a goal. If I see this situation developing, I may be able to anticipate the pass and, by coming out of the crease, either intercept the pass or check the offensive player's stick.

But there are two things to remember if you leave the crease area. First, when you decide to come out, there is no turning back. The move must be quick; you cannot hesitate. If you go, go all the way and don't worry about what might happen if you are too late. Second, come out stick on stick, body on body!

There are other times when I, myself, will come out, although many goalies wouldn't agree with me. Dodgers from behind the goal can be discouraged sometimes if I come out and double team the dodger with my defenseman. Sometimes I fake this move so well that the fake pulls the dodger out of his dodge. I only execute this move when the dodger is close to the crease, and I have to do it before he passes the pipes. (The best time for the move is *just before* he reaches the pipes.) *[Of course Elf makes sure there is not an open stick on the crease before he goes. He also knows the attackman has committed to the dodge and is not going to flip off inside.—G. F.]*

Also, I will come out when a dodger begins an inside roll, provided I can come out at the precise moment when the dodger begins his inside roll and his head and back are turned away from the goal.

As you can tell, many times I will make the gamble play rather than stay in the goal. Even though the percentages favor staying in, I would rather go for the interception or break up than stay in and let a good, *hard* shooter take a pass and rush in unmolested for a blazer.

Drills

The best basic drill for a goalie, especially preseason, is to get in the cage without a stick, hold your hands behind your back, and let a teammate throw balls at you. Try to save each "shot" by getting your body behind the ball. This drill helps reorient you and is best done with tennis balls. But as the regular season approaches, begin getting yourself used to being hit with and saving the hard ball.

Right before a game, the best drill is to be shot at by a hard shooter or shooters. There is no substitute for the real thing. I, myself, do not like a long warm up. I prefer a short, intense warm up of approximately 10 or 15 minutes. Then I'm ready!

Future of Lacrosse

I hope the game stays the way it is, although from what I hear, I would like playing under international rules. The after goal faceoff should remain part of the game; I think it will be reinstated on the college level.

Book Orders

Additional copies of **Star Sticks** are available directly from the publisher. Simply write to the address below:

Summer House Publications
P.O. Box 16257
Dept. B
Baltimore, Maryland 21210

Photos!

All the exciting photographs printed in **Star Sticks** are available as 9" x 12" full color prints (black & white if original not in color). Each print comes to you mounted for instant display.

Bring all the action, glamor and excitement of lacrosse into your den or bedroom for only $9.95 per print (postage paid).

Simply indicate which photograph(s) you'd like to have (indicate page number and player's name) and include a check or money order made payable to:

Summer House Publications
P.O. Box 16257
Baltimore, Maryland 21210

Your prints will be mailed to you directly by the photographer.